"Cunningham has searched and found a powerful response to one of the greatest questions of our time from the deepest part of herself and expressed it with eloquence and wit and discernment, taking the reader along with her for a marvelous ride into a greater state of awareness."

—SUSAN MURPHY, author of *Minding the Earth, Mending the World*

"*Ocean Country* is a book about the art of the possible. How it is possible to protect the planet's glorious richness of sea-lives and the life of fisherfolk? How can we harvest the sea without emptying it? How is it possible to bear the oceanic consequences of run-away carbon catastrophe? How is it possible to write a book that both celebrates and informs, calling us to respond with hearts and minds to the crises of the life-sustaining seas? In her book of underwater adventures, Liz Cunningham shows us how."

—KATHLEEN DEAN MOORE, author of *Great Tide Rising*

"Better than any book I've read recently, *Ocean Country* captures both the dilemma faced by every individual in a world that has lost touch with nature—How can I be part of the solution instead of being part of the problem?—and the only rational response—to re-establish your personal connection with it and with like-minded people wherever you live. Liz Cunningham's journey is remarkable not only in itself, but because it also symbolizes, and summarizes important aspects of the journeys of everyone concerned about the fate of our planet. Truly, we all live in Ocean Country."

—NORMAN MACLEOD, author of *The Great Extinctions*

"How we're changing the oceans—and can fix them—can seem all too abstract, until you read Liz Cunningham's powerful story. She takes you inside her heart as she witnesses a huge coral reef go from vibrantly and colorfully alive to bleached white death over just a few days, and as she feels the splendor of swimming with whales. Her message comes through loud and clear: through our individual actions, each doing what we can, we can nurture the seas we all depend upon, and where we've already damaged them, we can nurse them back to health."

—ANTHONY BARNOSKY, author of *Dodging Extinction*

"What a journey this is—both personal and planetary! These are the kinds of stories we need right now because they help us move from despair to hope. *Ocean Country* will change the way we look at the seas."

—MARY EVELYN TUCKER, co-coordinator of the Yale University Forum on Religion and Ecology and coauthor of *Journey of the Universe*

"Liz Cunningham takes us on a journey from the Turks and Caicos to the California coastline, to the Mediterranean, and onto the Coral Triangle of the west Pacific. We observe amazing creatures, explore unique habitats and ecosystems, and learn a fair amount of history and science. But the real reward of our adventures is the heightened appreciation we attain for the wonder and beauty, yet fragility, of the world's oceans. We recognize just why we must fight to defend them against the twin threats of heating and acidification caused by our ongoing burning of fossil fuels. If you were looking for another reason to take action to defend our oceans against ongoing environmental assaults, then *Ocean Country* will provide it."

—MICHAEL MANN, director of the Pennsylvania State University Earth Systems Science Center and author of *Dire Predictions*

"The ocean is medicine. That's what Liz Cunningham's book shows us. It describes the winding, unpredictable neurological cascades that happen when we connect deeply with our waterways. We experience awe, wonder, purpose, insight, calm, excitement, solitude, romance, empathy, creativity. We become advocates, warriors, custodians, fixers, champions—we become unstoppable. In *Ocean Country* we meet people where they are as they heal and are reminded how much we all need such healing now."

—WALLACE J. NICHOLS, author of *Blue Mind*

"If a pilgrimage is a transformative journey to a sacred place, which I believe it is, Cunningham's quest is a tale of sacred travel at a threshold point in human history. While the oceans are in peril we have it within our power to save them if we humbly recognize our reliance on them and truly experience their miraculous beauty."

—PHIL COUSINEAU, author of *The Art of Pilgrimage*

"For those who think the oceans are too vast, too remote for us to irreversibly delete their biodiversity, *Ocean Country,* is a sharp rejoinder. In her very personal account, Cunningham shows how we attack the oceans' species on every front. 'Biodiversity matters' she tells us—and provides compelling firsthand accounts of why."

—STUART PIMM, author of *The World According to Pimm*

"A vivid picture of Earth's ocean biodiversity. This is a beautiful book that will make you go do something about preserving that diversity for future generations."

—MARK WILLIAMS, coauthor of *Ocean Worlds*

"The wreckage we humans have caused in the ocean is monumental and dispiriting, its seeming inevitability enough to sadden and immobilize compassionate people who've come to feel there's no longer any meaningful way for them as individuals to help. Liz Cunningham faces this tragedy unflinchingly and, working painstakingly through her own personal loss, finds healing and hope in the sea. Bringing us to places of continued abundance and fertility—an Indonesian reef sparkling with life, a fishery restored through a collaboration of fishermen and scientists, a humpback whale nursery where mothers gently tend their calves—her stories are oases of hope, shimmering with the possibility of restoration for the larger, life-giving sea."

—DEBORAH CRAMER, author of *The Narrow Edge*

OCEAN
COUNTRY

Twenty-one percent of author royalties will be donated to con-servation organizations. This amount was chosen to highlight the fact that the percentage of oxygen in each breath we take is twenty-one percent and more than one half of that oxygen comes from marine plants and algae in the ocean.

OCEAN COUNTRY

*One Woman's Voyage from Peril to Hope
in Her Quest to Save the Seas*

LIZ CUNNINGHAM

FOREWORD BY CARL SAFINA

NORTH ATLANTIC BOOKS
BERKELEY, CALIFORNIA

Published by
North Atlantic Books
Berkeley, California

Cover photo © iStockphoto.com/Ethan Daniels
Cover and book design by Jasmine Hromjak
Printed in the United States of America

Cover photo: A school of blue-green damselfish spreads out above a coral reef in Raja Ampat, West Papua, the world's epicenter of marine biodiversity.

Ocean Country: One Woman's Voyage from Peril to Hope in Her Quest To Save the Seas is sponsored and published by the Society for the Study of Native Arts and Sciences (dba North Atlantic Books), an educational nonprofit based in Berkeley, California, that collaborates with partners to develop cross-cultural perspectives, nurture holistic views of art, science, the humanities, and healing, and seed personal and global transformation by publishing work on the relationship of body, spirit, and nature.

Poem on page 86 used by permission of Coleman Barks.

Portions of *Ocean Country* appeared previously in *Earth Island Journal* and *Times of the Islands.*

North Atlantic Books' publications are available through most bookstores. For further information, visit our website at www.northatlanticbooks.com or call 800-733-3000.

Library of Congress Cataloging-in-Publication Data
Cunningham, Liz.
  Ocean country : one woman's voyage from peril to hope in her quest to save the seas / Liz Cunningham.
    pages cm
  Includes bibliographical references.
  ISBN 978-1-58394-960-3 (pbk.) — ISBN 978-1-58394-961-0 (ebook)
  1. Marine resources conservation. 2. Ocean. 3. Ocean. 4. Environmentalism.
5. Cunningham, Liz. 6. Journalists—United States—Biography. 7. Women—Biography. I. Title.
  GC1018.C86 2015
  333.95'616092—dc23
                                2014043822

1 2 3 4 5 6 7 SHERIDAN 19 18 17 16 15

Printed on recycled paper

to Charlie

Contents

Foreword

Carl Safina, founding president of the Safina Center

In college, I asked a friend, "How do you get the energy to do so many things?"

"You *do* things," he said, "and that *gives* you energy."

In that moment, my life changed.

And so it is with hope. Doing things creates hope. You don't wait for energy, you don't wait for hope: you do things.

Liz Cunningham realizes this. In these pages, she takes us on that realizing, doing journey. We are flying over the ocean, looking down at remote coasts. We are plunging through the surface of the ocean, and the sea is revealed. Soon we are out past our known and accustomed world, traveling to remote corners with unpronounceable names, among strangers, and sometimes feeling very much alone.

The problems mount. The problems, we realize, are bigger than imagined. They are overwhelming. They are too much.

Liz Cunningham takes herself far outside her comfort zone. And she takes us along. Her time becomes our time. Her chronicle is a chronicle of our shared world. It is her story. It is our story.

Who has not felt, on our frightened necks, the heat of that dragon who breathes, "Don't bother." Who has not wondered, "Why care?" I know I have. That dragon is always there, looking for an opportunity. Why is that dragon sometimes so strong? Because we feed it. Because it takes courage to admit to ourselves that all is not lost. It takes courage because "Why bother?" is the easy conclusion. Doing nothing is also the answer that brings zero satisfaction to the human spirit. And so, the quest.

Liz Cunningham makes the quest because she must.

We often hear, or think, "I'm just one person. What can I do?" Can I refill the seas with fishes great and small? Not alone, I can't. Can I put the rising, island-drowning seas back into their genie bottle? Not by myself. But it's the wrong question. The question isn't, "I'm just one person; what can I do?" Everyone who has ever lived has been one person. The question is, what *can* you do? And who can you do it with? Who do you need? Who needs your help? Where *will* you start?

Slowly, as Cunningham looks deeper into the gathering pit of despair, we realize that we are learning of big problems, yes, but we are learning of the problems from people who have the solutions.

All solutions have the same first steps: someone realizes the problem, someone cares, someone shares the experience and the realization. Then, solutions start to come.

Cunningham is no superhero, thank goodness. Like us, she struggles. At times when she is nearly overwhelmed, she reaches for strengths to hold her and to guide her on. The philosopher Joanna Macy reaffirms, "Hope is something we *do.*" And so, in hope, Cunningham continues to do.

But aren't the problems *truly* too big? If you look at it that simply, yes. The trick to fully seeing an overwhelming problem is to keep looking at it long enough to find its weaknesses. We all feel overwhelmed at times. We all feel like it's "too depressing." But those are just excuses to hit the snooze button. Look a little longer, look beneath the surface, delve deeper, and you'll realize you know about the problems only because other people care. The people who care could use your help.

Hope is the ability to see how things can get better. The vision of what "better" would look like inspires all good work.

Author Cunningham begins to realize that solutions are coming in many small doses. That everywhere there are already people who understand, who are willing to help, to do what it takes. The problems are the attention grabbers. The problem solvers are more subtle, but there are more of them.

Seeing the positives requires recognizing how the actions add up. And so Cunningham writes to herself, "Don't discount the invisible plus signs. Even if you can't do the math, don't quit."

To feel fulfilled, we must find something outside ourselves, bigger than ourselves. Then we must devote ourselves to that thing, that need, that opportunity, that cause.

And if we don't?

If we don't, life will pull away, with or without us. Better to be aboard. And so, in a torrential downpour on a remote island, Liz Cunningham's guide is yelling to her, asking if she realizes that the boat they must be on is about to leave. "Yes!" she screams, louder than she'd ever done in her life, "but I have everything I need!"

Get your stuff; let's go!

Hope is a verb with its sleeves rolled up.

—David Orr

Introduction

When I was twenty-two, I packed some books into a bunch of cardboard boxes and rolled them with a hand truck to a post office on West Eighteenth Street in Manhattan. I posted them to an address in California. I was moving. In my mind the place I was going was "ocean country"—a long, slender state the shape of a caterpillar whose entire westward edge was nothing but coastline.

I had no idea that little bubble of a phrase would undergo a profound quickening: that some day I'd realize the entire planet was "ocean country"—a vast interconnected archipelago of continents and islands—because the life of the seas is so critical to each and every form of life on earth. Nor did I understand how deeply the life of the sea was in peril and how deeply that placed all of life as we know it in peril. What I also didn't know was how possible it is to change the course of our collective lives, if we have the audacity, the daring, and the wide-eyed courage to face that perilous truth and work together. This book is the story of these discoveries.

Halfway through my research it became clear that I couldn't write about the ocean unless I wrote about a sense of home, a sense of family, of community, of truth and hope and innocence, because these elemental experiences are so deeply intertwined with how we connect to the seas: our use of them, our love of them, and our hope for them.

I started out writing about the ocean, but the sheer facts that I encountered refused to be boxed up into my narrow-minded pursuit: the truest rendition would be the story of a journey deeper into life as a whole. For me that journey revolved around the life of the seas.

Beginnings

I'd love to say that this book began with an epiphany. But it didn't. I do know now, though, that when things end, they don't totally end. We, our words, our actions, all the gestures, small and large, they stream out into the future in ways we'll never fully fathom. Life has a habit of pushing through, like the juicy energy of the tomato seedlings my husband placed on the kitchen counter near a window this morning. They draw water into their limbs; they lean toward the light. I'm learning to trust that. That phrase, "It's over," I take that with a grain of salt now.

But beginnings? Well, the moment that most resembles a beginning was a sunny August day on the California coast. There was a crisp wind and big waves. I was surfing in a whitewater kayak. I wove out past the breakers, my torso held snug in the cockpit by a neoprene spray skirt.

I turned around to catch a big wave. It was a real wingdinger. My kayak took off like a glider in free flight, a silent, soaring ease. But just as I finished riding the wave, I felt the rear of the kayak veer sharply. I looked back: a rogue wave towered above me. I dug my paddle in, trying to ride the wave, but it was too late. The kayak pitch-poled forward with a harsh snap. I was knocked unconscious for a few moments.

When I came to, I was upside down, facing the bottom of the ocean. It was like being inside a water turbine, water rushing fast in all directions. I kept trying to move my arms to release the spray skirt and push my torso out of the kayak, but I was paralyzed. The wave had hit me with such force that it damaged my spine where the nerves ran to my arms.

"This isn't happening!" I thought. I tried to move my arms, but they were completely numb. "Come on! Come on!" I said to myself.

But my arms did not respond. My mind thrashed like a fish in a bucket, and then slowly the thrashing subsided. "This is really it," I thought, "I'm going to die."

The fierce rush of blue and white water went to gray and then black and then to nothing. I sank into a place where there was no sense of sight, not even darkness. But I could still hear.

"Do you want to live?" a voice asked.

"Yes," I answered, "Yes .... " And then with a jolt, like a strobe light being thrown on in a dark stadium, my eyes snapped open and sensation rushed through my hands.

I groped forward, yanked the spray skirt off, grabbed the edges of the cockpit, and pushed. I slipped free and floated to the surface. My life preserver buoyed me like a cork. Coughing water from my lungs, I sucked in air like a wheezing asthmatic.

I touched my hands to my face, felt my cold skin, the blood racing through my palms.

What was that voice? Was it inside me, like a dream? Or from somewhere else?

Salt water stung my eyes, dripped off my eyelids, and sparkled in the sun. I was breathing. I was alive.

Bonus Minutes

"You'd do better to manage the pain." The orthopedist squinted at an x-ray through tortoiseshell glasses. "We'd have to do an MRI to be sure, but these are possibly hairline fractures." He pointed to some thin whitish lines in several vertebrae in my neck. "See here at C5? Right? And C8."

"C?" I asked.

He pushed the reading glasses onto his forehead. "The cervical vertebrae start with the letter C, each one gets a number. C5, C6, C7, and C8—that's where the nerves run to your elbows, forearms, and hands."

"And my arms?" I asked. I was having bouts of numbness in my arms.

He put his hands on my spine at the base of my neck. "These thoracic vertebrae—T1 and T2—that's where the nerves run to your arms." He tapped the x-ray again. "There's a twist in your spine where they are, that might account for the numbness."

He pulled out his prescription pad. "With surgery, there's always a risk of further nerve damage or paralysis."

He described how just the year before, Christopher Reeve, the star of the *Superman* movies, had become a quadriplegic after being thrown from a horse and fracturing two vertebrae in his neck. "The fractures were at the top of his neck, C1 and C2," he sighed. "Just a few millimeters difference, and he'd have regained the use of his limbs."

"Is it possible," I hesitated, "I might become paralyzed again?"

"Yes." He started writing on the prescription pad. "It could get worse or it could get better. But I'd stay away from surgery." He paused and grimaced at me. "You're very lucky."

"But the numbness," I said. "What do I do about it?"

"If it's intermittent? Nothing." He tore off a wad of prescriptions for painkillers. "As long as you can play Parcheesi, you're fine."

When I woke up, my arms would often be numb. I'd roll side to side and feel the welcome tingling as the sensation returned. The hitch was that as the numbness subsided, it was replaced by pain. I learned a new language: ibuprofen is generic Advil; acetaminophen is Tylenol; carisoprodol, Soma; meperidine, Demerol. Painkillers got me through the night. During the day, pain was the price I paid for sensation.

In the midst of that, each moment was unspeakably heightened. And all those moments streamed together like a mysterious, near-seamless string of beads: time. The present was the most remarkable bead of all—it glistened with possibility—even in the midst of rush-hour traffic in a heat wave, with sooty air and a big-rig honking its horn, even then, just a sheer moment of sensation seemed miraculous. I was alive.

I was also disoriented, as if the accident had rattled the shoebox of my life so dramatically that all the parts inside fell out in disarray. I had been building a career as a journalist. My first book was about television news and presidential campaigns and featured interviews with prominent broadcast journalists.

One night a colleague called. George Schultz, the former secretary of state, was giving a speech. There was going to be a private reception after. "Would you like to come?" he asked.

"Sure!" I said and went to my closet, thinking about what to wear. I pulled out a floral-print silk blouse and scanned the suits I had for a good match.

He rattled off the names of other guests: members of Congress, senators, foreign-policy wonks. I reached down to the floor of the closet. There were several pairs of high heels: blue, beige, black, all to match different outfits. I picked up a pair of studded suede heels. A lump formed in my throat—I didn't *really* feel like going. The reception didn't hold the allure that it would have in the past.

"You know, I think I'll pass," I muttered, looking at the shoes like they were foreign objects.

"Are you nuts? Do you have any idea how many other people would kill for this?"

When we finished talking, I lay down on my bed. My dog, Skippy, jumped up. I stroked his back. He nestled into my side and rested his head on my chest.

I kept up work, but I was plagued by the bouts of numbness in my arms. And the voice. And death. And the ocean I loved, which nearly dished me up as chum.

I was thirty-six years old. Dozens of radio interviews had been scheduled before the accident. Radio stations piped me in from home by telephone. The gloves had come off in the last stretch of the 1996 presidential election. Bill Clinton, Bob Dole, and Ross Perot were slugging it out. Politics fascinated me, but there was no soul in it for me anymore. One day I was on the radio with another political commentator, and in the midst of the banter, I thought, "What is this? Is this my life?"

A few weeks later I was setting up a telephone plan with AT&T, and the saleswoman chirped, "With this plan you'll get bonus minutes!" It was too funny. She'd nailed it. My life: *bonus minutes.*

We settled on the "small-business, preferred customer, premiere premium plan," with five hundred bonus minutes per month.

"Can I do anything else for you?" the saleswoman asked.

"Oh, no, thank you," I said. "You have no idea how helpful you've been."

The orthopedist proffered one boorish nugget of advice. "Try anything but me—physical therapy, yoga … hell, even crystals, for all I care," he said sarcastically. "Anything but my knife." I did yoga. Between that and chiropractic care, the bouts of numbness became fewer. And a parallel thaw occurred—a deepening. Yoga felt like a place I could go where, in the silence of movement and breath, I could settle into the mystery of just being alive.

I puzzled over the voice I'd heard during the accident, but the metaphysics made me queasy. So I let it rest as it was, with all its incumbent meaning. I told myself a voice was a voice, whether it was the last synaptic gasp of what oxygen remained in my brain or whether it came from an unknown world beyond my comprehension.

About six months after the accident, I drove out to the coast with Skippy. On the way out I stopped several times and got out of the car to stretch my back and ease the pain. It was the first time I'd been back to the ocean.

The horizon was a steely gray-blue. The wind was so strong it swept up the sand. A little over a mile down the beach was the spot where I'd been in the kayak accident. When I dipped my bare feet in the ocean, a shiver of fear rippled through my spine.

A few weeks before, a tsunami had hit the coast of Peru. The radio waves were filled with cautions about how tsunamis can hit with unexpected force, that water weighs sixty-four pounds per cubic foot and a tsunami, clocking in at 450 miles per hour, can crush a village in a blink of an eye.

Skippy plunked his ball down and barked, waiting for me to throw it. I scooped the ball up with a squash racket and hit it again. He tore after it.

Had I been viewing the sea through rose-tinted glasses? For years the water had been my happy hobby. Whenever I had free time, I found something to do with water: swimming, sailing, paddling, or walking the beach. When I learned to scuba dive, I finally felt fully transported into the world of the sea. I felt that the ocean put me in touch with some important essence. But now Mother Nature, or Mother Ocean, didn't feel so motherly anymore.

Skippy raced back with the ball and skidded to a halt. I hit the ball again.

What had ocean been about? Peace, connection, joy, wonder. And now? Fear, suffocation, death.

I knelt down, scooped up a bit of wet sand, and felt its grainy, water-saturated weight in my palms. Skippy's paws sounded against the sand. He pushed the ball, dripping with salt water and dog drool, into my chest, as if to share it with me.

"Okay," I said to myself. "I need to get back into the water."

A year later, I began training to become a divemaster. Don't think for a minute that I brushed aside my fear with understated bravado. It was more like Lucille Ball trying to learn synchronized swimming. I frantically fidgeted with my gear, lest one piece fail and strand me underwater with no air.

But getting into the water day after day, I started to feel the tightly wound fear begin to ease. And because I was weightless in the water, diving was one of the few things I could do with an injured back. I was still in a lot of pain, but swimming underwater seemed to help.

We did drills in pairs. Step-by-step, we took off fins, masks, buoyancy compensators, and exchanged them while passing one air supply back and forth. Throughout, one of us greedily drew a big breath from the regulator while the other blew a fine stream of bubbles, waiting to receive the air supply again—dress rehearsals for deeper acts of trust.

During rescue exercises, we practiced mouth-to-mouth resuscitation in the water. One of us would mimic a panicked diver so hysterical with fear that he or she would try to drown the rescuer. The last resort in trying to assist people like this was to bring them to the surface, inflate their vest, flip them on their back, stay out of reach of their flailing limbs, and wait for them to collapse in exhaustion so they could be towed in.

It was my first taste of the gallows humor of those who actually do rescue operations—paramedics, Coast Guard rescue swimmers, firefighters. We teased and joked as we worked through the exercises in which one of us feigned death, unconsciousness, or inhaling water. This was my first exposure to the understated courage of those who perform rescues. They do everything that they can, often risking their own lives, and then they have to let go. It's not just that they risk death; they also risk failure. Some of their days are bathed in the light of saved lives, others not. They have the courage to live with that.

Later that year, off the coast, we watched two rescue swimmers haul what looked like a corpse on board a boat, slice the wet suit open with the speedy precision of surgeons, and start two-person CPR. For twenty or so minutes they continued, shouting out the beats. We looked on in shock as it dawned on us that they were having no success.

They kept going in what seemed like an irrational, trance-like fervor. One onlooker's face turned ash-white. Another blurted out, "This isn't happening," went to the opposite end of the boat, and looked away. I remember thinking, *Maybe it's time to let it go.* Suddenly their patient lurched, threw up, and murmured a few garbled words. He recovered completely.

It was as if I'd gone all my life without a glass of milk. And then downed one big glass and realized, "This is the milk of life!" That milk was courage and love and a spit-in-the-eye-of-fate tenacity.

I dove the kelp forests off Catalina Island. Swaths of sunlight poured down through hundred-foot-tall wavy kelp. Orange, chubby-cheeked Garibaldi fish eyed us. Harbor seals swished by.

Have you ever had a moment when you recognized something about yourself that was painfully obvious, but it had taken you almost forever to get it? That's how it felt. I'd perpetually put aside how much I adored the undersea world. It'd been some on-again, off-again affair, soulful and rich, but relegated to the leisure compartment of my life. But not this time. I wasn't going to shove it aside anymore. "I am where I belong." That's how it felt when I was underwater.

That summer I met a man while riding my bike along a canyon road in the Berkeley hills. I would drive my car to the top of the hills and park, since I was still too weak to ride up a long, steep hill. In the canyon there was a nice ride that was less hilly.

The man had stripped all the paint off his home, a small clapboard house with green shutters nestled in a shady grove of redwood trees. He'd hung wildflowers upside down in his garage to dry so he could collect the seed. In the kitchen a marble rolling pin rested on a wooden cutting board. He'd baked cobbler with wild blackberries he'd picked in the canyon. He had a thick shock of jet-black hair and steel-blue eyes. He was so disarmingly sincere it was disorienting. My cleated cycling shoes wobbled awkwardly on the smooth kitchen floor.

Charlie is as true blue now as that first day I met him. When we got married, I wore a traditional gown with a veil and carried a homemade bouquet of bachelor's buttons and Queen Anne's lace down the aisle. We were madly in love. I felt wildly alive.

But in the midst of that, my health was in a slow decline. It had been five years since the accident. I suffered frequent bouts of dehydration and heat stroke. I was diagnosed with a rare form of diabetes and was unable to retain water properly. I came down with bronchial infections frequently. I wore running shoes under my wedding dress because of hip and leg pain from the back injury. The bouts of numbness in my hands lingered stubbornly. We arranged to kneel during part of the ceremony because it was too painful for me to stand more than several minutes.

I was scared my health would get even worse. But Charlie would often say what he'd told me when we first met and I described the kayak accident. He ran marathons and loved the fable of the tortoise and hare. He told me that, even if you've slipped behind like the tortoise, keep telling yourself, "There's still a lot of race left."

I let that empty space I felt after the accident stay open and searched for a new direction with my work. I worked as a free-lance editor, wrote poetry, drafted ideas for children's books. I found a chiropractor who practiced cranial-sacral therapy and the hip and leg pain began to heal. But my overall health continued to get worse. I was getting weaker and weaker. I felt like the walking wounded, marching from one endocrinologist to another.

One day my good friend Barb said to me, "Maybe you have Hashimoto's disease." She'd suffered from a respiratory illness. An engineer by training, she'd started reading about her condition and knew how hard it could be to get a correct diagnosis. "The symptoms are so wide-ranging," she said, "it can be confused for other things."

I found a thyroid specialist, and it turned out I didn't have diabetes, but Hashimoto's disease, a type of hypothyroidism in which your immune system attacks the thyroid gland at the base of your neck. Some people who suffer from it take thyroid supplements and barely have any problems. Others struggle all their lives with fatigue, joint pain, sensitivity to cold or heat, and vulnerability to infections. I was mired in that second group. The thyroid medication helped and I stopped getting so dehydrated, but the other symptoms continued to plague me. The cold Northern California waters were too much of a shock to dive in anymore. When we traveled somewhere warm and I dove, I almost always got ill, a viral infection or bronchitis or some intestinal bug.

I was tired all the time, achy and weak. In the middle of the night I'd often wake with a wheezing, dry cough. I felt like an ailing mountaineer who longed for the Himalayas. And my mountains were the undersea world. But one thing about illness, it gives you time to think. It makes space for the gnawing, indeterminate hungers in one's heart. And one had been in my heart for many years—longing for the ocean. But I'd never asked, "What does it mean to me? To others? *Why is it so important?*"

So I decided to have one more go at getting back into the undersea world. I thought about going back to the place where I'd fallen in love with the undersea world, the Turks and Caicos Islands. "Maybe go there, quietly ..." I thought, "and just get in the water." And bring a notebook. Write. Ask, "What is it with water?"

"You're stronger than you let on," Charlie said when I told him what I wanted to do. We decided I'd go alone, take time to write in solitude.

My doctor wrote prescriptions for everything from pneumonia to cholera. It had been twelve years since the accident. I was forty-eight years old. My dive equipment was old, but I didn't replace it. If I got really sick again, I was going to hang it up. I stuffed the frayed, salt-worn gear into my bag.

PART I

The Turks and Caicos Islands

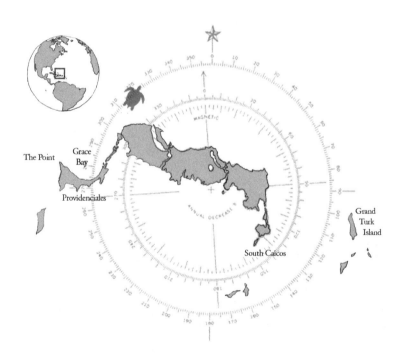

I

Beauty

The Turks and Caicos Islands are a tiny crescent of islands just north of Haiti and the Dominican Republic. As the plane descended, the sea turned a dark violet-blue at a spot where the island of Providenciales meets the Atlantic trench, which plunges seven thousand feet. On the opposite side of the islands were sand flats so turquoise green I kept taking my sunglasses off to check if the color had been doctored by the tint of my lenses. But the colors were just as vibrant to the naked eye—swirls of green and blue and turquoise intermixing with chalky sand.

As I walked down the stairs of the plane, I delighted in the warm blast of silky, moist wind. In customs, I chatted with an elderly woman who lived on the islands.

"Lived here long?" I asked.

"Thirty years," she said with a British accent.

"Changed much?"

"Yes," she said, a ripple of sadness in her voice. "The developers are destroying it." With that, she bolted off to get her passport stamped.

The cab ride from the airport revealed a new four-lane highway. The last time I had visited, over a decade before, there had been only narrow roads, most of them unpaved, weaving through miles of jungle. Slick high-rises had sprouted up, their ultramodern facades a surreal disjuncture from the jungle. Across from a luxury mega-resort with a guarded gatehouse were stalled building projects with rusted rebar gaping from cinder blocks and vacant lots littered with garbage.

We drove slowly through a cut in the road that revealed

stone with thin layers like baklava—eolian limestone. Named after Aeolus, the Greek god of the winds, *eolian* refers to the wind's ability to shape the earth through erosion. Limestone is formed from calcium carbonate, most often from the skeletal fragments of marine organisms such as coral, mixed with sand and compressed over millions of years.

The earliest inhabitants of the islands, the Taíno Indians, migrated from South America around 750 AD. They were seafaring people—hunter-gatherers and fishermen. Few of these indigenous settlers survived the brutal Spanish massacres and enslavement. Most of the people who now call the islands home are the descendants of slaves and call themselves "Belongers." Along with them are many Haitians and immigrants from other countries who came there searching for work.

The local economy evolved from the slave trade to the salt trade and fisheries, peppered with drug trafficking and offshore banking. Tourism boomed during the 1990s, with the building of large-scale resorts populated by thousands of cocktail-sipping guests. Indeed, I had first come as one of those rum-sipping tourists in search of refuge from an over-compartmentalized life.

I settled into a small resort on Grace Bay, a quiet cluster of low-lying buildings. That afternoon I fell into soft sleep, the warm, sweet, and humid air wafting in through the windows. Mixed with the wind coming off the ocean, it seemed to soften one's edges and render one's body more porous, open.

❧

The next day, our boat motored to the Northwest Point—nicknamed "the Point"—where the violet blue of the Atlantic trench almost touches the island. The number of buildings slowly thinned until there was practically no sign of civilization, and the shoreline was just a narrow slice of green jungle. A tern hovered above the bow. A school of flying fish darted across the water's surface.

My dive buddy that day was a woman from Paris. She explained to me in broken English that she would need a few moments in the water to get used to her gear, as she had not been diving for several months. "I will need the moment," she said, "to recover my sensations."

I smiled. Who could have said it better?

After jumping in the water and finding our equilibrium as "weightless aquatic mammals," we swam to what was called the "wall," where the reef descended to the continental shelf. Then, with a long outbreath, we sank in silence into that luminous, deep blue.

Once we were a hundred or so feet deep, something changed, as if we'd let go of terra firma and its last vestigial remnant, the water's surface, and abandoned ourselves to the open, watery realm. Its sensations were at once foreign and yet hauntingly familiar; it seemed to wake profound, archaic memories.

We descended through a narrow, vertical corridor of coral like the fluted vault of a cathedral. It was filled with thousands of tiny silvery fish—silversides. The beauty was overwhelming. For a moment, my body felt like a tuning fork; the beauty was so resonant that it reverberated through my breath and bones.

As we descended, the life of the reef changed every ten feet or so, the shape of the coral becoming wider until, at close to 130 feet, they were wide platters, expanding to collect as much light as possible, like solar panels, in the darkening depths.

To the east, the ocean went on for thousands of miles—next stop, North Africa. Just the open sea and the life for which it was home. We hovered weightless over a large knob of plate coral. Below us were thousands of feet of water. The reef wall receded with undulating arcs that reminded me of pen-and-ink Chinese landscapes in which mountains fade in successive layers into almost infinite distances. With each curve, the coral wall became more opaque, but seemed to go on forever.

A small dot appeared in the blue depths to the east. It got larger. It had fins, thick ones. Now I saw a roundish head and wide paddle-shaped front fins propelling an oval shell with the grace of a long-distance swimmer. It was nearly two yards long, with a short, stubby tail—a female green sea turtle. Migrating thousands of miles, they always return to the beach where they were born to lay their eggs.

We followed her up to shallower waters and lingered at about sixty feet as she slowly ascended to the surface to take a breath, her body a silhouette in the bright blue waters.

Each coral head was covered with clusters of fish nibbling and chasing and darting in and out of intricate tunnels and archways. A mosaic of shapes flashed in the distance. It was a school of horse-eye jacks. As we got closer, they did look horse-eyed, their eyes bulging out of their silvery bodies. Every few minutes the school would quiver and reorchestrate itself into a new shimmering shape.

The beauty of the undersea world was not just the beauty of *seeing,* it was also *being seen.* Hovering in the midst of the jacks, with their alert but calm gazes, I sensed them allowing me to *just be* in their midst.

There were damselfish and grunts and snapper. Gobies. Octopuses. Angelfish. Trunkfish. Pufferfish. Butterflyfish. Trumpetfish. There was no way to grasp it all.

At the end of our dive, we ascended slowly to about fifteen feet and floated peacefully near the boat. We would stay there for a little over three minutes, doing what's called a "safety stop." A grouper with puffy cheeks and bulging round eyes hovered beneath the boat. The water was dotted with hundreds of yellow grunts. My whole body was smiling. Diving opened up so many unexpected worlds for me, not just the ocean, but also my own body and how my breath was connected to the world as a whole.

The technical details of the safety stop are like "Breath 101: What Does Air Do When It Goes inside Your Body?" First stop: lungs. Then bloodstream. Then everywhere: brain, eyes, hands, legs. Your blood is primed with the air you breathe.

The safety stop is sometimes called a "papal decree" because of its importance. The deeper you dive, the more the water pressure compresses the air you breathe, which means that each lungful contains more air than you'd breathe at the surface. Since air is 78 percent nitrogen and 21 percent oxygen, each breath at depth contains not only more oxygen but also more nitrogen. Excess nitrogen in your blood can cause the dreaded bends—decompression sickness—which can result in paralysis.

You can get decompression sickness if you ascend too quickly without letting the nitrogen evaporate from your blood stream and tissues slowly. So as an extra precaution, at fifteen feet—where the water pressure is less, but not completely gone—divers stop and hover for three minutes to give the nitrogen in their blood time to off-gas further through their breathing.

If you dive a depth and time that is within "no-decompression" limits, the stop is done as a precaution; it is not mandatory. Most people dive with a computer, and when you get to fifteen feet, the computer bleeps at you and displays "three minutes." Then it counts down the time like a kitchen timer.

Technical stuff aside, the safety stop has always been like a bridge between worlds for me. The first time I surfaced after a dive I was flabbergasted by the simplest thing: there was air everywhere, not just in my tank! In the past, I'd carried around this assumption that the atmosphere was an infinite blank space. The revised view? A thin glaze of life-supporting gases around the earth that makes life possible. Oh, and it's in my bloodstream. So "honor thy safety stop" is a decree for divers, but the sensations riveted me—hovering weightlessly, feeling each breath fill my lungs, knowing there are chemical processes enacted in my body in each moment that allow me to stay in what was, ever since the kayak accident, the "land of the living."

⚬～

I dove for five days. My medical kit remained untouched—no infections or flu or heat stroke. I had braced myself for getting ill. Maybe, I mused, there was still a chance to get healthier? I still felt weak, was careful about what I ate, and turned in early. But I was healthy enough. And good enough was great.

Each night I hungered to get back into the reef, its vast spaciousness, that everything-is-alive feel of it. Drifting off to sleep, the ocean rivered in my veins. At sunrise it pulsed through my body like a soft, almost inaudible drum. I'd roll over, thinking of the first shafts of light hitting the salt flats. I felt steeped in some beautiful, uncharted mystery.

On the last day I sat at the bow of the boat and chatted with a retired pilot from Chicago.

"Beautiful out there, isn't it?" I said.

"Yeah."

"But I noticed, there's not many grouper. Last time I was here, there were tons of them, and big!" I remembered a grouper that was almost a yard long, so placid that I was able to stroke its fins.

"Well, the fishermen, they know where they gather to spawn," he said, "and there's like hundreds, even thousands of them all in one spot, and then they fish the hell out of 'em."

We paused and looked out at the ocean.

"It will all go to hell soon," he sighed.

"You think so? Don't think we can preserve it?"

"Nope," he said, "overdevelopment, overpopulation, even if we could turn them around, by time we did, it'd be too late."

He'd been diving all over the world, in Thailand, the Maldives, the Seychelles. He told me how many places had been gutted by dynamite fishing and coral bleaching.

"But the sea here," he mused, "it's like a little pristine pocket of life that's survived." He waved his arms. "I mean to the north, in the Bahamas, and to the south, in the Dominican Republic, the reefs are thrashed."

"Don't think there's anything we can do?"

"Phewssh! It's a goner."

"I try to take my pessimism with a grain of salt."

"Sure, but you need to be pragmatic. Might as well enjoy it while you can."

That afternoon I went to my room to take a nap. As I turned the key to open the door, his words were stuck in my head like a car in neutral with the engine revving, "You need to be pragmatic." *Pragmatic? What does that mean?*

I went into the bathroom to take out my contacts lenses. *Man, had that guy got on my nerves!*

I looked in the mirror. *Maybe it isn't him that gets my goat, maybe it's me! What will I do?* Just enjoy the beauty of the sea, consume it like the last few truffles in a box, leaving it empty for the next generation?

One of the most insidious wolves in sheep's clothing is pessimism disguised as pragmatism. When Barack Obama declared his candidacy for president, I thought, "Not a chance in hell." Mind you, I considered myself savvy about presidential politics. And I loved Obama, preferred him. But I voted against him in the California primary because I didn't think he had a chance. I voted for Hillary Clinton, telling myself it was a pragmatic, safe bet. Boy, was I wrong.

I walked the beach for the last time that night, lingering to enjoy that last bit of the warm sea wind and the silky air on my skin. I fell asleep savoring the ocean currents still flowing in my body.

As I watched the islands disappear the next day, I touched one hand against the airplane window. Then the swirls of blue-and-green ocean vanished. We flew along the Atlantic seaboard, northward to John F. Kennedy Airport in New York. The brilliant light of the sea faded to a muted green, and then as we approached Long Island, the sea turned a steely gray, edged by a landscape of geometric concrete boxes. I imagined for a moment what Manhattan Island must have looked like five hundred years before. I remembered growing up along the Hudson River in New York, how we wouldn't dare dip a toe in that river, so rife it was with cancer-causing PCBs in the 1970s.[1]

I cleared customs and found the departure gate for my flight home to San Francisco. Then I did something I'd never done—not about the natural world, anyway—I found a place near a window away from other people and wept. For a long, long time.

In retrospect, it was high time I did. But at the time I wondered if I was being foolish and overemotional. I told my soggy, weeping self, who had already reduced several tissues to shreds, "You'll go back!" But the howling from my insides blurted out, "Go back? Going back is the problem!"

Go back, experience the beauty, and then leave again? Throw up my hands and say that there was nothing I could do to save the place? I didn't want to go back and feel that anguish again. Even if I went and stayed longer, I'd still feel the pain. I could see it in the faces of some of the islanders, their sadness at what development had done to the islands. Their dread of the future.

It wasn't about pain; it wasn't about pleasure. It was about beauty. I didn't give a damn how much anguish I felt. And screw pleasure; it's overrated. But *beauty*—the beauty of the coral reefs, their wild aliveness, intense abundance of life, that was something I wanted to know better, to become well acquainted with. Something was amiss in the world and something about that beauty felt terribly important—that "everything is alive" feeling.

Okay. The anguish is a given, I thought. *Now what?* I had two choices. Behind door Number One: never go back, spare yourself the difficult transition, re-acclimatize to the vicissitudes of civilization. My hunger for that wild beauty and my angst over its plight would shrink to a subterranean ache, a kind of acculturated Novocain of the soul.

Oh, forget that! That'll never work! That mysterious, sensate beauty I'd felt in the ocean, it would just keep turning back toward me, keep singing in my sleep.

So it would be door Number Two: I could go back, but not without working to preserve it. I had no idea what I would do. But it was clear that I had to do something. It was the only way I could know the beauty of the life of the seas. They had become a loved one, and if I abandoned them, what would their beauty or my love for them mean?

At the gate for my flight, there were loudspeaker calls and a baby's guttural cry. I stood in line like a stunned animal: my soul had been turned inside out.

"Your boarding pass, please?"

"Huh?"

The flight attendant snatched the boarding pass from the passport keeper around my neck and slipped it into its slot. It whizzed out with a thwap. I put it between my teeth while I tucked my passport away and walked down the ramp to my plane home.

2

A Body within a Body

Six months later I flew back to the islands. My bags were heavier. I planned to spend some time writing and painting. Along with scuba gear, I'd brought an underwater camera, a stack of fish identification books, and watercolors and brushes. Could I put the tools of my trade to use in service of ocean conservation? It felt like an elusive trajectory. I didn't know where exactly I was going with it. I just knew that I needed to do this. I needed to go and be in these waters and write. I'd never done anything like it before. I wanted to write—about the ocean and what felt like its elusive mystery—but I felt like I was slipping off the grid into wordlessness.

I take that back—I actually did know where I was going. It was just that it didn't fit with my typical brass-tacked Prussian-general style of marching toward a goal with strategic precision. Instead I was going … underwater, returning to a beauty that was so miraculous that I couldn't walk away from it. I didn't want to document it or even describe it, I wanted to *listen to it*. Perhaps I could be a translator of sorts—its truths could pour through me.

But about a month before, something happened that was a blunt-edged quickening—the Deepwater Horizon oil rig had exploded in the Gulf of Mexico, killing eleven people and injuring sixteen others. A cloud of soot and flames dwarfed the firefighting vessels.

Forty-two days into the oil spill, I arrived in the islands. I knew it was forty-two days, because everyone was counting. Public sentiment vacillated between hope and disappointment over and over again as each new attempt to halt the spill was formulated and then failed. People who didn't normally care much about marine conservation were anxious and even outraged at British Petroleum's blithe understatement of the scope of the crisis and their thinly veiled assurances that things would be under control soon. The public knew it was terribly out of control and had the potential to become what it did: the largest oil spill in history.

Over two hundred million gallons of oil would pour out into the Gulf, eighteen times greater than the *Exxon Valdez* spill. The economic fallout of the "black tide" would be staggering. Hundreds of thousands of people made their living from seafood on the Gulf Coast. Thirty-six percent of the federal fisheries in the Gulf of Mexico would eventually be closed, over eighty-six thousand square miles of ocean, an area the size of Minnesota. Tourism plummeted; tax revenues sank. Suddenly an issue that was normally peripheral to politics was front row and center: water was important.

As the plane flew south, my eyes went back and forth between a newspaper and the blue-green swirls of water and lace-like strips of land that formed the Bahamian archipelago. The newspaper had photos from the oil spill that were so disheartening that I had almost put the newspaper in a trash can in Miami.

I turned the pages slowly and allowed the images to reach out to me: a sea bird mired in oil, its beak and eyes barely visible; a dead sea turtle suffocated in a wetland blackened by oil; the hands of a Louisiana coastal zone director, holding up a handful of oil that dripped in long elastic strands. The oil was as thick as rubber cement.

A flight attendant swished by, grabbing the last cups before landing. The plane made a gentle arc over the islands, which sparkled like silvery-green sardines in the turquoise sea. Just before the plane touched down in Providenciales, a flock of birds took flight over Chalk Sound. The water glistened through the flutter of their wings. I sighed. I was so happy to be back. It felt like I was breaking a fast.

But I did not go back to Grace Bay. Instead, I rolled my gear to the other side of the airport, where there was a kiosk and a twelve-seat propeller airplane. I asked the flight attendant if I could keep my knapsack with my camera in the cabin. "Not a problem, madam," she said politely. I was the only foreigner on the plane. Local Belongers held paper bags bulging with groceries on their laps.

If an airplane flight could be the physical embodiment of a haiku, this one was it: lyrical, terse, profound. We flew low over green-blue seas for twenty minutes. The plane was a loud, rattling, metal bird, its path punctuated by pelicans and flamingos. The sea had a chalky, rich density that made it seem like some primordial brine of life.

I had contacted the School for Field Studies, which had a field station in South Caicos, an 8.5-square-mile punctuation point of an island. There were no resorts there, but real-estate developers were knee-deep in political and financial machinations to get in there. Conservationists were scrambling to implement a sustainable development plan. Just over a thousand Belongers lived on South Caicos, which at one time was a major producer of salt. Now most of the Belongers worked as fishermen or at a conch-and-lobster processing plant.

I was met at the airport by a woman in her twenties. Lizzie had just started as an intern at the field station. "I'm new, so I'm assigned to take care of you," she teased.

She peppered me with details along the way, weaving the car between wild horses on the road. "Queen Elizabeth brought the horses with her and left them when she went home." We rolled by a dingy bar. "Only place on the island you can get a cold beer." The ocean came into view. "That's the cut between South Caicos and Grand Turk Island. The whales come through there in March—they sing." Then Lizzie explained, "Whenever anyone says what time something happens, remember to qualify that with an 'ish,' as in 'We shall dive at eight-ish' or 'We shall eat at six-ish.'" She enunciated the "ish" thickly. "And oh!"

she blurted out. "You've got to meet the Turtle Man! He's this guy—he came to work with the turtle fishers."

The field station was an old concrete building on a bluff above the water. It was originally a hotel, rumored to have been bought by drug lords, then confiscated, and then the School for Field Studies picked it up at a fire-sale price. It had a wide, open-aired patio that looked out on the ocean, a small library, and a few offices. It had been retrofitted to minimize its footprint on the environment. The kitchen was meticulously clean. Meal scraps were composted; dishes were washed by rinsing them with seawater, dipping them in a bleach-and-water solution, and then rinsing them with fresh water. There were no plastic cups or paper towels. Fresh water, made by desalinization, was used sparingly, so a bath was a dip in the ocean with some biodegradable soap.

It was hot and humid. Lizzie took me inside the cooler to show me where the food was. "If you get really hot and need a break, you can come in here and cool off. And …" Lizzie spaced her words with dramatic flourish and opened the freezer, "the best treat is a frozen chocolate-chip cookie." We each had one raw restaurant-supply slice of frozen cookie dough. It was delicious. Context is everything.

Lizzie introduced me to some of the staff—the program director and Eva, one of the professors. The school offered semester-long courses for college students who wanted field experience. They were between semesters, prepping for the next wave of students.

After dinner, Lizzie flipped open her laptop out on the patio.

"If you want to be a fish dork," she said, "you spend your evenings looking at *ichthyology sites*."

I stared at her blankly.

"Ichthyology is the study of fish." She showed me databases like fishbase.org and sealifebase.org, which offered scientific catalogs of fish.

"So Lizzie," I asked, "what are those funny little black-and-white fish?"

"Little black-and-white fish?" She had a degree in marine biology, so she was well schooled in that habit of mind that kicks in when a scientist sees a new fish. Is it oval, oblong? Flat, round? Any distinctive markings?

"The ones like snow."

"Snow?" Lizzie gave me a look like: *is that the best you've got for me?*

I had a lot to learn. I explained being mesmerized by small blizzards of black-and-white fish. Lizzie pulled up a picture of a Princess parrotfish with cyan-blue scales and streaks of yellow and magenta. "A fish that's post-larval," Lizzie said, "is basically a baby fish or one that's not yet an adult. A juvenile." She pulled up another picture—a group of tiny black-and-white striped fish. These were post-larval Princess parrotfish, my "snow."

It was June, and the light lingered late into the evening. As soon as it was dark, the mosquitoes went on a rampage, so at last light we all turned in. My room had two large windows on either side, one overlooking the ocean. I draped a mosquito net in the bottom half of a wooden bunk bed and dozed off listening to the wind.

〜⌘

The next day we motored out to Long Cay. The outboard carved a path through radiant turquoise flats that stretched as far as we could see. Long Cay was a sliver of an island covered with mangroves. The staff wanted to do some surveys before bringing their students there.

As we geared up, I reached for my hood.

"What are you wearing that for?" Lizzie teased me.

"It keeps the hair out of my face."

Lizzie looked at Eva with a wink. Eva smiled. "Liz, this isn't Club Med." Lizzie showed me how she wrapped a bandana around her head to keep her hair back. "Don't worry, you'll get there. You'll be a fish dweeb by the time you leave."

We hopped into the water. "The mangroves," Eva explained, adjusting her snorkel, "are nurseries for juvenile fish. You might see some when you are snorkeling." I'd seen mangroves many times before and thought nothing of them; they seemed like scruffy bushes. But now I was primed to pay attention.

The roots of the mangroves arced above the water and then descended vertically. The reflections of their leaves flickered on the surface, casting a deep-green hue. I peered underwater into the labyrinthine root system: hundreds of baby fish hovered skittishly.

It was like a "fish kindergarten" or an incubator—the roots formed mazelike bassinets or cradles that protected the young fish from larger predators. Those miles of milky blue-green flats that the two-prop plane had flown over were dense with mangroves and seagrass, nurseries for millions of juvenile fish.

I stood up and pulled my mask off.

"Nice, huh?" said Lizzie. "The juveniles, they feed on plankton until they grow large enough to go out on the reef."

"And plankton are …?" I didn't really know what plankton was.

"Organisms that drift in the current. Some are microscopic, others are big, like jellyfish."

"What kind of fish?"

Lizzie smiled. The partial list: angelfish, grouper, grunts, snapper.

"Liz!" Eva called out. She was carefully holding a sea urchin in her hands. Its spines were sharp. "Just touch it very gently."

I felt one of the smooth spines quiver. Urchins have light-sensitive molecules in their spines, similar to the photoreceptors in our eyes. Researchers speculate that they may "see"—as in "detect shapes of light"—with the whole surface of their body.

On the way back from Long Cay, we snorkeled at an island called HDL just across from the field station. It was a striking outcropping of stone. It seemed a contradiction that such a beautiful island would be named HDL. But scientists do have very dry wits. Maybe HDL was named the way a ravishingly beautiful woman named Joanna might be nicknamed Joe.

HDL teemed with juvenile fish too. May and June were "juvenile season"—swarms of tiny fish filled the water. Sometimes adult fish would circle and nip each other and then leave behind a plume of eggs and sperm. After the eggs hatch, the new larvae then drift in the currents and find safe havens in the mangroves and the seagrass.

That night I cooked for Lizzie and the rest of the staff. And we baked the cookies. We turned in early. I zipped into my mosquito net and sighed. Alone now, I remembered the oil spill. The weight of it felt like the leaden shield a dentist drapes over you before an x-ray.

Back home, I'd been horrified by the disaster, but I'd compartmentalized it. I got on with my day. But there, poised at the edge of an immensely beautiful sea, so dense with life, it was impossible to pull the shades down. I imagined just the twenty square miles of ocean encircling South Caicos, the rich milky flats we flew over, the vibrant schools of fish, the dolphins, the turtles, all of that life—obliterated.

Just twenty square miles was horrific. What exponential quantity was now being devastated in the Gulf? As I lay there, I knew thousands upon thousands of creatures were dying. The final tally a year later would be grim. Over eight thousand birds, one thousand sea turtles, and six hundred dolphins and whales would be found dead or injured. And those were just the ones that washed up.

It was too warm to pull even a cotton sheet over me. I lay back and closed my eyes and felt the air river over my body. I dozed off to the sound of the wind. In the middle of the night the wind started to howl violently. A storm was about to hit. I almost got up to close the windows, but the wind blowing through was such a relief from the heat, I left them open. The air was deliciously cool.

My thoughts drifted to our fantail goldfish at home. Glasgow was bright orange and Ying-Mei white with orange markings and a delicate, swishy tail, as ethereal as a little wedding veil. I got them from a well-known goldfish keeper in San Francisco, Steve Jue. When I went to pick them up, he asked me to bring him a bottle of tap water.

"So what's with the water?" I asked.

Steve poured some of the water into a plastic tube. "You have to test the pH." He added a few drops of fluid with an eyedropper, capped the tube, and held it up to the light. The water turned yellow. "It's the acidity of your tap water. It's too high."

"So?"

"So … that will kill your fish. When a goldfish is sick, it's almost always the water that makes them sick." He plunked down a small bottle of powder that would stabilize the pH to 7.0, which was best for goldfish.

Ocean acidification is exactly that: all the carbon dioxide we've pumped into the atmosphere and that the ocean has absorbed is changing the acidity of the ocean, lowering the pH. Goldfish keepers have known for a long time how toxic that is. The goldfish will gasp at the surface; their eyes will bleed or bulge; their fins may become streaked with blood. Eventually they will die. Oyster farms in the Pacific Northwest were already smarting from its effects. Oyster larvae were stunted by the acidic waters.

"Keep your water healthy, and they'll do fine!" Steve called after me when I left with Glasgow and Ying-Mei in a plastic bag. That night I skimmed through goldfish care instructions with a furrowed brow. Preventative care was the trick—weekly water changes. Are your fish listless? Do their gills pump awkwardly? Emergency water change! It was as if the fish had two bodies, the fish body that stretched from tail to snout and the body of water that they lived in. Both needed to be healthy.

The storm hit. A blast of wind roared in off the open water, and the rain pelted down.

God, I feel like I'm on another planet.

The field station's generator was turned off at night, so there were no lights. It was pitch black. At the edge of the island we were in the thick of the roaring wind and rain and tides.

But maybe it's this—that I'm finally feeling this planet.

In the months before, I'd pored over books about the ocean. Over 70 percent of the planet's surface is covered by water; 96 percent of all the water on earth is in the oceans. The earth is essentially an aquarium-terrarium. And the health of the water is in decline. The cultural revelation was slow and painful. It is easy to understand a pond or a river being poisoned—like the pollutants in the Hudson of my childhood. But for many, the ocean seems too big to be polluted in the same way. But it's not, and just like goldfish, sea creatures need healthy water to survive. And there is no other planet we can race to with a siphon to perform an emergency water change.

The wind whipped up stronger, thrashing through coconut trees. I remembered a NASA visualization of the currents in the Atlantic, swirls of currents and micro-currents, seas and subseas, all intermixing—each body of water flowing into its neighbors. And in those seas? Countless whales and turtles and sharks and tuna, riding the currents—their "second body"—from the Azores and North Africa to the Caribbean and northward to Newfoundland.

My heart beat and my blood pulsed through my arms and hands. A fact was surfacing as a sensation: I too was a body within a body. And a body of water at that. Our blood is 92 percent water, our brain and muscles, 75 percent. And all that water moves and moves and moves—circulation. That night it was wildly tangible, as real as the zipper on my mosquito net, as the rain pelting down, as the salty wind blowing through like some long-forgotten memory of our origins.

Bright light woke me. No wind. Birds singing. There was HDL, the ravishing island with its understated name. The light was so bright that the limestone was a white silhouette against the cobalt sky and turquoise sea.

On my last day we motored to an underwater wall that edged a deep trench between South Caicos and Grand Turk Island. I brought my bandana, which by that time I'd figured out was also my tissue, towel, and napkin. I folded it, laid it on my forehead, and tied a knot at the back of my head to keep my hair back.

Lizzie and Eva watched this operation, then hooted and whistled. "Check it out! You's ready to go!"

I'd made another journey. It had been a big effort, I still felt weak at times, but I hadn't got sick. I wasn't sure exactly why—maybe the thyroid supplements were helping me heal or maybe I'd learned to manage my health better. But it was a huge deal. I felt something inside me like a knot starting to loosen.

We dove in. The trench was a vast violet-blue. It was where Lizzie had said you could hear the whales singing when they migrated to and from their breeding grounds just to the south, called the Silver Bank. I was reminded of the feeling I'd had the night of the rainstorm, my body, a body of water within the larger body of the world. It was a simple, straightforward synchrony.

I packed my bags that afternoon. I left first thing in the morning. I'd fly back to the main island, Providenciales, and then home. Hadn't met the Turtle Man, but what a trip. I scrubbed down the bathroom in my room, emptied the trash can. The field station had been organized in such a way that in a couple days I'd generated less than a fistful of garbage. I was embarrassed. I imagined how much I generated at home—paper towels, plastic baggies, twist ties, scrap paper. And where did all that stuff go? And how much was extracted from the earth and the seas to make it?

The oil spill said one thing to me: there have got to be better ways to do things. What if I lived as if I were indeed a body nested within the larger world? What if I kept that in mind as I moved through my day, the way a navigator keeps a compass close by? I'd recycle more. I'd save more water. I'd reuse plastic bags. What else would I do? How would it change things?

But I'd known all this before, didn't I? Why did it seem different now? Now I knew it in my bones and blood. My edges had been redefined.

3

Water Garden

"Just mow down the mangroves for the ministry!" Marsha said, mimicking an exaggerated southern drawl. It was blazing hot and humid. Marsha Pardee, a marine ecologist, zigzagged her truck around potholes on a dusty dirt road surrounded by jungle brush. I didn't mind it that much, because the previous day another resident had driven me around the island hitting the bumps at such a speed that the clips of the truck's battery cables kept flying off. Marsha's slow, whirligig modality meant that not once did we have to stop, pop the hood of a steaming hot engine, and reattach the cables.

It had been a year since I'd been here, and I'd started to write about ocean conservation. I was fascinated with the juvenile fish I saw in the mangroves in South Caicos. I tracked down Marsha, who had spearheaded several mangrove restoration projects. She was explaining to me that several years back the government invited Al Gore to host a climate-change conference, and while officials were having their photos taken with Gore, government cronies were selling off national park land to developers and keeping the cash.

One of these sales was to a Christian ministry that planned to bulldoze one hundred square acres of mangroves to create, of all things, a spiritual retreat. Thankfully, Marsha added, the cronies were stopped before the bulldozers arrived, and the only remnants of the construction were survey lines that cut through the mangroves.

Because mangroves are where millions of juvenile fish take shelter, they're key to healthy fisheries. They also protect islands from the large waves generated by hurricanes, tropical storms, and tsunamis. During the 2004 Indian Ocean tsunami, many people's lives were saved because mangroves acted as protective buffers. Mangroves also store fifty times more carbon in their soil per square meter than the same amount of Amazon forest, a potent counter to climate change. So rip those out so you can create a place to commune with God?

The road wove through jungle characteristic of the islands. One day I drove with the Department of the Environment's Bryan "Naqqi" Manco through miles of mangroves and jungle brush on one of the neighboring islands, Middle Caicos. Naqqi rattled off the names of plants as if they were beloved grandchildren: black torch, crab bush, gum elemi, locust. Some developers viewed all that open space as a blank canvas on which they could ink in cash-cow luxury homes. But it wasn't blank! It was busy: pumping out oxygen, sequestering carbon dioxide, and harboring juvenile fish.

Marsha, in her late forties, with dirty-blond hair pulled back in a ponytail, worked as an environmental consultant in the islands. In her free time, she spent hours on mangrove and coral-reef restoration projects.

"So where'd you grow up?" I asked.

"South Carolina. I preferred putting fish in formaldehyde to playing with Barbie dolls," Marsha said. "Hang around me long enough, I'll get you into the plant stuff."

"Oh no," I held up my hand as if to block any talk of plants, "You got to understand, my grandma was a horticulturist. So what was I supposed to do when I grew up?"

Marsha stiffed her arms on the steering wheel and chimed in with me as I said, "Be a horticulturist!"

"So you're saying," Marsha asked, "you want to stick with the fish?"

"Serious avoidance issues with the plant stuff. My grandma had a watering can in my hand by time I was three, like it was a Stradivarius," I said.

"But the juvenile fish, they hide in the seagrass too," Marsha said and raised her eyebrows, knowing it was the juvenile fish that yanked my chain. "Statistics vary, but over 50 percent of the oxygen in each breath we take comes from plants and algae in the ocean. Some scientists say it's over 70 percent."

"Okay, keep working on me," I said with a grin.

"Well, hell! Where did life come from?"

"The ocean …" I knew that much.

"A plant," Marsha continued, "is a *photosynthetic organism*. That's a category of organisms—plants, algae, cyanobacteria, other types of bacteria."

I had a feeling of a sudden rash coming on, that I might be trapped in the truck for hours sweating in the heat while Marsha dragged me into a vortex of scientific minutia.

But she got right to the point. If she'd talked fast enough, she could have fit it into a thirty-second sound bite: the first of these organisms, she explained, were some of our oldest ancestors, cyanobacteria. They were at the base of the Tree of Life.[2] Over two billion years ago they made a unique evolutionary leap—they took water and light and carbon dioxide and converted it to oxygen and carbohydrates: photosynthesis.

It triggered a rather large balloon party. All the trillions of "photosynthetic guests" pumped out oxygen. That gave our atmosphere just the right life-support mix: 21 percent oxygen. And just like a Super Bowl party, the carbohydrates were the other must-have staple; they became the foundation of all the food chains. Those two things—oxygen and carbohydrates—formed the biological basis of the life we see around us.

Need to breathe? Need to eat? Photosynthesis is at the core of filling those needs.

Photosynthesis happened first in the ocean and cannot happen anywhere still without one thing: *water*. Even today, more than half of all photosynthetic organisms live in the sea—microbes, algae, and plankton. Imagine life on earth sustained by a gigantic air cylinder. Who refills that tank for us? Plants, algae, plankton.

"But I can't even pronounce it," I teased.

"What?"

"I had lisp in second grade. Couldn't pronounce S and TH sounds."

"And …?" Marsha said keeping her eyes on the road.

"I got over it, but even now," I said, imitating a cartoon character's voice, "it's like photo-*fin-fee-sis*."

※

A few minutes later we pulled into a harbor in the Princess Alexandra National Park. We walked over to a white clapboard building, the office of an eco-tour company called Big Blue Unlimited. One of the staff sat in the gear room, hands covered with grease, working on a motor.

"What are you two lovely chickies up to?" he asked with a British accent, lathering the words out slowly, like frosting on a cake. We were sticky with sweat and toting a hodgepodge of gear bags, slates, and cameras. I had bright-white zinc oxide smeared on my lips and nose. A wet bandana was draped around my neck and dribbled onto my t-shirt. Dust and gravel from the road stuck to my neoprene booties like wet grout.

"Just a little ground-breaking science," Marsha said, "nothing too earth-shattering. Can we use some of your kayaks?"

"Be my guests, ladies," he said with a wink, his eyes settling back on the engine. It was my first experience of something I'd encounter over and over again around the world—people and businesses lending support for conservation work. In this case, Marsha was able to use the kayaks without paying a rental fee.

I adored the pace of the islands. Where I came from, everything was "Go! Go! Tick-tock, clock!" This place was "Hello … and what's happening today? Oh, hmm …. Yes, we'll be on our way. In a bit."

We pulled two kayaks and some paddles from a bin and glided into the cool air of the open water. The water was crystal clear. I could see tiny tufts of algae and seagrass, schools of minnows darting about. We paddled alongside Mangrove Cay, which was thick with full-grown mangroves. Schools of baby fish hovered between the vertical roots—schoolmaster fish, pufferfish, and snapper. Several young herons with long green legs were perched on the roots.

"See that?" Marsha pointed to a sandy shoal. "That's Star Island."

As we paddled toward it, Marsha explained its history. In 2008 someone noticed a dredging rig with a crane scooping up sand and dumping it in the center of the channel to form an island at the edge of the nature preserve. Remnants of pummeled coral heads washed up around the perimeter of the harbor along with hundreds of dead conch; loose sand from the dredging smothered neighboring seagrass beds.

"They wanted to build a Dubai-style artificial island," Marsha said, her eyebrows rising for a moment. "You know, multimillion dollar homes, a luxury hotel, a marina." The then-premier of the Turks and Caicos Islands, Michael Misick, who would later be brought up on corruption charges and eventually even have an Interpol warrant put out on him, had signed off on the project without any public notice or debate.[3]

Princess Alexandra National Park was a "paper park." It was a protected area, but *on paper*, because regulations were not enforced or observed. But many marine parks are properly protected. David Helvarg, in his book *The Golden Shore*, documents the efforts that created California's network of marine protected areas (MPAs), the most extensive in the United States—16 percent of California's coastal waters.[4]

So what makes an MPA successful? Enforcement and collaboration. The State of California encouraged collaboration among the Department of Fish and Wildlife wardens, rangers in adjacent parks, National Marine Sanctuary personnel, lifeguards, and local citizens—all of them getting the word out about the aquatic havens, tracking activities in them, and enforcing the rules. Monitoring has found bigger fish and more of them inside the MPAs compared with similar habitats that aren't protected. And in California's Channel Islands MPAs, scientists had found that marine life increased not only inside the MPAs, but in nearby waters.

But the marine preserves in the Turks and Caicos were mere paper parks. The islands were a British Overseas Territory and at the time Marsha and I met, Britain was yet again attempting to purge the leadership of corruption. Misick began his political career as chief minister in 2003 with around $50,000 in assets. A year before resigning office in 2009, his assets were posted as $180 million. Misick and other ministers had accrued that wealth by selling off parkland to developers,[5] things like the hundred-acre tract of land that was slated to become a Christian ministry retreat.

But the dredging equipment gouging millions of square feet of sand from the harbor was in an area frequented by local islanders, including a cadre of well-organized residents. A petition circulated quickly, and between numerous court orders and growing public outrage, the construction finally halted. But by that time there was a lifeless island of sand over three hundred yards in circumference, surrounded by rocks.

So now what? Marsha described to me how she often strolled the beach at night to clear her head and would bring home cigar-shaped mangrove seed pods and let them grow in a glass of water. For Christmas she'd give friends a mangrove sprig in a vase, her signature twist on the yuletide wreath. So she put together a plan to plant five hundred mangrove seedlings on the new island.

The process started with mangrove seeds sitting in plastic cups of water until they sprouted. Then they were transferred to a gutter-and-gravel system that Marsha invented, then into floating rafts in salt water, and then, finally, planted on the island. By time Marsha was done, she'd marshaled the help of almost a hundred volunteers and financial supporters.

We beached our kayaks on the low-lying expanse of sand that was Star Island. Marsha wanted to see how the mangroves were doing. "So here's how it works," she told me. "We'll go in opposite directions. And we'll count mangroves." She handed me a slate and a pencil. "Make three lists—the dark shriveled stems are dead; not shriveled, green to reddish, that can come back; and green with leaves, that's healthy!"

We parted ways. I walked slowly along the shore, making hash marks for each plant I saw in one of those three columns. I marveled at what I saw, mangroves in all stages of development. First, a rod pushing up through the sand, then perhaps some leaves, then a shoot going out horizontally that would arc down into the water, the beginning of that remarkable maze-like root armature.

As I walked, I was struck by the simplest thing—my hash marks were documenting healing. Yes, there were some losses, and some seedlings were ailing, but some were surviving. Not only had I been oblivious to how much destruction was occurring, I'd also been oblivious to the possibilities for healing, how much can be done. There on that artificial island created out of pillaged ocean, in the new roots pushing out leaves, I saw it for myself—hash marks on a slate for each instance of life's resurgence. Later that week, Eric Salamanca, a scientific officer from the Department of the Environment, would take me to another shoreline where they had successfully planted over one thousand mangroves. They were literally reforesting coastal marine habitats.

I'd always thought of gardening as a terrestrial thing—carrots, corn, zucchini. My grandma had a garden in New Hampshire that woodchucks would pillage. She'd wake in the morning and screech "*Entsetzlich!*" No need to translate the German, right? The number of scratchy sounds says it all. But should you be curious, the corresponding English adjectives are "abominable," "horrific," and "appalling."

One thing about my grandma. She was "of the moment." Seeds went back in the ground. "Begin again" was the name of the day. And she wasn't exactly the product of glib aphorisms.

Widowed in her thirties, she survived a battle with cancer and then fled Nazi Germany with her children, escaping shipment in the cattle cars to a concentration camp. What had been her home would vanish behind the Berlin Wall.

I remember, as a little girl, staying with my grandma in her two-hundred-year-old farmhouse during a hurricane. The old building creaked as if it were on the verge of collapse. Time after time, the storm ripped open the tall casement windows and drenched the floor. Each time, her rotund seventy-year-old figure would stand up slowly, waddle over with an awkward limp and close the windows. And she'd calmly mutter, "*Ja, ja,*" as if to say to God, "Yeah, yeah, buddy, I've just about had enough of your hubris tonight."

Begin again. That's what I was looking at in the mangrove seedlings pushing up toward the sun. A small army of kind hands had nurtured them to get this far along. I suddenly understood the ocean was a garden in need of tending, nurturing—a vast, critically important water garden.

The ocean—to most of us, myself included—seems so vast and invulnerable. But I was learning it was so much more vulnerable that it appeared. It was sinking in that humanity, having expanded its influence so immensely as to be able to screw up the state of the oceans, now must live up to the task of stewardship. We need to see our oceans as water gardens, in desperate need of care. They are not so infinite as to survive all the damage we have inflicted upon them. Would I take motor oil or untreated sewage or the contents of a garbage can— things like dental floss, plastic wrap, bottle caps—and heave it on our garden at home?

We met on the other side of the island and walked back to the kayaks. "Okay, so we had a little look," said Marsha with a blasé yawn. Marsha had a steadiness about her—she seemed to have learned to moderate the highs and lows of work, the successes so uplifting, but the disappointments searing.

That evening when we said goodbye, Marsha rattled off the names of a few books I should read.

"Stay in touch," I told her as we hugged goodbye.

"I'll get you into it."

"What?"

"Photo-*fin-fee-sis*!" Marsha grinned and drove off.

～

"You should meet John," Marsha said. "He's flying in later this week." It was a year later, and we were sipping wine with her partner, Richard, on the porch of their house, an octagonal building nested in jungle. There were no glass windows, just screens for bugs and shutters for storms. Even on a hot summer day, the breeze blew through and cooled the air.

I'd published my first article about ocean conservation and had decided to write a book that documented the state of the oceans. I was back to do more research.

"John's from the Reef Ball Foundation," Marsha continued. "He's coming to work on one of the reef restoration projects." Marsha explained how she and John and Richard would salvage coral damaged by storms or dredging or pollution and bring the coral to an underwater nursery area. They'd nurse them back to health and then transplant them to "reef balls," upside-down concrete planters with holes for the fish to swim through.

The coral grew on the exterior of the reef balls, and when fully propagated, you'd never know the reef balls were concrete. And the fish liked them; they peered out from the interior with a sense of well-being similar to what you'd see in a coral reef.

Marsha said that if a piece of coral is broken off and falls to the ocean floor and its polyps fill with sand, it will die. But it also has the ability to continue to grow if it can find healthy, open water. "You have to handle coral really carefully," she told me. "If you handle it too roughly, you can damage it." She used a topical antiseptic to keep it healthy when she took it out of the water, keeping it out of the water no more than five seconds. "Temperature is a big care thing too," she told me, "you can't move it from colder, deep water to warm water right away."

I'd thought of coral as some stony, inanimate thing. As Marsha spoke, it sank in that what I saw as coral was a colony of millions of vibrant animals. Not plants. Animals. Each has tentacles, a mouth, and a stomach; each spawns and propagates.

This is not always apparent, because most coral tentacles come out at night when they feed. They sense the full moon and sunset and emit a chemical that allows them to smell each other during spawning.[6] Their mouths release bundles of eggs and sperm that shimmer in the richly dark nighttime waters. They mate and propagate, growing in colonies that form the limestone reef armatures that are intrinsic to life of the seas.

It makes you wonder about so much of our behavior that we think of as uniquely human—the full moon and sunset being so deeply entwined with our ethos of romance. A month before, my husband and I had climbed to the top of a ridge near our home with our friends Claudia and Miller, who were celebrating their anniversary. We drank wine, nibbled on cheese, and watched the full moon rise. Did the high we felt transport us into the deeper reaches, the very chemistry of our being? Was it something we shared with other creatures?

◜⤨

I left Marsha's place early, eager to get to bed, looking forward to diving in the reef in the morning. Before I fell asleep, I lay on my back and marveled at how much stronger I felt. I was no longer constantly getting infections and viruses, nor falling prey to heat stroke. It felt almost miraculous, because I had been ill for so long. But it can take a number of years for someone with Hashimoto's not only to learn to live with it but also to get the right thyroid dosage and for his or her endocrine system to stabilize.

I still battled fatigue from Hashimoto's disease, but if I ate pretty well, exercised, and paced myself, I was okay. For years I wanted the disease to go away, to be cured and be like a normal person again—or more correctly, to be the person I was before the accident, who could jump on and off red-eye flights, eat poorly, overwork myself to no end, and function on five or six hours of sleep.

One of the big pieces for the new me was to get nine or ten hours of sleep, which made me feel better and less vulnerable to getting ill. I stopped trying to function on less sleep, despite my envy of folks who could stay up late and pop up like toast in the morning.

My back still hurt at times, but most of the time it didn't keep me from doing things. Sometimes upon waking a few fingers would be numb. It'd startle me, but then the numbness would fade. Overall, I'd healed enough to tip the scale from fragility back to resilience.

It had also dawned on me that doing work that I felt a deep passion for was good not only for my soul but also for my health. The maxim applied to me in spades: if you do what you love most, you'll be healthier.

I was excited to get into the water the next day. Before leaving California for this trip, my husband and I had watched a documentary about Ansel Adams that described how Yosemite had inspired him to become a photographer. He vacillated between being a pianist and a photographer early in his life, and his experiences in Yosemite were ultimately how he found his calling. The reefs in the Turks and Caicos—they were my Yosemite, they'd had a catalytic effect on me.

Dozing off that night, my mind wandered back to my conversation with Marsha. Perhaps the reason I felt such a kinship with the reef was because it consisted of colonies of thriving animals. I imagined the light streaming down through the cathedral–like caverns, the schools of fish. I slipped into soft sleep, flush with anticipation.

4

The Truths of the Islands

"Liz?" the divemaster said, reading from a clipboard.

"Here!" I called out. It was the next morning. The roll call, both before and after the dive, was a safety precaution.

I loved mornings on a dive boat: the clank of gear being attached to aluminum tanks, the bursts of air as regulators were tested. The boat chugged out into the calm, turquoise waters of Grace Bay to a site called Boneyard. Oh, I loved that place! A week before, the water had been so crystal clear that we could see the contours of the ocean floor from the boat. A Canadian woman leaned over, saw the clarity of the water, and crooned, "Oh! This is going to be good!"

She had the distinctive habit of climbing out of the water and, dripping wet on the ladder, shouting out "I just can't get enough of it down there!" The guys on the boat couldn't resist teasing her that she was talking about sex. But who could deny that there was a hefty dose of Eros in our relationship with the beauty below? We returned to it again and again, our longing for it never fully satisfied.

I sat on the upper deck and remembered this spot from the week before. It was a series of deep sand channels, densely populated with coral. The finger coral were shaped like protruding stubby thumbs, and the large staghorn coral like the antlers of a deer. Hence its name, Boneyard.

Each cluster of coral had between twenty and a hundred finger coral and staghorn coral colonies, densely packed together. It was sometimes hard to even see the coral, because the schools of yellow grunts were so thick. There were hundreds of parrotfish in all kinds of colors—maroon and turquoise with magenta and yellow and deep blue markings—as well as damselfish and hamlets and grouper and neon-yellow trumpetfish. Turtles. Spotted rays. Sharks. As we motored out, I remember thinking that the waters of Grace Bay and the Point were the most deeply alive place I ever experienced.

The boat slowed. One of the divemasters used a long pole to moor on to a buoy. "Okay kiddo, get in the water," the divemaster said as he spot-checked my gear. I put the heel of my hand to my mask to keep it in place and took one long step off the edge of the back of the boat and into that world I so deeply cherished.

I exhaled and sank softly into the water. I closed my eyes for a few seconds to just feel the water river along my body.

Jeez, it's warm.

I looked at my dive computer: 82 degrees Fahrenheit. I turned horizontal as I sank and looked down at the site, about forty feet below.

Where am I?

It was almost unrecognizable. The sand channels were there, but hardly a sign of life. Everywhere the coral was white and brown, with green-brown algae growing over it. There were a few small clusters of fish and an occasional lone fish, looking out of place. The coral had bleached.

I paused at a bed of staghorn coral. The week before, it had been filled with so many juvenile parrotfish and blue chromis that the water appeared to be filled with the "snow" I had described to Lizzie. Tiny brown-and-white damselfish and bright-yellow conies had cautiously peered out from the shelter of the staghorn coral's antler-like structure. Small multicolored fish had darted mischievously, sometimes chasing each other, or had nibbled on a piece of coral, nestled in the safety of its tight matrix.

Now it was barren and whitish-gray, save for one oval blue tang that nibbled on the algae overgrowth. The other divers and I searched fruitlessly for a spot that might not be so damaged.

As I moved my fins slowly through the water, it felt as if I swam through the ashen remnants of a bombed-out cathedral. Each spot I remembered being deeply alive and illuminated with life. The mosaic of color was gone, only a white-brown monotone structure remaining, covered with algae. What was once brilliant was now muted and withered; what had shimmered was now grayed out; iridescent, now bleak and barren.

How could this happen in less than a week's time?

The devastation was unmistakable. We swam through a landscape of millions upon millions of near-microscopic animals, ailing and dead, unable to support the multitude of life forms they once did. I paused at a yard-wide knob of brain coral. The week before, small black-and-white gobies had sped across its Aztec-like patterns. Next to it had been some bright magenta sea fans. A large school of yellow-and-silvery-white schoolmaster fish had hovered there.

The schoolmasters were gone. The sea fans were tattered, with a blackish overgrowth. Almost all of the brain coral was covered with algae. A small portion of the coral's zigzag structure was visible, but it was a dark brown and white.

A French physician watched as I took a photograph of the brain coral. He looked at me with moribund eyes and then slowly ran his index finger across his throat from ear to ear, mimicking the slice of a guillotine. I opened the palms of my hands as if to say, "I'm not sure."

Before getting back on the boat, I keep looking down to the reef. I still couldn't quite believe it. It was incomprehensible.

That night as I walked the beach, the surface of the water glowed, illumined by a thin slice of moon. Below the surface, I knew the reef was fighting a terminal illness.

I asked myself, "What don't I know? What do I need to know?" So vastly had my view of things changed in less than twenty-four hours. All the data I'd consumed over months of research fitted together with new vividness and urgency. You can learn the physiological effects of a heart attack, but it's just data. But if your father later has a heart attack, survives, and is battling heart disease, all of that information registers at a new level. Every detail is alive. That's how I felt about the reef.

Coral reefs were in terrible danger from anchoring damage, overfishing, divers kicking delicate coral heads that take years to regrow, and nutrient runoff—that miserable hodge-podge of sewage, fertilizers, and other chemicals that is pumped into rivers and oceans daily. Coral bleaching was a sign that the global skeleton-in-the-closet, which humanity seemed immobilized to take significant action on, was on the brink of showing the fury of destruction it was capable of: climate change.

Fisheries had been declining in the islands for decades. The curator of the National Environmental Centre, Lormeka Williams, had described how plummeting fish populations were proportional to the destruction of coral reefs, seagrass meadows, and mangroves. She'd told me how the smallest fish in a catch used to be a foot long, and as fish populations shrank, the smallest were bait-sized sprats.

Many individuals have told me that at some point, they had gotten to the point where they understood that the earth itself was ill, like an ailing body. And what ails it? What limits its ability to renew itself? Us. *Humankind.*

If you'd asked me the day before, "Do you understand this?" I would have said, "Of course I do!" But in no way did I get it the way I did after seeing that bleached coral, which went on for miles. Now it was visceral. It was a window on the destruction going on *all around the world.* How could we pollute so vast a body of water so badly that it would run awry like an ill-tended aquarium? Could human beings really do that? The answer I'd been steeped in with each fin-kick through the water that day was "Yes."

I skipped dinner, went to bed hungry. An empty growl in my stomach was better than trying to digest food. I wrote nothing that night. I dozed off to sleep, with my journal at my bedside, a pencil aligned along its spine, holding open two blank pages.

⟨≋⟩

John Walch arrived to work with Marsha on the coral transplants. A few days later, I went over with video footage I'd taken of the bleached coral. By that time I understood there had been a four-degree spike in the offshore water temperature, from 78 degrees up to 82 degrees Fahrenheit, in the week between my two dives at the Boneyard. There was bleaching now all over the bay. NOAA, the National Oceanic and Atmospheric Association, would declare that month—June of 2012—as having the all-time warmest surface temperatures (of both land and sea) recorded for June in the Northern hemisphere.[7]

John and Marsha explained that the temperature change wasn't the only culprit, just the straw that broke the camel's back. In addition to bleaching, the reef suffered from coral disease and algae overgrowth. The tattered and frayed sea fans and the withered brain coral suffered from that tongue-twisting phenomenon called "eutrophication"—the algae that's been feasting on sewage and fertilizers and other chemicals begins choking the coral. It had been having a degrading effect on the reef for decades, but with the temperature spike, it reached a tipping point and became widespread.

Reefs all over the world suffered from similar toxic combinations of nutrient runoff, sewage, and warming seas. A global study by the World Resources Institute concludes that it is a major threat to coral reefs, noting that "many countries with coral reefs have little to no sewage treatment; the Caribbean, Southeast Asia, and Pacific regions discharge an estimated 80 to 90% of their wastewater untreated."[8]

Bleaching happens when the coral, reacting to environmental stresses, expels beneficial algae, with which it has a symbiotic relationship. "The coral basically gets sick and throws up the algae," John said, "just like when a person is ill and expels the contents of his or her stomach." This type of algae is different from the type that feeds on nutrient runoff and damages coral. The coral gets its nourishment from this algae's ability to make energy from light, photosynthesis. And it gets its green and rose and yellow hues from the algae's color. When it expels the algae, it loses its color and turns white. It can survive for a while without the algae, but not too long, and not if coral disease and algae overgrowth become predominant.

When coral bleaches, the fish leave, looking for healthier terrain. How far they go or where, scientists don't really know. John explained that if the temperature change had happened more slowly, in weeks rather than two or three days, the coral might have tolerated it. "Corals and marine organisms have evolved in the most stable environment in the world. They have no built-in mechanisms for rapid change. They can take change, but if we go too fast, that's where the problem is." The four-degree spike in temperature in less than a week is what the coral couldn't tolerate.

Marsha cleared her throat. "Take a cockroach in my kitchen. It can go through fifteen different insecticides in a year and get used to them all. Coral can't; they don't have the ability to make that rapid a change."

"There's no silver bullet," John said. "Everyone wants a silver bullet." Ocean ecosystems are so interconnected; you can't just cordon off a portion and preserve it like a pickle in a jar. Saving coral reefs isn't just about saving coral reefs. Their decline is about the quality of our water and the air we breathe. The damage I saw was a sign of massive destruction around the globe that was devastating fisheries, creating extreme droughts and storms, and polluting our waterways. The silver bullet would have to be a multitude of bullets: stopping overfishing, instituting proper sewage treatment, and limiting nutrient runoff and carbon dioxide emissions.

In the Caribbean, scientists had documented an 80 percent loss of hard coral over the last three decades.[9] The problems are so massive and so in need of international coordination that paralysis is often the reaction. What's needed? A vast collectivity of changes, equivalent to the damage that we've been inflicting. The possibility of change is in proportion to how many of us are willing to act. Think of slavery several hundred years ago. How ubiquitous was that? End slavery? A four-thousand-year-old tradition that was the very fiber of the economy? An elite class's grip on power?

Change came about because many people protested and voted and signed petitions and lobbied decision makers. Not to mention the courageous and steadfast souls who refused to be muzzled, risked death and imprisonment, and became the voice of generations. "Change," the social-justice activist Tom Hayden wrote, "begins in the individual lives of countless people when they no longer accept existing conditions as inevitable."[10]

Some of the most important tasks for ocean conservation would be to convince decision makers to do something about climate change, overfishing, and water quality. Of course, that pressure is often rebuffed with, "Oh now, that's going to be really complicated! And the economic fallout would be devastating." Just like a slave owner thinking how complicated it would be to run a plantation without slave labor. Okay, it's complicated. But more complicated than arctic oil drilling or fracking or fishing boats that drag fifty-five-mile-long drift nets at sea?

But that night my head just plain hurt. I sloshed down some wine to dull the pain.

Marsha gave me a soft-eyed look. "You hungry?"

"Yeah …"

She quietly cooked up some sausage and made a salad. She'd known all this for years.

While we ate, their yellow lab stretched out on the kitchen floor. None of us knew that night how extensive the bleaching would be or if the coral would recover. When we said good-bye, Marsha hugged me with a tight squeeze.

✺

I finally met the Turtle Man. His name was Amdeep Sanghera, and he was the project officer from the Marine Conservation Society's Turks and Caicos Islands Turtle Project. Often when he'd phone a local fisherman in South Caicos and tell him his name, the fisherman would draw a blank and then say, "Oh, yeah, dude! You're the Turtle Man!"

The goal of the project was to study the local turtle fishery and make recommendations to the Turks and Caicos Islands Department of Environment and Maritime Affairs for a sustainable turtle-fishery management policy. The current regulations were based on policies for fish, not turtles, and on an outdated idea that you could catch the big fish and leave the little ones. But it takes twenty-five years for these turtles to reach reproductive maturity; the largest turtles lay thousands of eggs. The nesting turtle population had declined in recent decades, largely due to the hunting of nesting females on the beaches, which had now been banned. The turtles' decline was not helped by the current turtle-fishery regulations. The plan was to revise the legislation to protect the larger turtles.

Amdeep wasn't a biologist. He was a sociologist. I was intrigued by that, because it seemed that our environmental problems could only be addressed by a cultural change. Not a top-down change or an us-versus-them confrontation, but a collective, cultural evolution.

Amdeep told me about the role turtle hunting had played in the islands since the Taíno Indians first settled there. A key element for developing a sustainable turtle fishery was to honor the age-old tradition of turtle hunting. For his first two years, Amdeep lived in South Caicos, fully integrating himself with the local community. Along with tagging turtles and monitoring catches, he learned to catch turtles with the turtle fishers. "If it's cooked right," he said, "turtle stew is very nice; it has a really unique taste."

"If you were to go into these islands with a purely biological perspective," Amdeep told me, "just finding out how many turtles are in the waters and how many are harvested and planning to base your recommendations just on that data, you would fail, because there's people involved here—there's fishermen, there's community members, there's families that have basically relied on turtles for generations. And to not consult them, it wouldn't be right, they've got a right to harvest and exploit their resources. They need to be involved in management discussions."

Sure, there's no silver bullet for the problems we face. But Amdeep's methodology showed a way to address them by honoring cultural differences and building consensus. Amdeep made a documentary called *Talkin' Turtle,* which featured local islanders and their views on turtle-fishery management measures. It was screened throughout the islands as a way to start conversations with turtle fishers and consumers about how best to manage the fishery.

Amdeep was born in Britain to Indian immigrants. Dark-skinned and in his thirties, his light, agile frame belied a rugged disposition. He told me how once, a few nights before a hurricane hit, he had gone alone to a beach on a small cay close to Grand Turk Island. The sea was really churned up. Amdeep came across fresh turtle tracks in the sand, illuminated by the moonlight. He heard a deep breathing sound and saw what he thought was the mother of all turtles, one of the last few breeding green sea turtles in the islands. He tried to catch her so he could tag her, holding onto her shell as she hauled him toward the surf. Before she got away, the turtle had dragged him, his cell phone, and his camera into the stormy night sea.

Twelve days later he went out at night looking for her. This time he brought help, Jodi Johnson, an environmental officer, and Ali Smith, a police force instructor. They spent the night waiting for her to emerge from the surf. Together the three of them intercepted her on the beach. "Shyvonne" was rigged with a satellite tag. She nested once more that season on the same beach and then migrated 780 kilometers to feeding grounds in St. Croix in the U.S. Virgin Islands, where she stayed until her tag stopped transmitting.

So why tag turtles? "Tagging Shyvonne is very special," Amdeep told a local newspaper at the time, "because, for the first time ever, we will find out where these big old survivors go after laying their eggs on beaches, and we'll identify other countries that should be helping us protect them."[11] And the tagging program showed what rich and remarkable lives the turtles led. The first turtle to be fitted with a transmitter was Suzie. A fisher had "landed her for the pot" in the summer of 2009. The Turtle Project bought her for five hundred dollars. It's not a typical practice to buy turtles, but in the case of being able to procure a rare adult female for satellite tagging, it is done.

The local fishers kept asking where she had gone, so Amdeep posted her tracking maps in public places around South Caicos. She ended up making international news with a six-thousand-kilometer migration through the territories of fourteen other Caribbean nations before returning back to the islands. Tagging and tracking Suzie enabled more and more of the islanders to appreciate their responsibility for protecting these big, egg-laying turtles.

One day Amdeep had found some weak and dehydrated turtle hatchlings stranded in a nest. They were too weak to crawl to the sea, unlike their siblings, whose tiny tracks fanned out down the beach to the surf. He put the baby turtles in a small food platter full of water and fed them tiny fragments of conch. He had to go back to Britain, so at a barbeque he asked a woman who worked at a local conch farm, Eiglys Trejo, if she would look after them. "Don't name them," Amdeep said, "since they probably won't survive."

You don't need me to tell you what happened next. For the record, their names were Daisy, Franklin, Joseph, Queen, Rocco,

Trey, and Vasy. I went to meet Eiglys and watched her clean out the turtles' tank. The little turtles were swimming swiftly, leaving small trails of concentric ripples.

Eiglys treated the turtles with the precision of a scientist crossed with a doting mother. An engineer by education, Eiglys was from Venezuela. She'd lived on the islands for several years with her husband and two young children. Somehow, between two jobs and caring for her family, she made time to take care of the turtles. Much of how she'd learned to take care of the turtles was by researching scientific papers at night once her kids had gone to sleep.

The turtles had become mini-superstars. At one point, with television cameras poised on them, preschoolers had transferred the turtles—then the size of chocolate chip cookies—into a larger pool at the conch farm. Local kids made collages from their turtle drawings and composed a turtle song.

"Rocco is always defensive, he puts his fins back on his shell," Eiglys told me while she scraped algae from the tank bottom. "Daisy is the biggest, Franklin is the sweetest." Their heads and fins were still slightly oversized, giving them a goofy look. The interlocking plate-pattern of their shell and fin markings and tiny beaked heads were already clearly defined, as if they were full-grown turtles in miniature. Holding one of these six-inch-long turtles in my hands, listening to its wheezy breath, and feeling the quiver of its soft, pearl-white belly, I couldn't imagine eating turtle meat.

But as I learned more from Amdeep about the tradition of turtle hunting, I began to appreciate more deeply the important cultural role turtle meat plays in the islands. The meat is gifted to various families when it is hunted, and no part of the turtle goes to waste. It is hunted with great care, respect, and skill. Alizee Zimmermann, the daughter of an expatriate, told me that when her mother was in labor with her, she was brought turtle soup, because it was one of the most nourishing and culturally valued foods that one could offer. It was always given to women in labor.

Eiglys and Amdeep could have been oil and vinegar, but they bounced their differences off each other like an inflatable beach ball. Amdeep was, at least on the surface, more detached. He worked with the turtle fishers, spent time at the docks monitoring catches, did autopsies on the turtles, and caught and tagged turtles himself. But Eiglys called the turtles "my babies."

One month all the baby turtles got a bacterial infection. "The vet never knows what I'll bring him," Eiglys said, laughing. "Can't I bring a dog or cat? No, no. Turtles!" To treat the infection, she went by the tank three times a day, dried each turtle off, applied Betadine antiseptic, and then put it back in the tank. *For a month.*

One day we'd gone to see the turtles, then a year and a half old, still waiting to be large enough to be tagged and released. Amdeep had added two more stragglers to the pool, so now they were nine.

We sat in the sun at the edge of a circular pool. A local conch farm had donated the space for the turtles.

"Shall we make a little soup tonight?" Amdeep teased.

"Stop it!" Eiglys giggled and slapped him lightly. "Would you please!"

Their good-natured banter was waking me up to something: not only can we respect each other's differences, but for meaningful social change to occur, we must. Eiglys herself told me that she wanted to see the turtles released, that they should live in the wild, that she'd rather "have one end up in a soup pot than die in a drift net needlessly."

A few days later, I had dinner with Amdeep, Eiglys, and Wes, a kiteboarding instructor and photographer. Eiglys explained to me that she'd always been afraid of the water. But the turtles would be released soon, so she'd pushed herself to overcome her fear and learn to scuba dive, so she could be in the water when they were released.

I imagined Eiglys diving there thirty years from now. What if, after migrating thousand of miles, one of the female sea turtles came back to lay her eggs? Would she recognize Eiglys?

If she had the wherewithal to find her way to the exact beach she had hatched on, would she recognize the woman who had held her when she was the size of a cookie, who had named her and cared for her for almost two years?

Before I left, the reef looked healthier at moments, if only because some of the fish came back. But the coral was not healing and the algae overgrowth was increasing. It was terribly in danger, like a car that teetered on a guardrail above a cliff. During one dive, a shark ambled by with a remora swimming in tandem, its rare majesty like an imprint from a time that seemed to be slipping away.

I'd put some flowers in a blue glass on a table by the window in my hotel room and placed shells from the beach in a circle around it. There was still no public acknowledgment of the coral bleaching in the islands. I wanted some palpable acknowledgment, like the roadside wreathes and crosses in Mexico at the site of an accident. Grief, like love, is an acutely necessary emotion. Its story is the story of caring; its chords— soulful lines of connection—situate us in the world.

On my last day, I rose and packed my bags slowly. I folded the nautical chart of the islands that I had scotch-taped above a desk and packed my gear. I pulled the heavy bag outside into the hallway.

Just as I was about to close the door, I paused. I went back in and sat down on the bed with a sigh. The room was bare save for the flowers and the seashells.

I gathered the shells in one hand and walked out to the dock. I'd brought a shell back each night until there were seven. Seven's my lucky number. It was Mickey Mantle's number, and when I was a kid, I wanted to play professional baseball. I spent hours refining my curve ball on a bounce-back. I didn't make it as a ball player, but that passion carried over into my writing. The clarity of the crack of a bat as it hits a home run—that's how I want to feel when I write. I want to pull up a truth that true.

I walked out to the end of the dock. Surrounded by the immense midday light and brilliant turquoise waters, I tossed the shells back into the waters, one by one. With each, I expressed my gratitude for a truth these seas had taught me.

First was the truth of beauty—beauty could be so much more than a passing, blissful apprehension, it could be a window into the very nature of life. When I tossed the shell, the wind was so strong that the tiny shell seemed nearly caught up by it before it reached the water.

Then the simple truth of connection, the truth of being a body within a body. We emerge from each other's midst. We have our boundaries, yet we live encircled by lives upon lives. The richness of that.

Then the truth that one can begin again. The simple act of volunteers planting mangroves on a pile of sand created by corrupt, greed-crazed politicians is proof of that.

I thought of Marsha and Amdeep and Eiglys. The truth that each of us can make a difference. Kids started picking up garbage around the island after meeting the baby turtles—they'd learned that turtles confuse plastic for food and that it can kill them if they eat it. And the turtle fishers had linked arms with Amdeep to craft a sustainable fishery. There was another truth: honoring each other's experience, no matter how different, is crucial.

I sat down on the dock and paused. Then gave another shell a gentle toss into the water: the truth within mystery, the truth of things yet to be comprehended.

I had one more shell. It was the size of a silver dollar— pearl-white, smooth rimmed. I stood up and bit my lip. These waters, which had given me so many truths, had given me one final truth that I would have so desperately begged and bargained and pleaded with them never to give me in such an intimate and devastating way: the truth of how deeply the life of our seas and the earth as a whole was in peril. Squinting in the bright light and open sea wind, I tossed the last shell into the sea.

PART 2

The California Coast

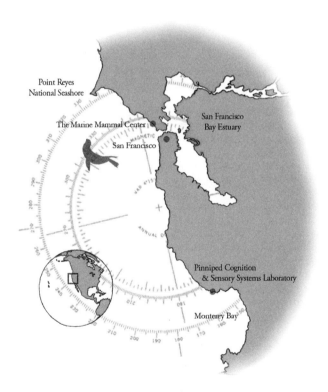

Point Reyes
National Seashore

The Marine Mammal Center

San Francisco

San Francisco
Bay Estuary

Pinniped Cognition
& Sensory Systems Laboratory

Monterey Bay

5

Second Thoughts

You know where this needs to go: insight leads to renewed dedication, and that leads to hope.

I didn't go there. I came home and came unglued. I got bronchitis in the middle of July. At night Charlie and our dog, Zack, retreated from my guttural cough to the haven of our living-room couch. One night, after an exasperating coughing fit, I went into the bathroom and splashed cold water on my face. In the mirror my cheeks were drawn and pale, eyes sour with pain and bloodshot. I saw in my face something I wished I'd never seen: resignation, a weary, beleaguered, "to hell with it, it will never change" despair.

I took some more cough syrup and peeked into the living room. Charlie was asleep on our couch, our dog stretched lengthwise next to him. I tiptoed back to bed, pulled the covers over me and lay on my back in the dark.

What do I do? What do I do with this kind of grief?

There were no Hallmark cards for these things, with inscriptions like "our thoughts are with you as you grieve the loss of your cherished place." This grief was categorically different. It was not *my loss*. It wasn't even the death of a place: it was the slow, gradual death of a home—or rather, home upon home upon homes—of fish and crabs and sea snails and sea stars and whales and sharks and dolphins and turtles. And the ripple effects touched the lives of thousands of people whose livelihoods depended on the ocean.

I was in over my head. Witnessing the coral bleaching had triggered a realization. All those things I'd read about—climate change, ocean acidification, toxic chemical loads, and marine-borne plastic—all of that fit together into a picture that made me understand that the oceans were on track to become a massive version of the toxic, garbage-strewn Hudson River that I'd grown up along.

I'd known about all of this for years, but it had been "information." Now it was visceral, witnessed: I was horrified. The term *environmental degradation* now meant something wholly different, in the same way that war correspondents understand that "lethal wounds to noncombatants" means the death of innocent civilians: mothers, fathers, daughters, sons.

Two months later, I had a date to interview Jenny Stock, NOAA's education and outreach coordinator. NOAA, the National Oceanic and Atmospheric Association, is one of the largest government agencies studying climate, weather, and the oceans. Jenny's office was located in the Point Reyes National Seashore, just over an hour's drive away. So I planned to take a quick dive in the ocean while I was there.

I went down to our garage to pack my gear. Our house in Berkeley originally belonged to my husband's great-aunt and great-uncle, and the garage has intricate built-in wooden cabinets and drawers, as if it were an oversized version of an antique toolbox. On occasion I'd pause in the cool, musty air and curiously open a cabinet to see what I might find.

I opened the back of our car and started loading my dive gear. The bronchitis had finally healed, but I still felt like I was moving in a slow-motion dredge of despair.

The night before Charlie and I had made chocolate-chip cookies. While I stirred the batter, he added ingredients.

"I know I'm in a real funk," I said quietly, "but I think I should just write through this."

"Yeah," he said matter-of-factly, breaking an egg into the batter. "Write through it." He didn't say another word.

But I had no idea how to "write through it." It was almost exactly a year before that I'd begun to write a book about ocean conservation. Sure, I'd thought when I started, I'd encounter sad and disappointing information. But I'd had no idea what an iron-cast stomach I was going to need to digest it all. And now I'd committed to writing a book about it! How was I going to do that if I could barely stand some of the most fundamental facts? The coral bleaching? The oceanic dead zones? The garbage patch floating in the Pacific the size of the state of Texas?

Couldn't I just focus on the beauty and importance of seas and avoid all the bad news? But what was I going to do, gloss over the pesky little detail that "ecosystem collapses" like the one I had seen in the Turks and Caicos had already happened all around the world? And that the remaining reefs were at risk of disappearing in the next forty years?[12]

Seventy-five percent of major marine fish stocks were either depleted, overexploited or being fished to their biological limit.[13] Each year, deforestation destroyed an area roughly the size of Costa Rica.[14] How much more bad news was I headed for? The book had seemed to hold so much promise, and I'd immersed myself in the research with such deep joy. Now that joy had vanished. Would the best I had to offer be a tragic tale of destruction and cultural blindness and greed? How was I going to inspire others when I was plagued by hopelessness?

The gear was loaded. I closed the hatch of the car and leaned against it, crossing my arms wearily.

I didn't sign up for this.

Every day I encountered more disturbing information. The sixth mass extinction, I'd learned, was underway. There have been five known mass extinctions. The sixth is due to humanity's destructive use of natural resources. Scientists estimated that as much as 30 to 50 percent of all species were headed toward extinction within decades.[15] I wanted it to stop. Stop!

When I'd first thought of writing a book about the ocean, I'd also considered getting a master's in nature writing. But the idea of writing a book as "citizen Liz" had captivated me—translating the issues into plain English. I'd looked at how much graduate school was going to cost and researching a book had a similar price tag. The idea for the book won out—it would be a grand adventure and an education, I thought.

But now I felt like I had a black eye—it made me sick to think about this stuff. And I was spending our savings, our rainy-day fund, on what? Adding to the heaps of information that already existed about bleached coral reefs? The details of how we ravage the earth? Facts, yes. But hope?

I sighed. *Maybe I should give the book a rest.*

I looked around. The garage was cool and dimly lit. I opened one of the wooden cabinets and peered in—some cloths for waxing cars mired in dust and cobwebs and some WD-40. I picked up the cool metal cylinder. After college I'd owned a small motorcycle and every week I oiled the chain. A mechanic in North Berkeley tuned it up every few months. The timing on the engine—the sync between the spark-plug ignition and the piston movement—astonished him. "It barely needs a tune-up," he'd croak. "It's just like a little clock!"

The first time I rode a motorcycle was just north of San Diego. A guy had a blue Kawasaki 250 for sale. "Want to take it for a ride?" he asked. I'd never ridden one before, but we were on a quiet road in the countryside. He showed me where the ignition was and the clutch, the throttle, and the blinker lights. I started the engine and opened the throttle slowly. I was off with a sputter.

It was a little motorbike with round rear-view mirrors, the kind you might own if you lived in Corsica. Small, but feisty. After a few minutes I felt comfortable enough to speed up a bit. The road undulated through a field of golden pampas grass. To the left, the Pacific sparkled. I opened the throttle a little more, the sputter of the engine evened out into a smooth whir. At 70 miles per hour, the spry little bike carved a path with the ease and sureness of a migratory bird.

Suddenly I thought, "Where are the brakes?"

He'd shown me a chrome lever on the handlebars, but that was the clutch. God forbid a stop sign or railroad crossing should appear. I had the sudden urge to close my eyes and jump off the bike. I eased off the throttle and gingerly peered at the other side of the handlebars. There was another lever, identical to the clutch. I waited until the momentum of the bike eased and gave the lever a gentle squeeze. Ah, the brake.

I was running late. I needed to be at Jenny's office by noon. I tucked the cloth and the WD-40 back into the cabinet and backed the car out of the garage. It was going to need to be like that with the book, I realized. I'd opened the throttle, and the momentum had been fabulous. All my passions were aligned in a way that felt so deeply heartfelt that it was almost intoxicating, like falling in love. Then I'd hit an experience so gut-wrenching that I had the urge to bail.

But I was going to have to see this through. Not because I knew where it was going, but because I couldn't walk away. I loved the ocean too much. If I walked away now, my soul would be sawed in half.

I was going to have to go left-foot, right-foot. One step at a time. And do it with open eyes: trust the momentum of that truth, the timing of that engine. This journey would come to a close when that momentum started to ease. And when that time came, I'd give the brakes a gentle squeeze.

6

Home

To get to Jenny Stock's office, I planned to take the freeway over the Richmond Bridge and pick up Highway 1 north, which ran along the coast to the Point Reyes peninsula. My favorite road from our house to the freeway was Marin Avenue. It cuts a straight downhill path through Berkeley's narrow, winding streets, descending around six hundred feet in less than a mile.

In low gear, the car engine emitted a tight mechanical whir. In the distance, sunlight bounced off the gray-blue mirror of the bay and sparkled through the canopy of green-gold sycamore leaves. Behind it, San Francisco was a pale-blue silhouette of rectangular shapes. In the distance, the red suspension lines of the Golden Gate Bridge linked that geometric cluster to the curves of the Marin Headlands.

"I want to see my home with open eyes," I thought. Not a cynical squint or the sardonic wince some people acquire with age, one eye closing halfway when making a point, as if to say, "I don't get my hopes up too much." I wanted whatever that openness would bring, be it destruction or terror or inequity, be it beauty or renewal or communion, or even those things that are hard to quantify, or better yet, even trust: "possibilities." Open eyes. The world "according to water."

So for starts, where in God's name did I live? *An estuary.* I knew what that meant, right? It was like that other word, *watershed.* Well, I was ... learning.

An estuary is a body of salt water partially enclosed by land, where the salt water of the sea mixes with fresh water of a river delta. In our case, the rivers are fed by rain and the snowmelt that roars down from the Sierra Nevada. So much of the magic of the San Francisco Bay is due to that—a little inland sea, at once intimate and expansive. Every day, the sea rises, and the water floods through the cut in the coast beneath the Golden Gate Bridge, sometimes moving as fast as 6 knots, almost 7 miles per hour.

The damage that chemical and sewage runoff did in the Turks and Caicos had sent me lurching at the cleaning supplies underneath our sink. What was in that stuff? Where did it go when we flushed it down the drain? The fertilizers for our front lawn? The insecticides? The watershed. A new column in the mental household budget appeared: the earth allocation. We started shelling out extra nickels for biodegradable dish soap and laundry soap. Instead of using fertilizers in our yard, we got a compost bin. I knew it would involve so much more. Things that had been of little consequence started to pop out: solar panels on homes, hybrid and electric cars.

We all live in some kind of watershed; water is always flowing into a bigger body of water. Even if you live thousands of miles from the ocean, the water around your home flows to a stream or a lake or a river or an aquifer, an underground layer of water-bearing rock.

Driving over the Richmond Bridge, I saw that the water was dotted with sailboats, a moored oil tanker, and tugboats. After a few miles, I turned onto California Highway 1, which winds through redwood trees and then along the coast. The road carves a path along hillsides that tumble precipitously into the sea; the highest point is the summit of Mount Tamalpais. To the left, cliffs dropped several hundred feet. Tall outcroppings of stone jutted out of the sea like spires, wet and sparkling from the spray of the waves.

The Pacific Ocean has an especially wild, rough-hewn roar to it—a straight-up blast of sea and wind. The sand on its beaches is coarse, not powdery. In some places there's no sand at all, just glass-smooth stones polished over millennia.

It is the earth's biggest, deepest, oldest, and arguably, wildest ocean. And the most unpredictable—the "ring of fire" around its borders is home to over 75 percent of the world's volcanoes and produces 90 percent of the earthquakes. Most tsunamis occur in the Pacific. But even your above-average Northern California winter storm is impressive. Every year, when the surf is deemed sufficiently stoked, a famed big-wave surfing contest is held: "Mavericks." Like ants to sugar, surfers rush from around the globe to Pillar Point, just south of San Francisco. The surfers look like toy figurines in proportion to the waves. The average wave crests at over twenty-five feet. The big ones? Over seven stories tall, eighty feet.

Yup. That's the Pacific. The Pacific is just "too much" in the best sense of the word, so overwhelming that all you can say sometimes is "Yup." If you hold a globe in your hands at a certain angle, the Pacific will cover almost all of what you can see, with just a few scraggly hints of continents at the periphery. It covers around a third of the earth's surface. If you took all the landmasses in the world and squeezed them like puzzle pieces into the Pacific, you'd still have room for more. Flip Mount Everest upside down and drop it into the Marianas Trench, and it would sink over seven thousand feet before hitting bottom.

At one point the road wound so tightly it was almost a 180-degree change in direction. Railings showed evidence of being perennially reinforced to keep cars from accidentally plunging down the steep cliffs. During especially wet winters, whole portions of the craggy hillside occasionally slide over the road. It felt like a place where the continent came to a plain old-fashioned screeching halt. So much mystery at the edge—that mysterious push-pull, that vitality, that life force.

Driving out, I remembered the first time I met Jenny, just before my last trip to the Turks and Caicos. We sat at a picnic table outside her office with some tea on a foggy spring day, and she told me about something that illuminated that sense of wild aliveness: "the upwelling." She had the overflowing zeal of a storyteller, as if everything she was telling me was something she was explaining for the very first time.

"The West Coast is incredible. It's one of four special places on our planet that have a tremendous amount of marine life. And that's attributed to the current system we have—the upwelling current that's called the California Current." Jenny sipped tea from a handmade ceramic mug that had a whimsical whale figure for a handle. Her cheeks were flushed from time spent outdoors. She described how every spring, as the days get longer, more energy from the sun is available for phytoplankton. The winds blow south along the coast and, because of the rotation of the earth—the Coriolis Effect—the surface waters are pushed offshore. Up surges cold water in its place, right at the edge of the Continental Shelf, where the seafloor descends to over five thousand feet.

"With that cold water," Jenny told me, "comes this infusion of nutrients that have been sitting on the seafloor. Everything that dies and decays—fish, whales, seabirds—becomes detritus on the seafloor, and the plankton basically use it like fertilizer and bloom." Jenny's eyes sparkled; she was getting to the best part. "And this is the *stimulus to the food web*. It supports all this plankton growth in the surface waters. Lots of fish and invertebrates eat this plankton, and in turn, they reproduce and release their larvae. And these are forage fish! Tightly schooling animals. Billions of them out there. They are food for larger animals like sea lions or elephant seals, the big whales. It just becomes a big party out in the ocean. I always get so excited in the springtime, like this is the beginning! This is where all the food is! Many animals will be coming here soon!"

The upwelling is an oceanic "spring fever," a resurgence of life, and it has a ripple effect all around the globe. Only three other places in the world have that kind of intense food-web event: the Humboldt Current off Peru, the Canary Current pushing downward from the Canary Islands to northwest Africa, and the Benguela Current on the southwest coast of Africa.

And on the Pacific coast that intensity of biological activity at the Continental shelf is only twenty or so miles from the shoreline. Hence the sense of a nearby "vital edge." On the Eastern Atlantic seaboard, it's one hundred miles away.

"I remember when I used to volunteer on whale-watching trips on the East Coast, we'd have to go forever!" Jenny said. "Because it's that edge where a lot of activity happens." South of Point Reyes, in Monterey and Carmel, the three-thousand-foot-deep Monterey Trench runs even closer to shore. All it takes is a five-minute boat ride to go whale watching. One day when I was scuba diving less that a hundred yards from shore, a humpback whale languorously rose and then descended, its torso, over forty feet long, disappearing like a submarine.

After Jenny had explained the upwelling, I never saw the greenish density of the spring seas the same way again—the food web was a dynamic spiral of life, beginning with plankton, those tiny microscopic plants that drift in the ocean. "Plankton are organisms that can't swim against the ocean's current, they are at the mercy of the movement of the water," Jenny had explained, "There are two groups. Phytoplankton are the plants or algae organisms that use photosynthesis to make energy and oxygen. You can only see them if you look under a microscope. Zooplankton are microscopic animals that float and drift. Some of them are really fish and invertebrate larvae that will eventually grow into larger organisms, but others are just microscopic animals. They don't necessarily swim in any direction, they kind of float in whatever direction they are taken." Jenny giggled. "Kind of a nice way to go once in a while."

Propped up on my desk at home was Ernst Haeckel's book, *Art Forms of the Ocean*. On the cover were enlarged, embossed illustrations of plankton, elegantly shaped, near-geometric creatures. In the late 1800s, Haeckel sailed around the Mediterranean and out to the Canary Islands with a microscope, studying and drawing these intricate, microscopic sea creatures. It was Haeckel who coined the German term *oekologie* from two Greek words—*oikos,* "household" or "home" and *logos,* "knowledge." Haeckel's definition was "the relation of the animal both to its organic as well as its inorganic environment."[16] We know it in English as *ecology*; we might think of it as the study of home.

Home. Imagine it. What words come to mind? Love? Peace? Safety? Family? Children? Sometimes in the early mornings, our dog, Zack, will gently paw at our bedside until one of us pulls him up into bed, and then he will snuggle between Charlie and me. We bug in together, a happy, soft place, that "everything is okay" feeling. We are full of warmth and quiet and love. Home matters. It's what we take care of.

⁓

I pulled up to Jenny's office, which was in an old red barn near the Point Reyes National Seashore visitor's center. It is NOAA that methodically collects data about the ocean and the atmosphere. After years of meticulous research, it concluded that climate change does indeed exist and that extreme weather events will become more frequent. Fossil-fuel companies—coal, gas, and oil companies—pumped ungodly quantities of money into public-relations campaigns to paint NOAA and other scientific organizations around the world, such as NASA and the World Health Organization, as a bunch of hand-wringing quacks.

I brought lunch. We sat at the picnic table again. The sun was out, and we munched salad and chicken from take-out boxes. Jenny apologized—she had been rushing her toddler son to day care that morning and forgot to bring the cucumber salad that she'd made.

As we chatted, I told Jenny about what I'd seen in the Turks and Caicos and how it drove home what a tremendous impact climate change was having. Jenny didn't mince words: "We are not going to see a change in policy in how we approach energy in this country until there is mass death and devastation. And there sure is a big gap between the policy makers and reality, because there already is mass devastation."

Bees were hovering over our food. We ate quickly. "Go, go!" Jenny said to the bees, teasing, "pollinate something!" Jenny had just been to a conference on ocean acidification and told me how being there in person and listening to scientists she especially trusted made the consequences of it even more sobering.

The unprecedented quantity of carbon dioxide being pumped into the atmosphere from the burning of fossil fuels was being absorbed by the ocean and making it more acidic, changing the pH—a global version of an aquarium gone awry. Organisms who have calcium carbonate shells or skeletons now are suffering from a kind "osteoporosis of the seas." Oysters and crabs and corals may not be able to form their shells and skeletons in the future. And when those creatures suffer, what's at risk? The entire food web: that crucial resurgence of life that's in high gear during the upwelling, all the way from plankton to harbor seals and blue whales.

Even just one slice of this problem was alarming. The Hog Island Oyster Company just up the road in Tomales Bay was already experiencing the economic fallout. Ocean acidification had been linked to large-scale collapses at oyster-breeding operations. "We've been having issues with sourcing what we call seed, or baby oysters, from hatcheries up and down the West Coast," Hog Island's cofounder, Terry Sawyer, had told a reporter, "They've been having crashes or die-offs of their entire inventories." Scientific studies demonstrate that ocean acidification can cause oysters to grow smaller, thinner shells, which are more vulnerable to predators. If Sawyer continued to have problems finding seed for his oyster beds, it would devastate his business.[17]

"I felt kind of stunned," Jenny said, describing how she felt after the conference. "I mean honestly, I still feel extremely deer-in-the-headlights about this entire topic. I think as a collective group of communicators, we are struggling with how to empower people to do something positive. *Especially having a little boy, I look at the timeframes of this stuff and think, He's going to be alive for this!* Just what is he going to see in this world? Things are not going to be the way they've been in the past. I've heard that and accepted that: we are no longer living in the same world that we've had in the past, in terms of the ecosystem."

Jenny marked a few spots on a map where I could dive along Tomales Bay. "I have a really close connection with Tomales Bay," Jenny told me. "I love swimming there. It's such a special place to me."

We said goodbye, and Jenny enviously eyed my gear in the car. "Sometime I'll come with you!" she said with a wink. I drove a few miles, and then the road descended to one of the spots Jenny had recommended, Heart's Desire Beach. Long before the Europeans arrived, the Coast Miwok had villages in Point Reyes. They would have foraged in Tomales Bay for oysters and clams and limpets, mussels and abalone. Their civilization was long gone, extinguished by the European invasion. Some of the Miwok's descendants still live in the area. A few hours drive up the coast will take you to an area where the vibrant cultures of over two dozen tribes work to maintain and revive their age-old relationship with the sea.

I popped on my gear and slipped in the water, into that silky, salty brine that was so thick with life. A group of silvery juvenile sea perch eyed me cautiously at the edge of a huge eelgrass bed. No longer than an inch or two, their bodies were still slightly transparent and their oversized eyes caught the sunlight and sparkled. A bat ray swam by. A snail ambled along the sandy bottom. I could still hear Jenny's voice asking, *Would snails be able to form shells several decades from now?*

I kicked out deeper into the channel. At around twenty-five feet, there were some white ghost anemones. From a short, cylindrical stem, wispy tentacles waved in the surge. When I placed my hand close to them, their tentacles retracted with a snap. Tomales Bay was Jenny's haunt, her inspiration. Would it end up a barren underwater landscape?

Yes, no, maybe. Tomales Bay would already have been pillaged if not for the hard work of dedicated individuals. In his book *Saving the Marin-Sonoma Coast,* Marty Griffin tells the story of how—through grassroots networking and fundraising during the 1960s and 1970s—the Point Reyes National Seashore and Tomales Bay Park were formed, despite plans for a coastal freeway, housing developments, and the filling-in of lagoons. All those unspoiled coastlines in the Ansel Adams photographs? Someone had saved them.

I kicked up to the surface, inflated my buoyancy compensator, and leaned back in the water, as if floating on an inner tube. The water was a glassy, calm blue. A few weeks before, Jenny had told me, "We went out to Chimney Rock and saw a grey whale. It was this gorgeous whale! It was this incredible day and the sense of place was overcoming me. I just felt so re-inspired."

I felt less lonely. Jenny hadn't tiptoed around the tough subjects or how she herself felt about them. At the same time, she retained her energy and inspiration. "I really am amazed by some of these incredible groups that get urban kids out into nature," Jenny had told me, "so that's where I place a lot of my hope. And that's what I love, to be a part of that, in terms of helping people, helping kids build a relationship with nature, so that they care." She'd mentioned a video series by author Lynn Cherry called Young Voices for the Planet, which empowered kids to take action on climate change. In one of them, a thirteen-year-old boy, Alex Loorz said, "Kids are the ones who will be most affected by climate change. By the time we are middle-aged, climate change will be a huge crisis if nothing is done today to help us."[18]

I took off my mask and rinsed my face. Some river otters, who sometimes venture into coastal waters, surfaced and playfully chased each other, splashing and squeaking.

Okay. If I want to keep moving forward, maybe it's time I take a hard look at just what the future holds.

It was time to ask what our world might look like by the end of the century.

⟨🐟⟩

I spent the next week reading environmental reports. I had plenty handy—ones I didn't finish reading in the previous year because they were "too depressing"—scientific studies from the IPCC (Intergovernmental Panel on Climate Change), the National Research Council, NOAA, the U.S. Geological Survey, and the World Bank. The last thing I wanted to do was fall prey to exaggerated predictions, so I'd chosen sources that had a reputation for being precise and conservative in their findings.

It was like the parable of the blind men and the elephant. Each piece of research revealed a part of the beast. One might say, "I feel a skinny fuzzy tail, so this is a mouse problem." Then one might say, "I feel something cylindrical; that's a tree-trunk problem." But gradually it become clear from reading diverse sources that climate change and environmental degradation had reached a tipping point such that these would not be mouse-sized or tree-trunk-sized problems we'd see in the next fifty years: they would be mammoth. To top it off, scientists warned that the interactions of various crises would fuel one another.

The operative word in these forecasts was "more." More collapsed fisheries. Unless there was dramatic change, we were on track to trigger a global collapse of all species currently fished.[19] Stocks of large fish—cod, grouper, marlin, swordfish, tuna—had already fallen 90 percent since 1950. More coral reefs lost due to eutrophication, ocean acidification, and warming seas. Three-quarters of the world's coral reefs were already "at risk," which meant ailing and on the verge of death; most studies predict all of them will be at risk by 2050. And since one-quarter of all the fish in the sea spend a significant portion of their life in coral reefs, they are also at risk. If fisheries collapsed, food shortages would dramatically increase; one-fifth of the world's sources of protein come from the sea. That feeds a lot of people.

Add to that the laundry list of other problems we face, from acid rain to marine-borne plastic to radioactive waste to oxygen-depleted aquatic dead zones to biodiversity loss. Climate change would lead to more wildfires, more droughts, more heat waves, hurricanes, tornadoes, cyclones, and more coastal erosion and flooding. Ask anyone who lived through Hurricane Katrina or Hurricane Sandy to describe how extreme weather affects medical care, food supplies, transportation, or water supplies. The ripple effects were staggering.

As I read through report after report, I wondered what would happen to our home. Would there still be fisherman on the West Coast? And what would happen to the San Francisco Bay? Would the beaches be underwater a century from now?

The National Research Council reported that sea levels could rise almost a foot over the next two decades. That means flooding in low-lying areas built on landfills. What was in those areas? Airports, schools, police stations, fire stations, public housing.

By end of the century, NOAA predicted sea levels would rise between 2.5 and 6.23 feet (75–190 cm) on the California coast.[20] And more firestorms? The 1991 Oakland Hills firestorm blazed within five miles of our house. It took twenty-five lives, spanned 1,560 acres, and destroyed over 3,500 dwellings. Rescue workers described finding a car engine melted on the pavement.

It was mind-boggling. I understood all the more why there was still significant public doubt about these predictions and why scientists were accused of exaggerating their findings for dramatic effect: it is a stunning, almost-unbelievable situation.

In *Collapse: How Societies Choose to Fail or Succeed,* University of California scientist and geographer Jared Diamond documents how some civilizations, such as the Maya and the Easter Island inhabitants, collapsed due to the destruction of their natural habitat—deforestation, soil damage, and overfishing. Diamond found similar patterns—food shortages and struggles over natural resources due to drought, deforestation and overworked soil interwoven with overpopulation—in the social collapse leading up to 1994 Rwandan genocide. But now, Diamond explains, because our world is so globalized, if we do not make a large-scale shift in how we use our natural resources, we are at risk for a global collapse of civilization. Added to that is a searing caveat: widespread environmental damage and struggles over resources can be early warnings for genocidal military campaigns.

This may seem shot through with apocalyptic mythos, but what Diamond means by "collapse" is not an apocalyptic Big Bang, but a dramatic collapse of populations and cultural activity due to environmental degradation, disease, scarcity of resources, and violent struggles over those resources. The difference between the present crisis and past collapses is that now our entire global civilization is at risk.

Scientists around the world had been facing an uphill battle to get climate change at the top of decision makers' agenda. Politicians were wary, because the remedies would require limits on industry, "hampering" economic growth. The irony was that while so many politicians ignored climate change, U.S. military intelligence had already classified it a "profound strategic challenge."[21] More violent storms, droughts, pandemics, mass migrations, struggles over food and water and shelter—all that "more" created more political crises, terrorism, and warfare.

That was the gist of it.

I felt so tired, like a towel that you just could not wring the sadness out of. My grief wasn't grief anymore. It was excruciating sorrow morphing into a sensory fog. I wanted to numb it with something—alcohol or an escape to some little pocket of island beauty, some distraction that would yank me out of it for a while.

I went to see a therapist. I explained seeing the bleached coral reef.

"That must be really upsetting," she said. She was listening intently, but that word *upsetting* almost made me laugh. It felt like standing in front of a demolished skyscraper and saying, "I'm not sure the elevator is working."

"Doesn't get near describing it," I told her. I explained that what I saw went on for miles and miles and how I understood this type of devastation was going on all over the world. My grief was about something that not only had happened but also would keep happening—something so global and pervasive that I couldn't wrap my head around the scope of it.

"So it must be really depressing," she said.

"*Depressing* doesn't get near it either." At that point we laughed for a moment. We went back to talking about the reefs in the Turks and Caicos. I told her how the destruction had exceeded anything I could imagine, a wasteland of dead and dying coral that once teemed with life.

She shifted in her chair. Her eyes narrowed and then widened again. "Are you telling me," she said slowly, "that this might be like being in Hiroshima after the bomb had been dropped?"

"Yes, an underwater Hiroshima." I paused for a moment and then continued. "But not necessarily all at once; it's a slow-acting blight taking hold over decades."

We talked for a while. She peppered me with advice: stay active, don't spend too much time alone. It was good advice, but it still felt like treating a yard-long gash in the hide of a buffalo with a Band-Aid.

Something else had happened though: listening. The alchemy of that. One thing about talking to a therapist is you can talk without fear of blowing them out of the water by how upset you are. No friendship will be put on ice; no colleagues will become less chummy since you vented your despair. Her listening helped my unconscious get some traction. Walking down the stairs from her office, an impulse surfaced. *I know what I need to do. Buy a surfboard!*

Something ratty. Old. Beat up. So thrashed no one would think of stealing it from the back of our jeep. An hour later, a saleswoman waltzed me into a dilapidated, corrugated-metal shack overflowing with used surfboards. The wind whistled loudly through the walls. She eyed my body up and down like a tailor and bellowed over the wind, "A short board would be good."

The top was down on our jeep. We strapped the board into the passenger seat with the seatbelt (to make sure it wouldn't take flight and impale someone's windshield). Just before I left, she yelled, "When you get out of the water, don't forget to lick your car key!" Salt water can cease the ignition.

I drove my favorite windy road to the beach. While I was driving, I remembered a story a therapist had told me years before. She had a pilot's license, and one day she was flying alone in a small plane and went into a nosedive. There she was, headed for the ground faster and faster. No matter what she tried, nothing worked. Finally she thought, "Damn if I'm gonna spend my last minute white-knuckled!"

So she let go of the controls. And the plane righted itself. Turns out that that was a last-ditch technique for righting a plane.

The road made a sharp turn that fed into a short straight-away rimmed by fir trees. The afternoon sun flickered through their towering trunks. Like some mysterious object pulled up by a lead line from the depths, one new thought surfaced: maybe this isn't something I need to fix.

Maybe sadness will always be there. But how that sadness figures into my life, that could change. When did it start? Long before I saw the coral bleach. That was just the last straw, the one that forced the issue. My first taste was when I began to feel more connected to nature and sensitized to its destruction. My sorrow was a consequence of connection, of being more a part of the whole of life. The process of anguish could become a step in opening up more deeply to life.

I pulled the car over and turned off the ignition. Bumblebees hummed in the tall grass. I thought about that mysterious synchrony I'd felt in the water in the Turks and Caicos, *that beauty*—moments of such pure apprehension and connectedness—myself, a part of the larger body of the world. I so desperately wanted to retain that. Now I realized all the anguish I had found so difficult gave me the link I needed. It had been pounding at me like a sledgehammer, driving a truth deeper and deeper until I finally got the point. I felt like bellowing back at the universe, "Okay! Okay! Alright already! I get it!"

Four words sufficed: home is bigger now. Home isn't just a house or an apartment or a family or a neighborhood or a community or a religious group or a nation. It's bigger than we can imagine, *and we share it*. And that means not only that there are things that affect us all, but also that we need to care about each other and the earth more, in a bigger, wider way.

I started the engine and turned back on the road. A few more turns, and the road led out of the forest into grasslands and then descended to the shore. It passed tidal flats and came to a harbor with a few old, brightly colored fishing boats, the entry to a lagoon. A white egret stood elegantly in a broad stand of tule grass.

I'd arrived at my destination. The road didn't go any farther. In front of me was a small concrete breakwater. Beyond a long sand spit, I could hear the surf's low, thunderous boom. I slipped on my wet suit, tucked the surfboard under my arm, walked barefoot to the end of the sand spit, and stood at the edge of the water.

It was one of those moments when you have no idea of the enormity of what you're doing and at the same time you know exactly what you're doing. You just don't want to think about it. Right in front of me was where I'd been hit by the rogue wave in the kayak accident. I had not set foot in that surf since.

Another surfer came up behind me, munching on an apple. "Hey, you're shivering and you're not even the water yet!" she teased.

I peered at the big breakers where I'd been hit. Anywhere in the world would have been fine to go in the water, *just not this place*.

"Buncha churn," she said, squinting at the waves. She munched noisily, words fitting between chews, "but the tides *[chomp]* goin' out … it'll settle *[chomp]*." She stopped chewing and looked at me through the corners of her eyes, curious. "You surfed before?"

"… Ahh …"

"Super! You're gonna love it." She took one more bite from the apple and tossed the core into the brush. "Tell ya what, we'll go in together."

"I'll just … just … just stay here, you know, watch you?"

"Okay, see ya out there." She flopped onto her board with abandon and paddled confidently out into the waves. I sat on the beach, teeth chattering in the bright sun. Finally I stood up and pushed my board into the water.

As I paddled out, the front of the surfboard pitched upward to rise up over the green-blue waves. I reached a calm flat of water outside the breakers and just sat on the board for a while. On the way back in, I tried standing up on the board. I rolled in the foam of the surf, a momentary spin in that forceful, underwater turbine. Then the waves pushed me toward shore. I stood up waist-deep in the water and took a deep, happy breath. The most intransigently complex thing had been simplified: I was alive. What next?

7

The Longing

I'm bad at remembering certain things: zip codes, phone numbers, items to pick up at the supermarket. I once left a silver flute in a phone booth (I called the police; it was still there); one of my college roommates fumed at being woken in the morning by the high-pitched whistle of an espresso pot (I'd get up, put coffee on, and then bolt out the door to class). Every year I write my husband a poem for Valentine's Day. One year I hand-bound a "ten-year anniversary" book of poems for him. There were eleven poems. Oops.

So how is it that sometimes when you don't know what you need, or when you can't articulate it, memory shuffles through time and coughs up some crucial tidbit? Different threads from different times in one's life come together to form new meaning.

I strapped the surfboard back into the passenger seat and drove home from the beach. The traffic came to a halt as I was approaching the Richmond Bridge. I turned the radio on—there was an accident right before the bridge. It was dusk. The road was a field of red brake lights flashing in the dim light.

It wasn't words of wisdom that came, or even an image. Out of memory and out of that dark well in which my hope had vanished, it was one sound: the clank of a fork on a china plate.

I remembered something that had happened four years before. A few days before Christmas, Charlie and I were eating dinner.

"He might have a day or two," Charlie said, his eyes narrowing with a wince. "But he's gonna die stranded out there." He nudged a piece of food with his fork, then pushed the plate away and let the fork drop with a clank.

Charlie was telling me about a sea lion trapped in the estuary across from his office building, several miles in from the coast. No one could get close enough to see what was wrong, because the wetland was behind a Homeland Security fence erected around the Oakland Airport.

Some of Charlie's coworkers said, "Don't do anything. Let nature take its course." Others said, "Excuse me? We built the airport, we put up the fence. How natural is that?" Charlie had called The Marine Mammal Center rescue hotline, but they were not sure they could assemble a rescue team. It was, after all, the holidays. It seemed almost inevitable that the sea lion would end its days starving behind that metal fence.

The next day Charlie called a local television station, and they dispatched a reporter. Then a white van from The Marine Mammal Center van pulled up—they'd assembled a volunteer team. "I don't think we're gonna be able to cut a hole in this fence," the team leader told Charlie, "we got to get clearance from the Port of Oakland and the airport." The rescue team left.

A cluster of people gathered next to the metal fence. The cold air was filled with the sounds of intermittent shotgun fire. Riflemen were shooting blanks at Canada geese to keep them away from departing and arriving airplanes. Then from a distance, from the inside of the airport, the small Marine Mammal Center van, escorted by a Port of Oakland security vehicle, drove out on the runway.

They parked at the edge of the runway. The sea lion was on a patch of tule grass that was separated from it by a passageway of water. The volunteers slowly waded through the water carrying a huge metal crate, what looked like an oversized fish net, and some wooden boards.

Frightened, the sea lion lurched away from them. They carefully corralled him into the crate, using the boards as shields—marine mammals can bite when resisting capture. They carried all 210 pounds of him in the crate through the chilly, waist-deep water and back to the van.

The next day, after a good night's sleep, a medical exam, and a couple of nice meals, the juvenile male sea lion, nicknamed "Saps," was deemed good to go. There was nothing wrong with him other than being "hungry, tired, and in the wrong place at the wrong time."

It was Christmas Eve. Just before sunset, The Marine Mammal Center staff wheeled him in the crate down to Rodeo Beach in front of their headquarters. The beach was a broad expanse facing the Pacific. No narrow inlets to get lost in. They slid open the crate, and Saps waddled toward the water. At the water's edge he paused for a moment and gazed back at his rescuers. Then he plunged into the surf.

The next morning we made blueberry pancakes with Vermont maple syrup. We sat on the couch with our dog and opened gifts. It was one of the best Christmas mornings I could remember, because I imagined Saps swimming through kelp forests, feasting on sardines, and finding other sea lions. He was home too.

At that time, I'd just returned from the trip to the Turks and Caicos Islands on which I'd resolved in that gut-wrenching revelation in JFK Airport to get involved in ocean conservation. I could still feel the warmth of the Caribbean sun on my skin.

How I would have loved it if someone had invented a little spray that would extend the life of an epiphany. You know, something romantic sounding, like "eternal epiphany"—or even better, in French, *épiphanie éternelle*. Anything, please, to make the clarity of the epiphany last. I'd had that bright flash—I couldn't partake in the beauty of the seas any more without being involved in their preservation. Clear. Salient. Lucid!

That lasted a few hours.

Then confusion, longing, ambivalence. Just how exactly was I going to live out my love for the seas? How was I going to earn a living? And would anything I did make a difference? I was healthier, but would it last? The whole thing reeked of change. Change is good? Sure—just not my life.

Charlie did nothing but push back at my ambivalence. "When are you gonna do what you want? It's as if you've got a pot cooking that you'll never let come to a boil."

The nerve of that man.

Some wild, passionate energy inside me was surfacing, waking up. It felt marvelous, but inchoate, visceral. The energy was so outrageous that I joked to myself, "You don't wanna go there."

At the same time, I had this interminable, subterranean longing for "it." And I didn't know what "it" was. It was this "thing"—this "thing-thing"—that had surfaced when I went back to the Turks and Caicos.

I can write about almost anything. Sex, love, beauty, horror, hypocrisy, depression, you name it. I love a good challenge. But not that thing, the "longing." My tank was empty. I resigned myself to a list of words in my journal: beauty, mystery, sensation, wildness, edge, waking. It felt like a horse that wanted to kick a barn door down.

I felt such a deep kinship with that warm-blooded, mammalian swimmer who took a few wrong turns and ended up stranded and hungry. On Christmas Day, we went out for a walk and looked out at the Golden Gate Bridge. "Where did Saps go? Was he somewhere out in the ocean past the bridge?" I wondered. Had he swum to Pier 39 in San Francisco, where groups of sea lions haul out?

I started reading about marine mammals. I learned that they are warm-blooded like us, and they are extraordinary divers, able to dive over seven thousand feet. A few months later, I went to a Marine Mammal Center volunteer meeting. It was in an airy hall with high ceilings and wooden beams. I'd never seen so many green fleece vests and pullovers in my life. These folks worked in the cold, damp conditions … and it was Saint Paddy's Day.

Everyone was cheerfully nibbling on snacks and sipping drinks. I got in line for some food and chatted with one of the volunteers, a broadly built man with gray hair.

"This sure is a lot of volunteers." I said. There must have been at least three hundred people in the room; the chatter was so intense it was hard to hear.

"Tip of the iceberg," he said, raising his voice to make it audible, "it's actually over a thousand volunteers." I told him about Saps getting stranded in the estuary. "Yeah, yeah," he had a strong New York accent. "Those folks are the stranding volunteers. Then you've got the animal-care folks and the research folks and the education folks, you know, who do the docent tours." He beamed with pride.

"There was something about Saps," I said, "and the rescue .... I got curious."

"Well, yeah," he said, eyes creased slightly in the corners, "you gotta jump on the moments, you know, when the dots connect."

I strolled through the crowd, as if floating through a new school of fish, sponging in snippets from conversations: "The enzymes were sky-high." "We got a good biopsy, so we knew what we were dealing with." "The interesting thing about that parasite is that it likes to live in the diaphragm."

Two women talked intently, their heads leaning toward each other. "He was a feisty little bugger," one of them said, describing a harbor seal that came in with a gash in its side. "And the maggots and flies and the discharge! But once we got him cleaned up ... no damage to vital organs." She was matter-of-fact. She rattled off details, which seemed to have been bottled up and fizzing inside her. Then she paused suddenly. Another fellow volunteer had arrived. "Oh sweetie!" she squealed. "It's great to see you!"

More and more people arrived until the hall was roaring with chatter: histograms, protozoan, EKGs, mediastinal ligaments, necropsies, scope tubes, methicillin-resistant staphylococcus, epithelial cells.

"Hello everyone," a voice said through a loudspeaker. "Welcome to the Year in Review!" The director Jeff Boehm was starting the meeting. "Or rather," he deadpanned, "what the heck did last year mean?" Boehm made a few comments and then handed over the podium to a man with brown hair and a wide grin—Bill Van Bonn, the chief veterinarian, or as many referred to him, "Dr. Bill."

"Okay!" Dr. Bill grinned like he was revving up a football team for a game, "We've got a lot of stories to tell. But why are all the veterinary interns in the back row? You wouldn't be trying to get away from me?" Giggles came from the back of the room.

Dr. Bill put up a pie chart on a big screen. "So ... we treated 998 animals last year" he said slowly. The pie chart had three sections: released, died in treatment, and euthanized. "I'm particularly interested in doing a couple things." He pointed to the died-in-treatment and euthanized sections. "I want to make these as small as possible. I don't want my patients to die. And," he pointed to the released section, "I want to make this one as big as possible, because that's released, went home."

"So let's talk about some of the cases," Dr. Bill continued. Each description started with the name of the animal, then a description of its condition, diagnosis, and treatments. Some of the names were pretty mad-dashed. If you've got to name nearly a thousand animals a year, you get creative: Huberschmidt, Zina, Prosecco, Chai, Boondoggle, Pelee, Lapawi. When you name something, you rescue it from indifference, you commit to it the energy of your attention. Eiglys had named all of her baby turtles, after all.

Dr. Bill worked through case after case—a harbor seal with a hind flipper that had infected wounds; a sea lion with leptospirosis, a severe bacterial infection; another sea lion with a fungal infection. Dr. Bill put up a photo of a young sea lion whose entire head was wrapped in fishing line. It was gruesome. As the sea lion had grown, the fishing line had bitten into him, leaving horrific red-brown scabs and lesions.

"Tromar," Dr. Bill said the name quietly. "Yearling. Starving, weak, malnutrition, severe trauma, and inflammation. We didn't know if the eyes were okay, there was so much trauma to the face." But they were able to remove the fishing line, and his wounds responded to treatment; he even kept his vision. Two months later he too waddled out of a crate and plunged back into the surf. "Pretty nice to see him go home," Dr. Bill said quietly.

Dr. Bill often remarked that his patients told more stories than their own. Tromar's was the story of marine debris. He was victim of what is called *ghostfishing:* abandoned and lost fishing gear—traps, fishing line, nets—that catches and strangles marine creatures over and over again.

When I was training to be a divemaster, my instructor, Tim, told me to buy a dive knife, a "nice sharp one." Knife? "Fishing line," he explained, "is designed to highly resist breaking." Some fish will snap it at the right angle, like barracuda, whose razor-sharp jaws are often referred to as a combination of scissors and a steak knife.

"Buy it!" Tim had growled at me. I bought a six-inch knife with a black handle and a serrated blade and strapped it to my calf. There! Now I was outfitted for a scene from *Lord of the Rings.* I mean, what were the odds of my getting tangled up in fishing line?

Significant: sixty tons of lost gear was retrieved by the California Lost Fishing Gear Recovery Project between 2006 and 2012. That's ten tons a year and just a drop in the bucket of what's out there. Several times I've hacked away at fishing line with that toothy, serrated blade. The sensation is that of being snared in a spider's web made of titanium filament. Tromar, the yearling sea lion? He didn't have a knife.

The ghoulish sidekick of lost gear, Dr. Bill explained, is marine debris. Death by entanglement in or ingestion of plastic debris—things like six-pack rings, bottle caps, swizzle sticks, and straws—had increased by 40 percent over the last decade.[22] It's estimated that thousands of sea turtles, marine mammals, and birds die from eating it every year, because they mistake it for food.

I flashed back to the day my dog Skippy came up to me, his body trembling. The vet couldn't find anything wrong, and if Skippy had swallowed something, it should have showed up on an x-ray. They put Skippy on antibiotics and an IV, but he just got weaker. Three days later the vet said, "It's very possible he's eaten a piece of plastic."

That evening, after an exploratory surgery, the vet handed me a baggie with a quarter-inch fleck of a plastic Mr. Snowman toy that Skippy had chewed to pieces. It had punctured his small intestine and triggered an infection, which was spreading through his body.

Dr. Bill was whistling Dixie. Name: Orange Vest. A subadult sea lion with pneumonia who wasn't responding to treatment. "So we had a look," he said, which was short for "did a bronchoscopy." He put up a video taken during the procedure. And there in the lungs—mites!

"Anytime an animal doesn't respond to treatment," Dr. Bill slowed his speech and raised his voice, "we're missing something. And the most common reason for missing something is?"

A chorus came from the interns in the back of the room, "Not looking!"

"Yeah! Go look! And yeah! We look a lot!"

⁓

It had been four years since that meeting. Now I was remembering Dr. Bill's words, sitting in a traffic jam on a damp beach towel with a surfboard jutting out of the jeep. I'd had a dunk in the surf without breaking my neck, and I'd realized I didn't need to wring the sadness out of my system.

When I saw the coral bleach in the Turks and Caicos, I felt that part of me was dying, and now I understood, yeah, part of me *was* dying! So many living creatures on the brink of extinction. The "me" that I thought I was wasn't "me" anymore. The world was a part of me, and I was a part of it. But now what? And where was the hope in all this?

Now the clank of the fork on the plate had new meaning. And the garrulous call and response between Dr. Bill and the interns: The most common reason for missing something is? Not looking!

The cars began to move. A state trooper waved traffic by a tractor-trailer on its side. A car was crumpled like a beer can. Two paramedics lifted someone on a stretcher.

Not looking: what was I missing? That many people had already arrived at the place I'd arrived at, the place Charlie had arrived at just a few days before Christmas. We push our plate away and drop the fork: our personal well-being is not enough. *It's not about us anymore.*

All those volunteers at The Marine Mammal Center—it wasn't about them, it was about each animal's struggle to stay alive and about the health of the seas it came from. It was about rescuing those animals, rehabilitating them, and releasing them to their home, where they belonged. The volunteers worked in cold and wet conditions, scrubbing out holding pens, sterilizing feeding tubes, making special fish formulas for each type of animal.

When I went to that volunteer lecture four years earlier, I'd had no idea how crucial their rambunctious, MASH-unit mentality was, that they had to summon emotional discipline to work with emaciated and wounded animals and not make eye contact with them, otherwise those animals would never be wild again. And they had to stomach losing some 40 percent of their patients and yet every day to care for each new animal with renewed hope, vigor, and focus.

In the center's early days, they used car headlights to illuminate nighttime tube feedings and took animals to human hospitals for x-rays in the middle of the night, during the hospitals' "off hours." They were better equipped now, but still they grieved their losses, celebrated their successes, and constantly sought to find better ways to do things. They kept looking: for clues, answers, possibilities.

The traffic accelerated onto the bridge. The gray-blue water of the bay flickered through the suspension lines. A half-hour later I pulled into our driveway. The garage door was open. Charlie was at a workbench with a light on. I'd tell him what I did, but he could already see it in my eyes.

He looked at the surfboard and smiled. "I see that you've been busy."

⌇⤳

Still morning. Raven calls. I pulled out an old scrapbook. On one page, some pressed wildflowers, a snapshot of me at age four with my favorite teddy bear, and on a piece of paper with torn edges, a poem by Rumi:

You're song
a wished-for song

Go through the ear to the center
where sky is, where wind,
where silent knowing.

Put seeds and cover them.
Blades will sprout
where you do your work.[23]

The word *ocean* is derived from the Greek word *okeanós*, which means a "river circling the earth." The oceans: one big river. Even the dry stems of a wildflower were connected to the sea, to plants that sprouted from the ground and drew water into their veins. If that water came in the form of rain, only a few days before, it might have been in the sea. Seed, sky, wind, sprouts. They were "of ocean" too.

And the seas sponged up whatever we pumped out into the world: carbon dioxide, PCBs, plastic. The health of the seas was dependent upon the health of the world as a whole. I'd listened to that connection I felt to the sea, and it had dropped me with a plunk on the doorstep of the plight of the whole planet.

Some thread of clarity had surfaced when I remembered the Marine Mammal Center staff. It hadn't vanquished my despair, but it had put a dent in it. Dr. Bill's credo stayed with me—keep looking.

It'd been several weeks since I'd bought the surfboard. The autumn light had deepened, succumbed to a season of shadows, of early night.

I ran my hand over the worn pages and the stubby photo corners of the scrapbook. Next to the poem I'd glued a snapshot of my grandfather's brother, Kurt Hahn, who was a well-known German educator. Uncle Kurt wrote little, but when he spoke, he didn't mince words. The Third Reich imprisoned him after he said in a speech, "Hitler isn't a Christian. He's a fascist." Uncle Kurt escaped to Britain and founded one of the first experiential education programs, Outward Bound. His statements had an old-school, pithy heft. The task of education, he wrote, "was to insure the survival of these qualities: an enterprising curiosity, an undefeatable spirit, tenacity in pursuit, readiness for sensible self-denial, and above all, compassion."

He championed the idea that "service to one's fellow man" should be integral to education, that there was something in that act of saving—in the passion for rescue—that was crucial. Australian lifeguards, he pointed out in a speech, "devote to the art of lifesaving a meticulous care such as is generally only associated with the art of killing."[24]

Before he died, I promised him I'd go to Outward Bound. I remember him chatting it up. I was sitting in his study in his apartment in Germany. He scanned me like a Geiger counter, looking for signs of life inside my shell: I was ten years old—sickly, skinny, pale. I wore a kilt, white blouse, white socks, and loafers with tassels, my small hands quarantined inside white gloves.

"If you went to Colorado Outward Bound," he exclaimed, "you could learn an ice-ax arrest!" He reveled in it as if talking about a beloved poem or a Bach cantata, as if it were the $E = mc^2$ of the human spirit. If a mountaineer is slipping down a steep slope of snow and ice, he or she thrusts an ax into the ice to halt the slide.

Four years later Uncle Kurt died. I started running. The first evening I didn't get farther than a hundred yards before my lungs wheezed me to a halt. Each evening I ran farther. Two summers later I finished an Outward Bound course in the Smoky Mountains of North Carolina. I'd never experienced such deep camaraderie with others before, how we were able to do things that seemed impossible, because we came together in such a true and open and vibrant way.

That word: *impossible.*

Hard not to think about the kayak accident. Elisabeth Kübler-Ross, the psychiatrist who wrote extensively on death and dying, spoke of five stages of death—denial, anger, bargaining, depression, acceptance. While I was paralyzed underwater, I'd whizzed through those stages in high speed: "This isn't happening!" "Oh, please! Come on, come on!"

I wanted to live, but the situation was one big No. No sensation, no air, nothing. It was a slam-dunk no. The last stage, acceptance, came speedily: "This is really it. I'm going to die."

But then in the middle of all that no, no, no, there was a quiet yes-note. What little oxygen was left in my brain, what neurons could still fire, cobbled together a few threads from memory—some letters of the alphabet and the timbre of a voice—and carved a new neural pathway. A voice asked, "Do you want to live?" And I said, "Yes." And the gist of that yes, the feeling of it, was: I'm not done yet. This isn't over.

Really? Just who was I to have such audacity? Hadn't I accepted death? Who was I to pull a 180?

And what if I woke every day with that audacity? How would my life change? Those folks at the Marine Mammal Center? *They weren't done yet either.* Nor firefighters, nor rescue divers, nor aid workers risking their lives to bring food into famine-stricken areas. These moments of care, of saving, they are all moments when the boundary between the possible and impossible is fluid, changeable.

But the global destruction of humanity's life-support system—clear air, clean water, natural resources? Where was the hope in that? The statistics were so damning. Like so many who'd digested the scientific information, I struggled for any genuine optimism. I realized I wasn't just now being sucked into a nasty well of hopelessness—I'd always been there. I just hadn't given it the focus that I was giving it now.

About eight months before, I'd gone to a reading by eco-philosopher Joanna Macy. She'd just written a book with a doctor who specialized in behavioral change, Chris Johnstone, called *Active Hope: How to Face the Mess We're in without Going Crazy*. The bookstore, called "Mrs. Dalloway's" after the Virginia Woolf novel, was crammed with people perched on fold-out wooden chairs nestled between bookshelves. Copies of her other books were on display as well, including her memoir, *Widening Circles*. I thumbed through Rilke's *Book of Hours,* which Macy had translated with Anita Barrows. Rilke's piercing diction was unmistakable: "Let everything happen to you: beauty and terror. Just keep going."[25]

Macy had started a series of empowerment workshops called "The Work that Reconnects." One of her first books, *Despair and Personal Power in the Nuclear Age,* broke ground in its insistence that if we brush aside—ignore, belittle, play down—our despair about the destruction in our world, we also bury our power to do something about it. She often said that a phrase used by the French editor Gerard Blanc, *angoisse planétaire,* might be more apt: planetary anguish.

She was a ripple-effect person. She'd facilitated hundreds of workshops for decades and had trained others to do the same. Refusing to shy away from the darkest underbelly of our body politic, in 1992 she and her husband, Fran Macy, did a workshop in the Russian city of Novozybkov. After the Chernobyl nuclear accident, a plume of radioactivity drifted toward Moscow. Soviet military pilots seeded clouds to make the radioactivity precipitate before it reached Moscow. The people who bore the greatest brunt of that ferociously toxic, heavy rain—cancer, birth defects, homes bulldozed, and a beloved forest quarantined because it was so highly radioactive—were the fifty thousand citizens of Novozybkov.

If you'd asked me a few years earlier if nuclear energy was related to ocean conservation, I'd have said no. Yet one of Jacques Cousteau's early efforts as an activist was to protest the plan to dump radioactive waste in the Mediterranean in 1960. He organized a highly successful publicity campaign, and the train carrying the waste to the sea was stopped and forced to return to its origin by women and children sitting on the railroad tracks.[26]

The day I heard Joanna Macy speak was just over one year after the Fukushima Daiichi nuclear disaster in Japan, in which three nuclear reactors had melted down. The Japanese government estimated that each day, three hundred tons of radioactive water used to cool the reactors were being dumped into the Pacific Ocean.[27] The Woods Hole Oceanographic Institution would end up testing the waters of the Pacific—the largest and healthiest ocean in the world—for radiation.[28]

An adroit woman in her eighties with a lighthearted smile walked up to the podium. How could anyone dealing with this subject have such a cheerful demeanor? I'd imagined her face would have some kind of austere, ingrained grimace. A gangly, almost teenage joyousness belied the signs of age. She looked like someone who'd be fun to go out for ice cream with.

"Active Hope," Macy explained, "is something we *do* rather than *have*." It is *active*. Instead of asking, "When is the train coming?" you roll up your sleeves and say, "Let's build that train." It doesn't require optimism; we can even employ it when we feel hopeless. Macy thumbed through a copy of her book, which bulged with yellow sticky-notes. "Active Hope," she read, "involves identifying the outcomes we hope for and then playing an active role in bringing them about. We don't wait until we are sure of success. We don't limit our choices to the outcomes that seem likely. Instead we focus on what we truly, deeply long for, and then we proceed to take determined steps in that direction."[29]

One of the unique elements of Active Hope, Macy explained, was the "honoring of despair." She described how attending a Cousteau Society conference in Boston in 1977 drove home to her the dangers our world faced, from toxic waste to mass extinction. After the meeting, she took the subway home. As the train emerged from a dark tunnel and crossed over the Charles River, she asked herself, "How do I live with the horror of this knowledge? Do I go crazy with it or do I numb myself again?"[30]

This began a journey of inquiry; she answered those questions for herself, and ever since, through her writings and workshops, she has helped thousands of people answer them as well. "Pain for the world—the outrage and the sorrow—breaks us open to a larger sense of who we are," she writes. "It is a doorway to the realization of our mutual belonging in the web of life."[31]

Grief-work is healing, because in recognizing our grief fully, we regain our energy. Macy pioneered a parallel path for planetary anguish. In encountering what she called a nameless disease that was like a "hidden ulcer," that "dread-filled grief for our planet," we unleash new energies we might never have thought existed. "We all need to unblock our feelings about our threatened planet and the possible demise of our species. Until we do, our power of creative response will be crippled,"[32] she says.

The stiff-upper-lip approach to grief is about as effective as tying a noose around the neck of someone who's stopped breathing: "Maybe tightening the noose will revive him?" Macy's modus operandi is to pump new blood and air—attention, insight, care—into that oft-hidden corner of our psyche that is choking on anguish.

I was starting to see how pervasive the silence about our environmental future was. One day at a social gathering, I decided to set a mental stopwatch to see how long I could sustain a conversation with someone about our future without him or her sighing and changing the subject with "Oh, it'll work out" or "We'll manage." Two minutes was the average.

A month later, I took one of Macy's workshops. The first evening, Macy drew a diagram of what she called "the spiral of the Work That Reconnects." There were four parts or "stations": coming from gratitude, honoring our pain for the world, seeing with new eyes, and going forth. The spiral, Macy had written, "offers a transformational journey that deepens our capacity to act for the sake of life on Earth."[33] She explained that as our energies move from one station to the next, a momentum builds, and each time we experience the spiral, we do it in a new way.

I listened cautiously. *Was this a bunch of New Age fluffernutter?* The spiral idea didn't click for me; it seemed too conceptually tidy. But the conversations! The people! In the nitty-gritty trenches: social workers, urban farmers, a watershed manager, a filmmaker who worked with poor kids in New York City, a community organizer from Brazil, a professor who taught business ethics, a teacher who'd started schools in Tanzania.

Macy kept breaking us into pairs, peppering us with things to talk about that revolved around the elements of the spiral. Each time we paired up, it was with a new person. Our last exercise was with pen and paper. "Imagine a family member living seven generations from now—two hundred or so years—writing you a letter," Macy said. "What would he or she tell you? Would he or she thank you for things you might have done on behalf of future generations? When you are finished, if you'd like, share the letter with your buddy."

It was a gorgeous spring day. We bolted outside to soak up some sun. "Don't fuss, just free associate, write!" she called after us as we funneled out the doorway. My buddy, Laura Reddick, was a graduate student in philosophy. We sat in silence for a few minutes. How could it be that I'd never thought about how my actions would affect life two hundred years from now? *No one had asked.*

In my mind, I abbreviated the parts of the spiral: gratitude, despair, new eyes, going forth. I thought about Uncle Kurt. I was his grandniece. He was born in 1886. One hundred and twenty-six years later, Macy had dispatched us to write our letters on the lawn.

We scribbled away. My great-great-great-grandniece wrote to me: "Thank you for thinking of me and my generation. I know a part of your life was really difficult because of the accident, but because of your courage and your open heart, you became a person who opened to the world and loved and cared for others." I wept.

After two days at the workshop, we were a merry herd, hugging and swapping business cards as we said goodbye. Each person seemed to be making that spiral his or her own. It was not writ in stone; it was a catalyst for forging, for ourselves and for the sake of the world, our own version of Active Hope.

But then, five weeks later, I went to the Turks and Caicos and saw the coral bleach. And my hope collapsed. After that, I did all the research on climate change and what our world would look like fifty or a hundred years from now. *That buried it.*

Now it was early winter, five months later, and I was looking back on all of it—Joanna Macy's workshop, the coral bleaching, my conversations with Jenny and Marsha, Amdeep and Eiglys, my research into what the future held.

So? Who needs hope? Couldn't I just do what I thought was best, save what I could, live my life, and "let the rest go," that black cloud a century or two down the road? No! This wasn't about me anymore. I didn't want to live a shuttered life. This was about something bigger, the life of the planet, and it, not I, needed hope.

I remembered that on my last dive in the Turks and Caicos, a remora and shark elegantly swam in tandem around our boat. Remoras are a type of fish that attach themselves to a larger creature, a turtle or shark or even a whale. They hitch a ride on the larger organism's energy, sometimes traversing thousands of miles with it. I wanted that bigger hope, hope for the life of our planet as a whole, and I wanted to hitch my energies to it.

I kept thinking about what Joanna Macy did and what Uncle Kurt and Outward Bound did, that there was some special thread of connection. Well yeah, they helped people meet challenges, supported teamwork, communication, and so on. But still something nagged at me, something about Uncle Kurt and Macy's spiral.

I fiddled with it like an intransigent Rubik's cube. But it ended up in some pocket of my psyche reserved for perennial puzzles, right alongside that subterranean ache, the horse that wanted to kick the barn door down—that wildness and longing and hunger that I could make no sense of. I chalked that longing up to a rush of emotion, like a teenage crush, when your brain is so stoked on neurotrophins that every nanosecond is intensely heightened.

You have to write what is true, even if you hate it. That's what floats the boat. So for me, despite all the searching—the realizations, catharsis, therapy, and *New York Times* bestsellers on the state of the planet—despite all that, the global path of destruction we were on seemed unstoppable.

If push came to shove, and you asked me if there was any hope, I'd tell you hope was not in the cards. Save a little here, save a little there, but too much of humanity was conducting itself like bacteria in a Petri dish, which eat up all their food and then die. When it came to the big picture and the accelerating destruction, the odds for significant change stank.

⁓

"Liz! I'm on Grizzly Peak Road, but where do I turn to get to your house?" It was about two weeks later, and my friend Arlene Ustin was calling me. Arlene was a professor at Prescott College and had worked with Outward Bound for decades. She'd emailed that she was going to be in town. Joanna Macy lived in Berkeley, so I thought, let's get some Outward Bound folks together with Joanna, and they could chat about working with groups.

So Joanna, Arlene, Nettie Pardue, from the Outward Bound Center for Peacebuilding, and Nettie's husband, Jeff, came to our house for supper. It was a chilly evening in early winter. Charlie lit the fireplace, and soon the living room felt cozy and warm.

Risotto was the perfect dish—it needs to be stirred constantly for over a half-hour as you incrementally add water. I'd be glued to the kitchen for at least forty-five minutes. No choreographed conversational niceties—I'd let them mingle on their own.

I started stirring the risotto.

Joanna came in the kitchen with a mischievous grin. "So?"

"So?" I said, stirring with a flat wooden spoon.

"Show me where you work."

"Ah … sure, just for a minute."

"It feels like a boat in here," Joanna said. Next to the windows in my study were a National Geographic map of the oceans and a poster of the domes of basilicas and churches in Rome. She held one corner of the Rome poster in her hand and scanned the circular mosaics.

Joanna reminded me of Eiglys, who had taken care of the baby sea turtles. Funny. Her features emitted a wise innocence.

I pointed to a nautical chart of the Turks and Caicos Islands on the opposite wall. I told her how much I loved the islands and about the coral bleaching. The chart had hung on my wall for several years, and I took it with me to the islands, I explained. When I returned after seeing the bleaching, however, I couldn't bear putting it back up. But just several days earlier, I'd finished writing about the bleaching and put the chart back up.

"Of course, you remember your loved ones," Joanna murmured, gazing at the nautical markings, the names of passageways and inlets. "Even if they are ill or have passed away."

I remembered one of Uncle Kurt's pithy quotes, "The passion for rescue reveals the highest dynamic of the human soul."

God, what's with me? Why am I so goddamned hung up on Uncle Kurt and Joanna's spiral?

Joanna paused. A hint of sadness graced her eyes.

Alert! Alert! New neurological pathway coming through! Clear the road: *Why? Because that's how the horse gets out of the barn.*

That "thing," that impetuous, wild longing, the "thing-thing" inside me—that was the passion for rescue. That juicy, audacious force that pulled a 180 in the kayak accident. And yeah, it was like a horse—it chomped at the bit; it wanted to run to the limits of its endurance. But as far as my life went, it was stuck in a barn—the confines of short-lived, adrenaline-spiked episodes.

So how do you translate that fiery energy into years of patient, sustained effort? Well, what the hell was I doing going back into the water with the surfboard? Confronting my fear? Uh, uh! Gratitude, industrial-strength. "I'm alive!" Each moment: a gift. And what happened when I refused to mute my despair? Seeing with new, more open eyes. And where was that taking me? Going forth: action. The spiral!

Wait, wait, lemme get this right—that wildly alive energy inside me? Put it to work? Every day?

Yup.

The spiral was a floodgate for the passion for rescue, for that life force to flow through, over and over again. For the long run. We already did it instinctively. I'd been doing it, the folks at the Marine Mammal Center were doing it, Eiglys and Marsha and Amdeep and Jenny and Dr. Bill were doing it, the scientists who studied climate change were doing it—anyone seeking to make the world a better place was doing it. It was like that song: "birds do it, bees do it, even educated fleas do it" and then the refrain goes "Let's fall in love!" Even though we do it, we still need to sing about it. We want to do it more and do it better. What Joanna had done was name it, pay close attention to it, nurture it. And that helped us navigate our lives, the ups, the downs, the challenges, like a navigational chart.

"Liz!" Charlie called from the kitchen. "Do you want me to keep cooking the risotto?"

"Ah, yeah … thank you."

So how could I have hope? Nurture the passion for rescue! Give it room to run. That spitfire that barrels out of the gate, even though its odds are 100-to-1. And the so-called inevitable? The suffering? The starvation? The genocide? The destruction of seas and forests and mountainsides and river deltas, the vicious cycles of cynicism and hatred and indifference? You betcha, it's overwhelming! But does a lioness calculate the odds when she protects her cubs? No! She's firing on all pistons, on that pure, unmitigated life force, that milk of life. There is so much that can be saved. We're not done yet: *this isn't over.*

8

The Family Tree

The road to indifference is well paved. The aggregate of propositions are so familiar it's easy to mistake them for the truth: saving the environment is economically unfeasible; it's a dog-eat-dog world; destruction is unavoidable.

Stage left: enter the detour, the workaround, the unpredictable zigzag art of the possible. Okay, that's what you call it when the day's going well. On bad days, it's the art of the impossible.

It's not about heroes or martyrs or ideologues. *It's a process.* But the people? The unexpected, sweet pie in my face was that as soon as I set foot on that path, I started to meet more beautiful and kind people than I could have ever imagined existed.

Peter Cook held a bucket full of anchovies. There was so much splashing that it was like a pool full of kids who'd each guzzled a six-pack of Coke. Peter called out. The water settled, and a set of big round eyes with a shiny nose and long whiskers glided toward us. A sea lion leapt out of the water.

"Down," Peter said.

The sea lion stretched flat on the ground.

"Stay."

Not a quiver.

"Ronan was really into people," Peter said. "She was twelve weeks old when she was rescued. She kept coming up to people." He turned back to Ronan. "Sit," he said, and Ronan sat up, bright-eyed. Her coat was sleek and shiny.

Peter was in his early thirties. He had curly blond hair and wore jeans and waterproof sandals. "The pups will stay with their mom for six months," he told me, "even up to a year. They have a really strong bond with their mom."

He raised a hand, and Ronan lifted one of her broad flippers for a high five. Then Peter gave her an anchovy, which she swallowed in one gulp.

A few weeks after the volunteer meeting at the Marine Mammal Center, I interviewed Dr. Bill. On his desk was a manila folder with the medical records for Saps, the sea lion Charlie helped rescue. He explained that Saps had been screened for something called domoic acid toxicosis. If you've heard of someone keeling over after eating shellfish, it might have been that—it's also known as amnesiac shellfish poisoning. Domoic acid is a neurotoxin. It's produced by a type of algae bloom, and it gets into our food chain through seafood. It triggers seizures that, over time, damage the hippocampus, the part of the brain responsible for long-term memory.

They had feared that it might have been brain damage that caused Saps to get disoriented and become stranded. But he didn't show any signs of it, so he was released, with the hope that he'd just taken a few wrong turns and gotten lost and then hungry and dehydrated. I peppered Dr. Bill with questions about how marine mammals use their senses to navigate. A blindfolded seal can track a school of fish more than 120 feet away, sensing their wake with their vibrissae—ultrasensitive whiskers.

At the end of the interview, Dr. Bill put his stethoscope around his neck. He was off to make rounds. "They use their senses to survive. If you want to know more, Peter Cook is the guy to talk to." Peter was studying cognitive activity and sensation in marine mammals as part of his doctoral dissertation in cognitive psychology at the University of California at Santa Cruz (UCSC).

"Roll," said Peter. His voice was low. Ronan rolled sideways back into the pool.

The pool into which she flopped was at UCSC's Long Marine Lab's Pinniped Cognition and Sensory Systems Laboratory. *Pinniped* is from a Latin word meaning "fin-footed" and refers to marine mammals that are amphibious—seals, sea lions, and walruses. The lab is run by a leading expert on comparative cognition and bioacoustics, Dr. Colleen Reichmuth.

"Hold." Peter stood at the edge of the water. Ronan backed up a few feet and floated in the water. "Good one, Ro!" Peter threw her another anchovy. Then he called out "porpoise!" and Ronan burst into full form, carving wide, exuberant circles. She swam in undulating arcs above and below the surface, like a porpoise.

"For a sea lion," Peter said, "being in the water may be like a bat being in the air—really fluid three-dimensionality." An Olympic swimmer can manage 5 miles per hour. A sea lion? Twice that. They can dive to more than nine hundred feet and hear sounds over a mile away, not only above water, but also below.[34]

I was so envious. I mean here's the thing: we think sensation is "sensation." You see, you hear—on and on—that's the world. But other creatures sense the world differently. What I would have done to slip into Ronan's sensory suit and experience the ocean through her senses.

Pinnipeds live in both worlds. They give birth and rest in large social groups on land (they "drape over each other" Peter explained), but they feed and migrate in the sea. I recalled being riveted by a photo by the photographer David Doubilet, in which some sardines had formed a "mill formation"—a mesmerizing oval—around a sea lion. The sea lion hovered in a striking moment of poise.

A larger sea lion rested at the other side of the pool. She looked older than Ronan. "That's Rio," Peter said. "She's been here twenty-five years." Rio was the Barbra Streisand of sea lions; she had decades of stardom under her belt. "She's been on Nova and the BBC like … I don't how many times."

Rio had shattered her own type of glass ceiling: the idea that the human brain is the exclusive bastion of logical thinking.

She was the first nonhuman animal to demonstrate logical thinking, doing so in experiments with numbers and letters of the alphabet. "Rio's really, really focused," Peter said.

Rio had also displayed what's called *equivalence classification,* making the mental leap from "A goes with B" and "B goes with C" to "A goes with C." *Equivalence* means "a higher order logical relationship between category members." Humans view flowers as part of the same category, even though individual flowers look quite different from each other. At the heart of showing this in a nonhuman animal was proving that it's not just humans who conceptually order and segment the world to understand it better.

"You should see her running through an experiment," Peter continued. "She has had decades of work, and she knows 'I'm really going to put all my mental resources on that arbitrary stimulus, that random black-and-white picture you just showed me.'"

Peter called out to Ronan. She swam over and leapt out of the pool. Zip! Terrestrial mode: seated, poised, peppy. Peter squatted and moved his face closer to hers. Ronan put her nose to his cheek. Her tapered snout and big whiskers made her seem much more like a "sea dog" than a sea lion.

"Down." Ronan slid down and sniffed my sandals and looked up at me. Ronan was now three. She was rescued and released twice as a pup. When she stranded a third time, it was clear she wasn't going to manage in the wild. So she ended up at the lab, doing elaborate cognitive puzzles.

"Her eyes are so striking," I said.

"They have eye adaptations that allow them to focus both in the air and underwater," Peter explained. "Humans are near-sighted underwater. Without goggles, it's extremely blurry." A sea lion's eyes can also adapt to a greater range of light conditions. Underwater, a sea lion's pupils expand to allow them to forage in extremely low light. Above water, their pupils contract to the size of a pinhole to offset glare from sand or ice. Human pupils expand and contract as well to focus, but not nearly as much.[35]

"Roll," Peter said. This time Ronan did it slowly, seeming to enjoy the languorous flop into the water, yet one more improvisation on the choreographic possibilities of the space around her.

She hovered next to the edge of the pool. Peter stroked her back and her wide-palmed flippers. "They're remarkable climbers. They look awkward on land, because they're flopping all over the place. But they're actually super strong, and their back legs really are legs."

Peter continued to stroke one of her rear flippers. "It's almost like a skirt of skin that holds their legs together. When they walk, you can see that their legs are jointed like normal legs, and they really can run … like fast!" Their wrists and elbows, knees and ankles are held in a sheath of skin flexible enough to give them mobility on land, but which also allows them to propel themselves smoothly through the water as flippers.

Peter pointed to some small mammalian claws on her rear flippers. Marine mammals, he explained, were bear-like mammals living in coastal environments that, fifty million years ago, began to evolve to live in the sea.

Ronan rolled sideways slightly. Peter gestured to me. "Here, put your hand on her belly." I reached out nervously. "Firmly," he said quietly, "but don't startle her."

The water was cold. Ronan's furry coat was soft and warm. I felt her heart beat.

Peter was collaborating with the Marine Mammal Center on a study of domoic acid toxicosis in sea lions. We walked up a dirt road to where he had built what he called a "T-maze" to test the sea lions for memory damage.[36] He pushed his bicycle beside him.

"The Marine Mammal Center said, 'There's this neurological problem that a ton of our animals have, but we don't know what it means for a sea lion to have hippocampal damage. How is that going to affect them in the wild? Is it a death sentence?' "

Domoic acid toxicosis was becoming more common, and there was rising concern that pollution and climate change would increase the algae blooms that caused it. But Peter's study was a little unusual. He chuckled. "The Marine Mammal Center is a rehab facility, and they are really into research. But it's like ... psychologist? What's that?"

A psychologist being part of such a study wasn't typical. Peter spoke rapidly, his voice filled with fascination. "But the disease is neurological. From a veterinary perspective, it's a lot like understanding how an infection affects liver enzymes. They wanted to understand how this brain damage would affect behavior in the wild."

So a win-win scenario was put together. A sea lion was rescued and nursed back to health. If it was suspected of having domoic acid toxicosis, it might do a stint at "Club Cook"—pool, no predator threats, ample supply of anchovies. After several weeks of games involving fish, buckets, and opposing doors in a T-maze, Peter would have gathered behavioral data related to memory and spatial navigation and analyzed it in relation to data from an MRI of the sea lion's brain.[37] Each marine mammal was also assessed by the veterinary staff as to whether it could survive in the wild. Those who could were released, but sadly, any who were deemed unfit to survive on their own and had domoic acid toxicosis often had to be euthanized.

Peter's work reminded me of the concept *solving for the pattern*. The writer and environmental activist Wendell Berry coined the term. The idea is that there are three types of solutions to a problem: bad solutions that make a problem worse, bad solutions that cause more problems than they solve, and good solutions. A good solution doesn't just fix one thing; it has many positive outcomes in surrounding patterns of activity. Solving for the pattern is crucial in a world with overwhelming problems. It's like leverage: the longer the wrench, the more patterns you solve for, the better.

Do you know how, when you're shopping for a certain type of car, suddenly you start seeing it everywhere? And how a vehicle for many people is an expression of who they are? Well, that's how it was with the "art of the possible." Everywhere I went, I was starting to see it. If I were to assemble a toolkit for the art of the possible, *solving for the pattern* would be in it. And there was a lot of that in what Peter was doing.

In the case of Peter's study, you have the initial solution: sea lion rescued, treated, and either released or relocated. Add to that the increased knowledge about brain damage, which improves treatment of brain damage in both humans and nonhuman animals. Further synergies: greater understanding of early childhood development, amnesiac shellfish poisoning, and what climate change is doing to the oceans and our food chain.

As Peter and I walked, I could smell the fresh grass of spring and the salt air. It was very windy, and the fog was dense. The lab is located on a small peninsula, a two-hour drive south from San Francisco. As I drove there that morning, I could see green-brown patches of kelp on the water's surface, the top of the underwater kelp forests that sea lions make their home. It so embodied for me what it was like to be in California, to be in "ocean country."

Peter stopped for a minute. There was a twig wedged in the spokes of his bicycle. I felt so peaceful standing there watching him pull that twig out.

A couple years after I'd moved west, I was on the phone with a friend from New York. "What do you want to stay in California for?" she asked.

"Because I don't have to wear socks," I blurted out, before I had time to think.

Something about California was fundamentally barefoot. If civilization were a castle surrounded by a moat, California was as close to the drawbridge as you could get. But even though I'd moved to "ocean country" decades before, it was like my psyche had gotten stuck in the Dallas–Ft. Worth hub. The kayak accident brought it all to a head. Finally, all of me had arrived.

We started walking again. My pants were wet from Ronan's splashing and the water in my sandals squeaked. Things had changed. Bye-bye high heels, hello sandals. And no socks.

We turned off the road into a fenced area with a small pool. Another sea lion stood up and peered at us curiously.

"That's Midway," Peter said.

Midway was an adolescent male sea lion. He was three days into a two-week stint with Peter. Behind the pool was a rectangular structure cobbled together from weather-beaten plywood—the T-maze.

Peter picked up a plywood-framed mesh ramp and placed it between the pool and the entry to the T-maze. Midway let out a sharp, guttural call. "It's not nasty," Peter said nonchalantly. "It's just like barking, like a show of force."

Peter attached other plywood sheets vertically at the edge of the ramp so that it became a corridor to the T-maze. "One of the most surprising thing about the sea lions is their mobility on land. These really aren't land animals or ocean animals. They are both, which is very rare. I had to change all my experimental stuff after the first couple animals. I'd make the maze this high off the ground," he said, laughing, holding his hand a yard high, "you know, thinking, 'a sea lion can't climb that.'" Peter tugged at the plywood pieces to make sure they were firmly in place. "And they'd be running around on the top of it! I had to make everything higher, and then I'd get a better climber. It was like an arms race." I noticed that in one place the T-maze had extra slabs of plywood nailed to it, making it almost six feet high.

Three days in, Midway was already "working the T-maze." The training had begun with patient games of "hot and cold." Say, for instance, Peter wanted to train a sea lion to go down a ramp. So when the sea lion swam close to the ramp—thwap!— an anchovy would appear. When the sea lion put its head at the top of the ramp, another anchovy. On and on, until the sea lion worked up to more complicated tasks.

The last piece of plywood was in place. We walked up some stairs to a lookout post. Just like the Marine Mammal Center staff, Peter avoided eye contact with Midway. "We don't want to get them really into people," Peter said. "The less they can associate me with the food, the better." Peter hid behind a wall whenever he tossed Midway a reward, so that the fish seemed to plop out of nowhere.

Midway climbed out of the pool and headed down the ramp into the maze. He had two choices—the left door or the right door. He pushed through the door to the right. Peter threw a fish down.

"The basic task we do is called *alternation*," Peter explained.

Midway was back in the pool. Then he headed down the ramp. This time he pushed through the left door.

Ta, da! Another fish. "If you think about it, it's a pretty difficult thing to ask an animal to do," Peter said. "If you're foraging in the wild and you think, 'Okay, I found some fish over by that reef yesterday.' It makes sense to go there again to look for fish, right?"

Midway popped out the door to the right. Plop! Another anchovy. "But here what we're asking them to do is the opposite from what just got them fish," Peter said. "So the sequence is abstract, because you just went through the opposite door and got a fish! In animal-training parlance, that door is now primed. That's a good door, that's a tasty door—I want to go through that door."

Right. Left. Right. Left. Rather than one door, it's *the pattern* that becomes "primed."

After learning the basic alternation task, all animals were tested with a delay—they had to wait for a few seconds at the beginning of each trip through the maze. It was here that the effects of brain damage really showed, because of the extra stress put on memory by the delay.[38]

"Animals with hippocampal damage perform far worse," Peter explained. "This may be related to difficulty in spatial navigation in the wild and may be part of why they have difficulty surviving."

It'd been over a half-hour. Peter reeled in four buckets mounted on lines with pulleys. He put fish in one of them and then lowered the buckets to different locations. "This test is for spatial memory."

Midway started moving from one bucket to another, searching for fish. I couldn't resist thinking that the human form of this would involve car keys.

So all this study of the minds of animals, it takes you right smack to that perennial slippery slope, that gnarly cultural contradiction: how we feel about animals. We butcher them and expose them to horrible forms of cruelty, while others, such as household pets, service dogs, and rescue dogs, have a better standard of living than many people in the developing world.

In the midst of all the debates about this, research into animal cognition chips away at what Peter termed the idea that nonhuman animals are "soulless automatons." The more we know about what is going on in an animal's mind, the less easy it is to dismiss the question that's often brushed off because "it's too complicated": Do animals have a right to exist? Do they have a right to a habitat? Or is the earth and its creatures simply a provider of "ecosystem services," a resource stockpile, and waste-management facility for humans?

Personally, I was leaning in the "rights" direction but still feeling knee-deep in "it's complicated." One of the founders of the antislavery movement, William Wilberforce, also founded the world's first animal-welfare organization, the Society for the Prevention of Cruelty to Animals. That was no coincidence. He championed the rights of the discarded, the shunned, and the forgotten.

Midway found the fish in the second bucket to the left. Peter reeled in the buckets and put another fish into that same bucket.

It's easy to think the view of the earth as a stockpile for humans has to reign. I mean, we have to survive, right? But something nags at us. What breaks through, for so many of us, are the eyes. The eyes of animals awaken something in us.

Getting my first dog, Skippy, was like being doused with that mystery. Skippy was going to be "a pet"—fun, stimulating, like a hobby. Uh, uh. Within twenty-four hours, Skippy had permanently reset the tone: you won't be doling out love with a teaspoon, you'll be doing it with buckets. It was reciprocal. And so much of that was transmitted through his eyes. When that piece of plastic gutted his innards, and the vet explained an exploratory surgery was his only chance to live, I was bowled over with heartache.

"The surgery could be expensive," the vet cautioned me.

I'd been saving money for a car. Blink! Who cares about some thing-a-ma-gig with two axles?

"So ..." the vet paused. "I have your permission?"

"I just want my dog back."

Skippy was ragged and feeble when I carried him up the steps to my bungalow. The incision ran the length of his torso. At night I'd lift him into bed, and he'd rest his head on my belly, look into my eyes, and let out a deep sigh. He was family now. I would have leapt in front of a truck to save him.

Midway waddled over to another bucket. No fish. Peter watched carefully. Then Midway went to another bucket and sniffed. Still no fish.

"So all this work with the sea lions," I asked, "has it reinforced the perception that they have rich inner lives?"

"I'm almost certain nonhuman animals have emotional lives that are at least similar to what humans experience, but you do have to be careful when inferring emotion in an animal you're working with."

Midway was not finding the fish. Peter shook the line to the bucket with the fish. It clattered. Midway turned and headed toward it.

"There is the intuitive sense of that animal feeling something," Peter mused. "Then there's the practical sense, that emotion works in a certain way, and in this situation, it would make sense for the animal to feel a certain way."

Midway chomped down on the fish from the bucket.

"And then there's the neurological approach. Animals have the same circuits devoted to emotions, the same hormones, neurotransmitters, and peripheral nervous reactions to external stimuli that we do. And each of those supports the idea that the animal is experiencing something in the realm of what we experience when we have a thought or a feeling."

We were done for the day. Peter started to disassemble the plywood corridor. Midway jumped into the pool and swam a few small circles. Ten days later he'd depart his fish-wielding captor's accommodations. The veterinary staff would deem him fiddle-fit, and like Saps, he'd waddle out of a crate on the beach and return to his home waters.

"When our dog is having a dream at night," I said, "his paws quiver, and he'll bark in his sleep. I'm always wondering, 'What's he thinking?' "

"The one that is most tenuous, is that direct intuitive feel. There is a lot of good psychology research suggesting that humans are really good at painting the world around them with emotion, even inanimate things, totally inanimate things, like, 'That rock looks like it's smiling!' "

Midway watched Peter cautiously and then lay down and relaxed in the sun as Peter took the ramp apart. "Well, when we step back," he continued, "the rock doesn't have anything that would be required to have a feeling. Look at the neurocircuitry: we have parts of brain that deal with working memory tasks, and mammals have parts of their brain that also are active doing the same sorts of tasks. Parts of our brain dealing with emotional stimuli? So do they. The big difference is that we have this way of referencing things using language, and they don't."

I said goodbye to Peter. He and his wife had a newborn baby at home. He looked tired, but he still overflowed with enthusiasm. He seemed so "placed"—right where he needed to be, his love of working with the animals and his fascination with cognition all funneled into his research.

"Animal welfare is what drove me into psychology," he'd told me. "I thought that understanding how these animals work would help people be more disposed to treat them with respect. But then I started thinking in more applied ways. Like 'Okay, that's all fine, but what can I do, as a psychologist, to positively impact the lives of animals?' "

The work at Long Marine Lab fell into the category of "naturalistic noninvasive neuroscience," an alternative to what is delicately termed *invasive neuroscience,* which means inflicting damage on healthy animals in ways we can barely can stand thinking about. Mice are given domoic acid to induce seizures or parts of their brains are surgically removed, and the resulting brain damage is studied.

There is no official count of how many animals—cats, dogs, hamsters, mice, primates, rabbits—are used in medical research, but in 2014 the Humane Society estimated it at twenty-five million a year.[39] Years before, the woman who raised Skippy's litter told me not to leave Skippy outside when I left home, because she'd heard of a puppy that had been stolen and sold for medical research. That black market, I was now learning, involved millions of animals.[40]

Noninvasive neuroscience was a shift in a new direction, studying animals who had already suffered brain damage from natural causes. And the research is just a brief detour in the rescue and rehabilitation process, which will lead either to release or to a new home, if the animal can't survive in the wild. "I'm not so naïve that I think this type of research will replace the mouse model," Peter said, "but I do believe it's been underexplored and that it can make a valuable contribution."

The patterns Peter was solving for were even richer than

I'd thought: how we treat animals, and how we use them in our research to better our own lives. I wasn't just envious of Ronan, I was envious of Peter. I wanted to find a place in the world like that, where I put all my passion for the sea and all my skills to use.

⟜

There was a small museum next to Long Marine Lab called the Seymour Marine Discovery Center. On one of the walls there was a quote by the mathematician and biologist Jacob Bronowski: "That is the essence of science: ask an impertinent question and you are on your way to a pertinent answer."

Impertinent questions. Add to "art of the possible" toolkit.

Something caught my eye on the far wall in the gift shop, a pattern like a large leaf with multicolored veins. I walked over to have a look. It was a Tree of Life poster.

At the bottom were some of our oldest ancestors, whose wild and beautiful leap we still can't explain—cyanobacteria, those photosynthetic organisms scientists get so dewy-eyed about, because of the consequences of their ancient chemical innovation: all the life we see around us.

I ran my hand upward along the main artery of the tree. I wanted to find Ronan. First stop, a brown fish with four tiny paws—the Tiktaalik—the "fish with a wrist" that would allow it to walk on land. Above it, a branch went off to mammals, and from there, a secondary branch went to that group of mammals who'd taken an evolutionary U-turn and went back to live in the sea again, marine mammals. There were two branches. The first was cetaceans, which included dolphins, porpoises, and whales; the second was amphibious marine mammals, the pinnipeds. There was Ronan's spot. Not far to the left, along the main mammal branch, were those tool-wielding creatures that stood up on two feet, hominoids.

I'm not a big fan of Freud, but if there was ever a day when I made a Freudian slip, this was it. The cashier rolled up the poster and put two rubber bands around it. "I'm sure you'll enjoy this," she said.

"I've always wanted a family tree," I said.

The cashier giggled, "Actually, that's how I think about it."

I walked back to my car. Next to the parking lot was something that looked like the rib cage of an oversized wooly mammoth with elongated jaws. The lab staff had named her "Ms. Blue." She was eighty-seven feet long.

Ms. Blue had washed up nearby in 1979. She was not fully grown at the time, and it was not known why she died. Blue whales can grow to over one hundred feet long. They are the largest known animal to have ever existed, even bigger than any dinosaurs. The lab had reassembled her skeleton with wire scaffolding.

Most opportunities to see a whale skeleton are in a museum bustling with visitors. That day outside the lab, however, there was no one else around. The biting wind whistled through the armature of metal and bone. Right in front of me was one of Ms. Blue's fins. It had a wrist and finger bones.

Whales, like all marine mammals, are warm-blooded, and they surface to breathe. If I'd been able to put my hand to Ms. Blue's cavernous rib cage while she was living, as I'd done to Ronan's, I'd have felt her warm body and the beat of blood in her chest.

I sat down on a bench in front the skeleton and unrolled the poster. It was like being able to read a foreign-language newspaper after years of study. The poster "read" like a family tree: ostrich, dinosaur, butterfly, shark, trout, orchid, fern, snail.

But really, the whole Tree of Life—family? Sure, right. Sweet. Quaint.

Alright, family writ large. Extended. And thank God for impertinent questions. What if we started to think of the Tree of Life *as like a family tree?*"

Stage right: a chorus of invisible voices squeal, "But that's impossible! You can't think like that!"

Just keep going. What if one's sense of family expanded? That sense of a shared thread of vitality and nourishment. That we depend upon each other for our well-being. That rather than dominate and consume as much as we can of each other, we learn to get along better. The Tree of Life wasn't just a map of evolution. It was a map of our interconnected destiny. There it was: the biggest pattern to solve for. I was primed. I wanted to go through that door.

PART 3

The Coral Triangle

9

Divestiture

The plane shook as if it were cutting through a headwind. It was past midnight. Outside the window were miles of black sky with no lights in sight.

Three days before, Charlie had seen me off at San Francisco International Airport. We kissed and hugged over and over. Then Charlie waited while I stood in line at the security gate. I would be gone almost seven weeks. Just before I passed through the x-ray machine, I turned to wave one last time.

Charlie smiled, trying not to look worried. I'd just recovered from a massive dental infection and three root canals. Despite that and my struggles with Hashimoto's disease, well, I was "good to go," but Charlie bit his lip.

I walked into the scanning machine and froze with my hands over my head while a glass cylinder circled with an ultramodern whir. When it opened, I looked back again, but I could no longer see Charlie through the crowd.

It was a semicircular route—San Francisco to Hong Kong, then south to Indonesia, first Denpasar on the island of Bali, then northeast to Makassar on the island of Sulawesi and then my destination in North Sulawesi: Manado.

I wanted to stay with the simple questions. Why is the ocean so important? How can we live without leaving a trail of destruction behind us? And now there was that door I was primed to go through—if we really did share an interconnected destiny with other creatures, how did our lives need to change?

There was no better place to explore these questions than on the thousands of islands beneath the plane—the Coral Triangle, which stretches from Indonesia to Malaysia, the Philippines, the Solomon Islands, and Timor-Leste.

Names matter. The mad-dashed names of patients at The Marine Mammal Center sure drove that home—they are a registry of what we care about. Not a minute too late in the effort to preserve our environment, a new category of geographical names had emerged, forged not by military hubris or politics or property ownership or cultural or ethnic boundaries, but by virtue of biological processes: bioregions. The Coral Triangle consists of the Indonesian-Philippines bioregion and the Far Southwestern Pacific bioregion. It harbors the world's most biologically diverse marine habitats and the highest number of coral species and fish in the world. It is referred to as the Amazon of the underwater world and as the cradle of marine biodiversity.

A voice crackled on the airplane intercom. I only made the last two words, *terima kasih,* which means "thank you" in Indonesian. *Terima* means "I receive" and *kasih* means "love." A few lights appeared below, then more. Shaped like a Rorschach test squiggle, the island of Sulawesi is north of Australia and west of New Guinea. Manado is at the very northern tip.

Some personal divestiture beyond my understanding was occurring. I'd stripped down to one duffle bag and a small carry-on. The dive gear, cameras, and computer all had to fit in that. The remaining nooks were prized real estate for a medical kit, rain jacket, bathing suit, t-shirts, journal, and a few other must-haves. No shampoo. I had my hair cut so short that my ears seemed to jut out like a donkey's. It felt like I was shedding an unneeded skin and heeding some ancient, mysterious gravity.

The whir of the engines shifted, and the plane pitched steeply as we began our descent.

Humid air rushed in when the door of the airplane opened. At the baggage carousel, I felt like a giraffe in a herd of zebras. Most of the other women wore traditional Islamic headdresses. Indonesia is a primarily Muslim country. Out of deference to Muslim tradition, I wore pants and a long-sleeved shirt to cover my arms and legs. People cautiously made eye contact with friendly, shy glances. I felt awkward, but welcome.

It was a long wait for the baggage, and it was the middle of the night. I sat down on the metal edge of the carousel, and my mind sleepily drifted off. I remembered some jazz musicians I'd known in college. One of them, a bass player, drove a Volvo so old he used a screwdriver to start the ignition.

"It's gonna be an oatmeal summer," he said. They'd decided to share a secluded house in the countryside so they could play bebop morning, noon, and night. They'd pooled their cash for rent, gas, the occasional beer, and a big barrel of oatmeal, their symbolic disavowal of distractions.

One day after a concert, the bass player said, "Come by later, bring your flute."

I was getting into my car. "Yeah, right," I started rolling the car window up, "and some condoms?"

"No! We don't want you!" he called out. "We want your flute!" Explanation: the silvery flute would augment the brassy sax and trumpet.

I rolled the window back down, "You really know how to flatter a girl."

He put his hands in pockets. I started the ignition. "Okay, so if I wanted to ... when?"

"Whenever it's *now*," he grinned. "Just come."

"Okay, Zen man." I said as I pulled away. I couldn't sleep that night, so I drove out there at three in the morning. The push-pull beat was audible before I even got out of the car—acoustic bass, sassy drums, tenor sax, and a freewheeling trumpet—a racing, syncopated blood-beat.

Toward sunrise, we had one those feverish surges of energy that you get when you are so tired you can't be tired anymore.

"This one's for you," the bass player said, winking at me while he flipped through his sheet music. It was the Charlie Parker tune "Now's the Time." We played it as an orange glow dusted the green hills outside. The trumpeter wailed on it with such precise fervor I was surprised a light bulb didn't burst.

A grinding noise. I hopped up. The baggage carousel lurched. My duffle bag appeared. Then I felt a tap on my shoulder. A man with broad features showed me some car keys and asked, "Lembeh?"

"Lembeh!" I smiled. "*Terima kasih.*"

The lodge I would be staying in on Lembeh Island had sent a driver to meet me. We drove east across the top of North Sulawesi toward the port city of Bitung. From there I would cross to the lodge by boat. There were few road signs and few other vehicles, save the occasional motorcycle, in the pitch-black night.

The driver smiled. "*Ibu* Liz come long way?" In Indonesia, one is generally known only by one's first name, even on a business card. The literal translation of *Ibu* is "mother," but it is also used for "Ma'am" or "Mrs."

"Yes, San Francisco." I gesticulated "sleep" to him as I rested my head against the car window. Then I dozed off, doing something that I would learn to do time and again in this new and foreign place: trust.

When I woke, we were entering a small city.

"Bitung?" I murmured.

"Ya, Bitung," the driver said.

There were more road signs now and traffic lights. I saw a big concrete compound surrounded by metal fencing.

"Prison?" I asked.

"Fish factory," the driver said. Wresting myself from half-sleep, I vaguely remembered an article describing how, in a tuna-processing plant in Bitung, one worker can cut open four hundred tuna in the course of an eight-hour day.[41]

Another concrete complex, similarly barricaded, with dark, unadorned square windows.

"Prison?" I asked.

"More fish factory." The filleted tuna is vacuum-packed, blast frozen, and then shipped all over the world. The demand for fresh tuna had catapulted with the popularity of sushi. Twenty thousand tons of fresh and frozen tuna was exported by Indonesia to Japan in 2010, thirteen thousand tons to the United States. The numbers defied imagination.

We turned onto a narrow, bumpy street that led to the waterfront. There was a dingy food cart with a dimly lit lantern dangling from it. A man looked at us from inside a parked car with a penetrating gaze that looked like the glare of a rabid pit bull.

"Cops," the driver said quietly. "Place not good at night."

The driver halted swiftly. A small wooden skiff with two men approached, slowed down, and then idled next to the dock. The driver heaved my gear bag to them. I jumped in and turned around to say thank you, but the driver was already pulling away.

We motored out of the dark harbor. Suddenly all those numbers, all those thousands of tons of fish—I didn't need to imagine them anymore. For as far as I could see, loading cranes towered over rusty fishing boats and tankers carrying thousands of shipping containers. This was where the fish came in, bare, shiny, and wide-eyed, and this was where they left, shrink-wrapped and blast frozen. A plate of sashimi or a can of tuna would never look the same.

Our boat sped past more and more loading cranes and tankers, large fishing boats with steel hulls, and small wooden boats draped with nets. Then we glided out into the open night waters.

Now there were no lights in sight ahead of us. We streamed through silky, calm water. To the right, on the mainland, were the outlines of two volcanic mountains over four thousand feet tall, Lokon and Mahawu. To the left was the low-lying dark jungle of Lembeh Island. I had felt so haggard, even before I left home. But now, as the night advanced toward sunrise, under the luminous, velvet-black sky, I felt beautifully awake.

⟨≈⟩

An hour or so later we came around a bend in the island. A small figure appeared in a cove. I heard the sound of a dog barking. One of the staff had waited up to meet me. When I stepped on to shore, the dog sniffed my hands.

She led me up the hill with a flashlight and along a path through the jungle to a bungalow perched over a small, calm inlet of water. The sound of crickets and frogs and the eerie screeches of owls filled the dark air. We bid each other good night with a smile. She handed me a sandwich. I wolfed it down and unpacked a bit. I felt so hot; my body was still used to cool, foggy San Francisco.

A swim! I grabbed my flashlight and clambered down the narrow path to the water. The dog came alongside me.

There was a slip of sand dividing a serene, glassy inlet from the open seas. I dashed knee-deep into the calm inlet. The dog halted at the water's edge, legs stiff.

Maybe a cold shower would be better.

I walked back up to my bungalow, took a long, cold shower, and lay down. A gecko lizard chirped from the ceiling. I drifted quickly off to sleep.

⟨≈⟩

A chorus of birds woke me at dawn. It was my first sniff of understanding the term *biodiversity.* I'd been awash in all kinds of cerebral definitions like "the degree of variation in life forms."

But what was so urgent? Why was the loss of biodiversity so potentially catastrophic? I didn't get it.

But that morning I began to translate that word, biodiversity, into one of many phrases I would come up with. Not only did the Coral Triangle have the greatest marine biodiversity, but Indonesia was also ranked fourth in the world for terrestrial biodiversity, after Brazil, Colombia, and China.[42] As I walked through the dense green jungle, astounded by the cacophony of bird calls, I translated "biodiversity," into "richness of life." I could see it with my own eyes—more types of trees, ferns, flowering plants, more types of birds, butterflies, amphibians. The mosaic of life had more pieces. It was different now—me, us, and the "rest of life"—the Tree of Life was thick with the mystery of how much we have in common.

The manager of the lodge had arranged for a divemaster, Winston, and a translator, Upung, to take me to a nearby village named Kasawari to interview some local fishermen. We motored there in a small boat. Along the way I noticed many dark-brown beaches, made from volcanic ash. We were in the Ring of Fire. Three months later, one of the volcanoes on the mainland, Lokon, would eject a plume of ash into the air two and half miles high.

Several families lived in Kasawari in small homes they had built themselves from thin slats of bamboo and old plywood. Some of the roofs were thatched with a tall, coarse grass. Behind were hillsides dense with lush green plants and thousands of palm trees. A few hens and a rooster wandered about. It was drizzling.

Upung introduced me to a villager named Ronny. I nodded sheepishly, notebook in hand, while Upung explained what I was doing—"American journalist" here to "study marine biodiversity" and "how the condition of the ocean affects people in the developing world."

The look on Ronny's face was at once quizzical and respectful. His home was at the edge of the water. He showed me with pride fishing nets he'd woven by hand and several boats that he had built with other villagers—finely crafted outrigger sailing canoes, painted bright blue and green and yellow. Many fishermen build their own boats, and some of history's greatest boatbuilders came from Sulawesi.

"There are fewer and fewer fish," Ronny told me. "When I was a child, it was easy to catch fish. I was born in 1970. Now we take the boat and go farther and farther, and the fish, when we do get them, they are very small. Until around 1990 there were lots of fish, now there are very few."

The research on the Coral Triangle was grim: fisheries decline (industrial and small-scale overexploitation), poverty increases in coastal areas (lack of fish to eat or loss of employment in the fisheries industry), and access to clean water in decline (pollution, rising sea levels contaminating fresh-water aquifers, lack of waste management). But the research hadn't yet registered fully in me. I'd read it in the midst of days crammed with other things competing for my attention. And then there's the degree to which you can digest excessive horrors. By this point, I'd trained myself not to get too upset by what I read. There was a barrier between me and that data, like an impact-resistant windshield.

Ronny talked about garbage in the strait between Lembeh Island and North Sulawesi. The city of Bitung had begun a waste-management program, but for years they bulldozed the garbage of over one hundred thousand people right into the water. Twice on our way to village we had stopped the outboard motor to untangle plastic and fishing line from the propellers. And the big trawlers that cruised outside the straight, Ronny said, were pillaging the fish populations. When he was a child, there were whales and sharks and manta rays. Now it was years since he had seen any.

When we were almost done, I asked, "Is there anything else you would like to tell me?"

"Yes," he said. "We need water. There is no fresh water anymore." His wife and his kids were watching. His wife made eye contact with me.

"When we do have a good catch, when catch more fish than

we can eat, we sell it to buy petrol for the motorcycle," he explained. "Then we drive to the water plant, a desalinization plant, to buy forty liters of water. We try to make that last a week."

The windshield shattered. Forty liters? That was ten gallons. *Ten gallons a week?* They had three children. And that was the good week, when they'd caught more fish than they could eat. How much polluted, bacteria-ridden water did they drink in order to survive?

As we motored away, I clutched my notebook. I promised Ronny I'd make sure his words were heard.

One hundred million Indonesians lacked access to safe drinking water. That's the equivalent of everyone in California, New Jersey, New York, Texas, and Virginia combined.[43] UNICEF estimates that around the globe, insufficient access to clean water, lack of sanitation, and poor hygiene causes 1,400 children to die from diarrheal diseases *every day*.[44]

The village disappeared into the gray-green hues of the hillside.

We came to a small inlet and lashed the bow line to a tree trunk in the shade of some overhanging trees. The lodge had packed stir-fried chicken for us, along with some cookies. The five-gallon cooler of water on the boat now looked like a garish luxury item.

Winston put his palms together and next to one ear, gesturing "nap." I smiled and climbed on top of the tiny wheelhouse and dozed off, my head resting on a rolled-up t-shirt. In the tiny boat, everyone found a spot to sleep.

An hour later, we motored away from the shore a bit, and Winston and I slipped on our scuba gear and rolled backward off the side of the boat.

The ocean floor was like a black-and-gray moonscape of volcanic ash. Since the mid-Pleistocene, over 126 millennia ago, the nearby volcanoes had been pumping out silt so finely grained that it made a cloud in the water if your fin kicked it. All kinds of unusual critters had adapted to live in that volcanic ash.

A fish with broad, wing-like fins crawled across the bottom—a flying gurnard. It was almost the exact same color of the volcanic ash. It looked part bird, part fish, part animal. It used finger-like extensions at the ends of its wing-like fins to move itself.

A school of slender fish floated vertically, with their heads downward—rigid shrimpfish. A sea urchin had neon blue spots that radiated like a miniature Times Square on New Year's Eve. Something that looked like a small eel, with black-and-white bands, swam out in the open water. Later Winston told me it was a juvenile banded sea snake.

We came upon some anemonefish, often called "clownfish," the most well known being the orange-and-white-striped variety of *Finding Nemo* fame. Each type of clownfish lives in tight symbiosis with a certain type of anemone. As I got closer I saw that some eggs had hatched in the anemone. Several dozen newly hatched clownfish hovered inside the anemone like vulnerable bumblebees.

One of the adult clownfish swiftly swam up to me and hurled its entire weight at my mask. Thwap!

Huh?

Thawp! Thwap! Thwap!

Even though I weighed thousands of times more, the clownfish pounded my mask like a rubber mallet. The male clownfish defends the eggs and the new hatchlings.

I backed away. He swished confidently back to the anemone. There was something raw and unmitigated about this pugilistic little fish, as if he were taking on Godzilla with a golf club while his wife hovered in the bedroom with their newborn.

Foolish? Well, I backed off. And as far as that fish was concerned, that's all that mattered.

At supper there was a botanist who was visiting to research a rare pitcher plant. "It's like a giant Venus fly trap," he said calmly. He sat very upright and chewed his food slowly. "It's big enough to eat a rat."

In every part of the world, there's some subject that's endemic to conversations. New York City? Getting mugged. San Francisco? Earthquakes. In Indonesia, one of the most frequent subjects of late-night drinking banter is *venomous creatures*.

I got up to get another shot of rum. The laughter at the dinner table got louder. The names of the creatures just kept coming: stonefish (disguises itself as a stone, neurotoxins are fatal); scorpions (check your shoes in the morning before putting them on); and the banded sea snake, which I'd seen that day (their venom is ten times more deadly than a rattlesnake's).

I sat back down.

"But don't … but don't," an elderly Dutch gentleman chimed in, giddily, barely able to eke out the words because he was trying to contain his laughter. "But don't forget the jellies."

"Jellyfish?" I asked.

"Ja, ja …" he replied. "The moon jellies, they are not too bad, but the box jelly has been moving north, and we see them now in Sulawesi."

"Because of warming seas?"

"*Ja, ja*. And the box … it stuns the prey." His speech slowed as he cut into a piece of meat with the precision of a surgeon. "And the toxins, they attack the heart and the nervous system. The heart can fail before you even get back to the boat."

A British woman at the end of the table leaned forward and said with raised eyebrows, "It's said to be the world's most venomous creature, even more than the king cobra."

I took another sip of rum.

"The lagoon …" the Dutchman added with his mouth full, pointing his knife with a casual flick to where I'd waded into the water the night before, where the dog's legs had gone stiff. "The lagoon is full of them."

10

Heart

It happens not long after the beginning: the heartbeat. Each of us has our plankton-like phase in the nourishing brine inside the belly of our mother. When we're no larger than a drop of water, our heart beats for the first time with a primitive circulatory system. When we are born, the umbilical mother-breath that sustained us is swapped out for every breath we take in the world.

～

Two days later, a small plane carried me from North Sulawesi to West Papua, the western half of the island of New Guinea. We flew low over jungle islands that looked like droplets of green on the blue expanse.

I boarded a wooden schooner that was taking a group of divers and photographers into the Raja Ampat archipelago. If the Coral Triangle was the heart of marine biodiversity, then Raja Ampat was the "heart of the heart"—remote islands that had been determined to be the absolute epicenter of marine biodiversity.

When I boarded the boat, photographers were prepping camera rigs that looked like miniature Mars Rovers with strobes mounted on extension tubes and dome-shaped lenses as big as dinner plates. We motored south from the port of Sorong through a cut between the island of Salawati and the Doberai peninsula. Wavy patterns of clouds filled the sky with a magenta glow at sunset. Then the dark green of the islands merged with the darkness.

I unpacked my things, putting them into small wooden drawers with latches used to secure them in rough weather. I was giddy—I'd made it! Next to my bunk I tucked my journal, some antacids, and a bottle of probiotic capsules.

Two months of antibiotics to treat the dental infection had left behind a trail of heartburn attacks and a host of feminine biological woes. So what do you do when antibiotics gut your system and you're wondering when you will ever have unbridled sex with your husband again? Probiotics! At the pharmacy, the label read, "Live microbial organisms. Amount per serving: fifty billion organisms."

Organisms? Excuse me? Microscopic creepy-crawly things? I'm supposed to invite *them* to live inside my body?

Yes. Antibiotics kill off not only harmful bacteria but also "beneficial bacteria." Our bodies don't function well without those beneficial ones. The fix was to invite to specific bacteria to make their home inside my body.

The guest list? *Lactobacillus acidophilus, Bifidobacterium bifidum,* and *Lactobacillus plantarum.* There were three types of organisms in the "proprietary blend." So we had all arrived: me and my organisms.

A storm was brewing in, so the captain had chosen to motor overnight to one of the southernmost islands, Misool, where the weather might be better. There was a glass portal next to my bunk. I fell asleep to the sound of waves sloshing against it and the rumble of the engine. Just before dawn, the boat lurched in reverse and a metallic clankity-clank rang out loudly—the anchor line. Then there was nothing but sweet silence and the rocking of the boat.

⌇☙

A black backdrop for a photograph sets the colors in the image in sharp relief. The darkness rests the eye and makes it more receptive to what the image has to offer. Arrivals at night can be like that, especially if you're asleep and don't see the land-scape in the dark. Then, just after waking, your mind fresh from sleep and dreams, the place hits you all at once.

At sunrise there were footsteps and the sound of silverware in the galley above. A narrow, steep stairway led up to the deck and out into the light. My neck immediately craned upward, as if I were coming out of a subway station in downtown Manhattan.

Karst limestone islands over ten stories high towered above us, narrow pinnacles of jagged gray-black stone covered with jungle brush. A swarm of frigate birds circled over their peaks. The base of the islands jutted in from water erosion, as if a giant lumberjack had cut into them in preparation for felling them like trees. These were the green droplet shapes I had seen from the airplane—some towering pinnacles, others sloping like sleeping bodies, rounded and knobby.

We loaded our gear into a small boat and headed to a dive site. Then, all together, we sat at the edge of the boat and rolled backward into the water.

I've never been lost in a cornfield. I mean, I've heard stories about it happening. People wandering off and getting lost, en-veloped by thousands of eight-foot corn stalks, losing all sense of orientation.

It was like that. Nothing but fish. Iridescent, oval blue bodies with yellow tails called fusiliers. I looked up, and all I could see were their elegant cutout shapes against the rays of morning light. Above, below, side to side—the school just kept going and going.

A swarm of anchovies the length of a basketball court de-scended on us and hid the fusiliers like a sheath of glittering fabric, stretching and darting into all kinds of fantastic forms. It was so beautiful, so overwhelming, that all I could think was, *It's raining fish.*

Under the dark overhang of the limestone towers was coral that looked like huge tufts of cauliflower, in all kinds of colors—green, magenta, rose, orange. There was coral shaped like foot-tall flower petals, the thickness of leather, other coral like yard-wide platters. And everywhere, fish: blennies, gobies, breams, damselfish, anthias, a peacock grouper with a brilliant blue tail.

The anchovies were back, engulfing us. Finally they parted like a gigantic curtain, and I was lost again in the flickering, yellow-tailed blue field of fusiliers.

There were aboriginal petroglyphs, the crew told me, just around the bend from where we were anchored. One evening I paddled off in search of them. The glassy waters were only a few feet deep, and I could see coral filled with thousands of small fish. The limestone towers cast elongated green reflections.

It started raining. I slipped my kayak under some jungle brush for shelter. It was the middle of the southern monsoon season, which meant that it might rain every day, for a few minutes or an hour, or it might storm for days.

It was nice to pause and watch the rain pour down. My stomach growled. I pulled out an apple and nibbled on it. I'd arrived at the heart of marine biodiversity. Everywhere we went, we were bombarded by new types of coral and fish and sponges and anemones. "Don't try to figure it out," I told myself, "just sponge in as much as you can."

In my journal the night before I'd written, "This place is messing with my senses." But perhaps it wasn't vertigo. Maybe it was a reorientation, that I was acquiring sensations for things that I'd thought were only "ideas." Gravity's like that. It's an idea, but jump off a tall pier into the water, and it's a sensation!

The jungle was full of boisterous bird calls, caws and squawks completely unfamiliar to my ear. In French, the word *flash* is slang for a sudden moment of comprehension, when you suddenly "get it." To me the word *ecosystem* had always been a bit cone-headed. It's defined as "a community of living organisms (plants, animals, microbes) living in conjunction with non-living components of the environment (air, water, and soil)." There wasn't much life in that word for me.

Two hornbills flew over the open water with serrated black wings. The loud whoosh of their wings mixed with the sound of the downpour.

Flash! Healthy ecosystem. Vibrant community of creatures living in synchrony. Thriving, rich, overflowing with energy and activity.

I'd never seen a place so alive. The morning after I landed in Sulawesi was my first taste of it, when the jungle overflowed with bird calls. It was like gravity—I "knew of it," but I'd never jumped off the pier.

The hornbills settled in the brush. They had prominent curved beaks and orange-gold feathers on their heads. As the rain poured down, the barriers between sea and sky and land seemed to vanish.

One part of the apple was bruised and starting to rot, but I was so famished I ate it all. I peered out at the horizon through the silky downpour. There were over 1,500 islands in Raja Ampat. And then there were the islets, some no larger than a big navigational buoy. Sometimes a large stone jutting up out of the water had a small tree or bush on it that had managed to take root and grow, dwarfing the stone by comparison. It'd look like an oversized tuft of hair coming out of a bald-headed Dr. Seuss character. How did the seed get there? Bird? Current? Wind? How did it take root? Everything seemed set in stark relief. Hunger. A rotting apple. A seed finding the means to thrive on a rock jutting out of the sea.

The rain stopped. I pushed back out onto the open water. The sun came out, and everything glistened. Paddling a little farther around the island brought me into a lagoon; there was a huge patch of exposed stone with markings in black and rusty ochre. Pitcher plants, which did indeed look like cylindrical containers with leafy lids were nestled in the jungle, along with wild orchids.

The cliff went up twenty or thirty feet. It had a stark, almost magnetic presence. Some three thousand years ago, the early inhabitants of Raja Ampat had inscribed images of dolphins and fish and handprints on it and colored them with red betel-nut juice. I rested one hand on the stone. It was cool from the rain and rough, like sandpaper, with sharp edges in places.

I heard a wooden thump in the distance and turned around. On the other side of the bay was a dugout canoe fitted with a mast. A cloth sail flapped as a man pulled in a small fishing net. The very first settlers in Raja Ampat were the Ma'ya people, who arrived in dugout canoes and on bamboo rafts fifty thousand years ago. At that time, there was still a land bridge between New Guinea and Australia.

As the evening light faded, a school of flying fish broke the surface of the green-blue water with speckles of pearly shapes. And the bird calls grew louder.

"Would you help me with this?" I called out. My hands were wet and slipping when I tried to open the air valve on my tank. It was pouring rain.

"No problem, Ibu!" The divemaster opened it without a blink. A burst of air filled my gear.

Descending into the ocean, I looked up and watched the pellets of rain and the foamy sea surge disappear. The water felt denser than usual; it was full of small particles. The reef was darker, because of the rain; everything moved with heightened energy. A school of shiny, stout-bodied trevallies funneled upward almost vertically, as if shooting out of a gigantic waterspout. Batfish swam in the opposite direction, plunging downward. Anchovies collided with a swarm of jacks. The school of anchovies broke apart and reformed with an acrobatic snap.

A strong current carried four other divers and me along a reef wall. The boat captain would follow our bubbles and pick us up at the end of the dive. If he lost us, one of us would inflate a "safety sausage," a neon-orange six-foot tube that could be spotted from far away; each of us had one clipped to our gear.

The current surged and shifted, occasionally pulling us sideways or upward or downward. That intense mixing of currents is one of the main reasons Raja Ampat is the bull's eye of marine biodiversity. Currents shoot into the maze of the islands from the Pacific and the Indian Ocean and splinter into spidery configurations. The creatures that ride those oceanic superhighways are so varied and rich that scientists call Raja Ampat a "species factory," a region especially conducive for new species to come into being. "Heart" meant not only biodiversity epicenter but also "circulatory crossroads."

The waters grew denser and denser with skittish schools of fish that constantly changed direction. A horde of silvery barracuda mingled with a school of snapper. One of the barracudas ripped apart a snapper. Another lunged at the refuse of the snapper in the water.

Something approached in the distance that looked like a prehistoric bird with triangular wings—a reef manta. It swam closer, gracefully, with unfettered calm. Its underbelly was ivory with gray speckles. The top of its cape-like fins was black. Its "wingspan" was at least twelve feet. Its mouth was wide open and cavernous.

Hunting of manta rays was on the rise. Like sharks, who were hunted for just their fins for shark-fin soup, the mantas were hunted just for their gill rakers, which were used in Chinese medicine. The market for gill rakers was booming, and conservationists warned that mantas might be facing extinction. A single fishing fleet could wipe out an entire population within weeks. In some fishing villages in Indonesia, it was reported that fishermen caught more than two thousand mantas a year.[45]

The water was so cloudy with particles I didn't even reach for my camera. But for the manta, the dense water was a banquet—minestrone soup! Or rather, plankton soup. Tiny shrimp, krill, and crab. Those pesky specks that would have ruined my photos were what Jenny Stock had described with so much excitement: an upwelling. It was a feeding frenzy. Everyone was coming: zooplankton, copepods, coral larvae, fish larvae. Any one of these microscopic creatures might become a new, larger life.

Mantas are the object of much fascination because they have the largest brain-to-body brain ratio of any fish. Reef mantas make their home in shallow areas and can grow to eighteen feet wide. This one had likely lived its entire lifespan in the islands. Oceanic mantas—the largest type of manta—dwell in offshore waters and migrate thousand of miles. But they frequent Raja Ampat to feed on the rich currents. Their wingspan can reach twenty-five feet.

We came to a shallow sloping area. Thousands of reddish, translucent fish swam beneath the coral in an area no larger than two square yards—golden sweepers. They circled beneath the coral in the tightest formation of fish I'd ever seen, almost touching.

I'd always wondered what ancient seas looked like, before humankind began to deplete them—those waters from which the first "fish with a wrist" walked onto the land. That day in the storm might well be the closest approximation I will ever experience—the seas were such a rich, thriving brine.

Once, when Eiglys, Amdeep, and I had gone out to dinner in the Turks and Caicos, Amdeep and I chatted about diving and how amazing it was to be able to breathe underwater.

"It just takes me to this mysterious place," I said. "But then the feeling is gone; I can never hang on to it."

"Yeah, I know what you mean. What is that?" Amdeep raised both eyebrows.

"Maybe it's cellular memory? Something in our DNA? A little piece of evolution?"

Amdeep shook his head. "I don't know, but it's this archaic feeling."

We came upon a yard-wide gap in the wall. The other divers kicked through it handily. I kicked toward it, but another current was funneling through the gap toward me and kept pushing me back. I couldn't seem to swim hard enough to get through. I wheezed through my mouthpiece. Finally, near breathless, I managed to kick through.

On the other side of the gap, the current eased. A curved area sheltered us from it. We hovered together at exactly fifteen feet and began our safety stop. The divemaster unfurled his safety sausage, inflated it, and released it to the surface, keeping hold of its cord, so the boat could find us.

I caught my breath. My heart had been pounding wildly, but it now eased to a steady rhythm. One of the divers tapped his computer and held up five fingers to indicate he needed to do a five-minute safety stop. The divemaster nodded.

When someone dives especially deep, stays down a long time, or is diving many days in a row, his or her computer may prompt a safety stop longer than three minutes, based on calculations of excess nitrogen in the bloodstream. That stop is mandatory—unless you're in a life-or-death situation, you want to make sure to do it. It means you have done a "decompression dive" and if you don't do the stop, you are at high risk for decompression sickness. If you surface at this time, it's extremely dangerous. You don't surface unless you are out of air or there is another type of emergency.

So it would be a longer stop, but we were all together and protected from the current. Each of us settled into his or her own internal quiet, enjoying the sensation of weightlessness.

Thousands of silversides encircled us, breaking apart and reforming into schools. The waters beneath the karst limestone overhang were blue-black. The silversides looked like swirling, glittering slits of light against them.

The safety stop is at least three minutes, because that's how long it takes for an average person's blood to completely recirculate in the body. When I was diagnosed with Hashimoto's disease, I became acutely aware of my heartbeat. If the thyroid dosage wasn't correct, my heart would race or beat abnormally slowly and wreak havoc with my body—weakness, dizziness, indigestion, and vision problems. Every year or two, the thyroid dosage I needed shifted. After several cycles of this, I realized that my heart rate gave me a heads-up that I was becoming ill.

So most mornings, I put my hand to my neck and take my pulse. It is a daily reminder of that organ in my chest that pumps blood at five quarts a minute, of that oxygen-infused brine that travels an average of twelve thousand miles a day through my veins.[46]

The silversides moved with such acuity to each other's movements and that of predators—left, right, up, down, swish! I wondered if they sensed my heart beating, that muscular organ that had pumped blood through my veins ever since I was a multicellular speck of life.

At fifteen feet, we could see the storm surge smashing against one of the karst island overhangs. Everything was in motion. As through a ventricle or a valve or a vein, the life blood of the sea poured through the straits of the islands over and over.

When we surfaced, the rain had stopped. The sharp-edged cliffs were a shiny brown-black. Etched against the ruler-straight horizon was another storm front.

⁓

"Mind if I come in?" I asked.

"*Silahkan.* Please." The captain kept his hands on the wheel. The wheelhouse was perched at the top of the boat with view of the night waters. There was a large nautical chart stretched out on a wooden counter, held in place by several large seashells.

"I was just curious to see where we're going."

"Have a look." He traced a line with his finger on the chart from Misool north to the island of Waigeo. We were motoring away from a storm that was going to linger in the south. While I looked, he reached for a radio handset. He rattled something off in Indonesian and then put the receiver down.

"What's up?" I asked.

"See that?" He pointed to a dot of light on the far right of the horizon. "That's a trawler. We don't want to foul the lines."

"But that's like a mile away."

He pointed to another small light on the other side of the horizon, way to the left. I squinted.

"That's the end of the net," he said.

Oh, Lordy, this was where the cornfield of fusiliers, the engulfing veils of anchovies, and shiny, taut-bodied jacks met trawlers. I had just finished reading Charles Clover's *End of the Line,* a devastating account of how industrial fishing is extracting staggering quantities of sea life. The United Nations Food and Agriculture Organization estimated in 2008 that the global fish catch was 79.5 million metric tons.[47]

The age-old hunt for fish was now armed with military-grade, high-tech armaments—freezer boats equipped with spotter helicopters, space-aged binoculars, state-of-the-art sonar, and nets so gigantic that they could drape over several 747s. The boats can process 250 tons of fish a day. Industrial bottom trawlers decimate underwater habitats like gigantic bulldozers.

"Sometimes there are so many that I spend the whole night going around the nets," the captain continued.

"But we are in Raja Ampat?"

"Yes, Ibu, but we are not in the MPA anymore. When we get a little farther north, we'll be back in it."

Fish populations were plummeting at astronomical rates. But the number of MPAs—marine protected areas—was growing. In West Papua, a network of MPAs had just been established by Conservation International, the Nature Conservancy, and the World Wide Fund for Nature (WWF). It was called the Bird's Head Seascape. This, like the network of MPAs in California, was an extremely collaborative effort. The Bird's Head Seascape combined fisheries regulations and enforcement systems with empowering local communities to strengthen their rights to manage marine resources and sustainable development efforts.

Before I boarded the boat in West Papua, I chatted with Helen Newman and Simon Day, the founders of the Sea Sanctuaries Trust, which had just established a Marine Conservation Agreement (MCA) around the uninhabited island of Penemu in Raja Ampat. MCAs are private agreements between a local community and a nongovernmental organization, such as Sea Sanctuaries, with the support of the local government.[48] Helen and Simon spent more than a year talking with community members about a marine conservation project before gaining their trust and formalizing an agreement. The MCA gave Sea Sanctuaries the right to undertake conservation work for twenty-five years. In addition, Sea Sanctuaries helped the local villagers develop sustainable businesses, such as a coconut--oil company, to provide them with a source of income other than destructive fishing practices. And they trained the villages to patrol the MCA.

"The need for more MPAs is massive," Helen had told me. "Raja Ampat has survived so far because it's underdeveloped. There are not many places like this left. We're at the bottom of the barrel; we've got to save what's there."

For so many centuries, *ocean* was almost synonymous with *infinity*. But the oceans are now becoming so depleted that it is clear we have to protect parts of the sea as we do park land. Some 10 to 15 percent of all land has been set aside as park land.[49] But the ocean? When I spoke with Helen and Simon, it was 2.8 percent.[50]

Helen was cautiously optimistic about the MPAs. The work with local communities was progressing well, but not without some struggle. "As there are fewer and fewer fish outside the

MPAs, the pressure for fishermen to go into the MPAs and fish illegally gets stronger and stronger."

One the most obvious examples was that sharks were now rarely seen in Raja Ampat, because so many had been slaughtered for shark-fin soup—the fishermen often cutting just the fins off and then tossing the shark back into the sea to die a slow, horrific death. In contrast, almost every time I was underwater in the Turks and Caicos, I saw one or two sharks. They were endangered there as well, but not as acutely as in Southeast Asia, where the population declines were stunning—many shark species having declined over 50 percent to 97 percent in the last few decades.[51]

The cynic's vision could easily prevail—that no matter how hard the conservationists work, the MPAs would still succumb to overfishing and other forms of damage. But change doesn't happen overnight. In the early years after Yosemite National Park was established, there was still illegal logging. Eventually public consensus grew such that the park was properly protected. For the Bird's Head Seascape, it was a scramble against time to marshal enough consensus and collaboration to protect it.

I said goodnight to the captain and climbed up on the bow of the boat. I lay on my back and looked up at the sky. The schooner had been built in the tradition of the great boatbuilders of Sulawesi. Wooden ladders ran up either side of the traditionally rigged masts.

I was far from home. But for some creatures, the scope of home reached all the way back to California. Leatherback turtles off the California coast migrate over six thousand miles to sandy beaches in West Papua, returning to the exact beach where they had hatched to lay their own eggs. The protected waters of Papua were among the last remaining sanctuaries for the endangered leatherback turtles in the entire Pacific and Indian Oceans.

❧

"It's like gold," Helen had told me.

The water was clear. I was on a long, shallow reef at about thirty feet, lit by morning sun. And I couldn't help but remember what Helen had told me, because now I saw it with my own eyes.

"Please, layman's terms," I'd said. I'd asked her why preserving biodiversity was so crucial.

There were so many platters of coral stacked on top of each other it was like some fantasyland. Plumes of fish slipped through intricate crevices. Behind them, like a scrolling backdrop, thousands of fish swam by in schools. It was palatial—if I were a fish, this would be the most sumptuously magnificent abode.

"Biodiversity is like gold," Helen had said. "It's what you put away; it's what you rely on in tough times. Take rice—that feeds people, right? If you have many strains of rice, there is a lesser likelihood of mass starvation if a blight strikes the region, because some of the strains will survive. With climate change and rising sea levels, the more diversity of coral you've got, the more chance that some will survive."

Helen had tapped a spot on a map of Raja Ampat just south of latitude 0. "See this?" She ran her finger along a wide strait. "That's the Dampier Strait. It's one of the main arteries of the archipelago. It has extremely dense diversity." Water from the Pacific shot into the strait and accelerated through the forty-mile funnel between the islands. The strong offshore currents roared in and created a jet effect. Along with a rich brine of plankton and coral larvae, the swift and unpredictable currents brought large schools of fish. And it was a major migration corridor for mantas, sharks, turtles, and whales.

This was one of the reasons why the Sea Sanctuaries Trust had established their MPA where they did. It was right on the receiving end of that nutrient-rich current, at the western end of the Dampier Strait. "A lot of larvae are being generated in this area, because the biodiversity is so high," Helen had told me. "You have a sufficient size of a protected area where fish can reproduce. That means they are just chucking out lots of larvae, which restocks other areas."

The reef I was on was smack in the middle of the Dampier Strait, a little underwater ridge surrounded on all sides by deep blue water. The current was swishing me along so fast I felt like I was going to get a speeding ticket. Out of the corner of my eye I saw a black-and-white glitter. A shiver went down my spine. A banded sea snake came up from behind me and passed just in front. It was several feet long. Its black-and-white bands shimmered like a barber-shop pole. It terrified me, but it was also startlingly beautiful. It vanished into the coral.

I warily swam on. While the banded sea snake is highly venomous, it is generally said to have a "placid temperament." There are no accounts of divers being killed by them, but local fishermen have died while disentangling them from fish nets. The esteemed ichthyologist Gerald Allen adds one caveat to the "placid temperament" theory—a sea snake once chased a fuel drum he and his colleagues were transferring through the water to a boat. Greatly agitated, it repeatedly attempted to bite the drum, even as they hoisted it on deck.[52]

We came upon some staghorn coral. The last time I'd seen staghorn coral was during the bleaching event in the Turks and Caicos. There the coral had been covered with algae and bereft of fish, but here scores of fish darted in and out of the antler-like shapes. The coral was a healthy brown color with white tips.

To save creatures, you need to save their habitats. And pulling just one type of creature out of a habitat can cause that habitat to collapse. Coral is a keystone species. Like the hub of a wheel, if it is lost, it causes a collapse. If coral dies, it triggers a collapse. Mangroves and seagrass are similar keystone species.

When you save coral, you are saving the habitat that it forms: coral reefs are home to 25 percent of all marine life.[53]

And there was a compelling reason why the coral in Raja Ampat was such a focus of conservation efforts. "Raja Ampat," Helen had told me, "already has quite a lot of fluctuations in temperatures, so there is good chance that we have corals that are more resistant to climate change." Raja Ampat had over six hundred species of coral, ten times that of the Caribbean, as well as over fifteen hundred species of fish, four times the number found in the Caribbean. That's a lot of possible pathways to survival.

I was getting it. The more biodiverse an ecosystem is, the more resilient. The more spokes on the wheel, the less likely it is to collapse if one spoke breaks. The dazzling diversity of the reef wasn't surface beauty, it was *crucial beauty*.

The reef dropped several feet to an open plateau. The other divers turned around to stay on the reef. Curious, I kicked out onto the plateau, which was nothing but stubby white rubble. The reef had been dynamite fished, pulverized into small pieces like bones. Fishermen use dynamite or homemade explosives to kill or stun fish. Then divers collect the fish from the decimated ocean floor and the ones that float to the surface.

I kicked out another hundred yards; it was as barren as if leveled for an airplane runway. The bleached reef in the Turks and Caicos at least had some signs of life trying to eek out an existence, the occasional fish nibbling on some algae. But this reef had been completely obliterated.

It was a stomach-turning reminder of the sixth mass extinction, the outcome of the massive biodiversity loss occurring. Scientists estimate that we are losing species at over one thousand times the normal rate. Dozens of species are going extinct every day.[54]

I swam back toward the other divers. The current had kicked up, making it difficult for me to catch up with them. I reached down to make sure I had my safety sausage and felt the roll of nylon clipped to my gear. "If the current sweeps you off the reef," the divemaster had told us, "do a blue stop and inflate your safety sausage so we can find you." A "blue stop" is a safety stop in open, blue water where you have no topography to orient yourself. While you do the stop, you keep your eyes on your depth gauge to make sure you stay as close as you can to fifteen feet.

I wasn't too thrilled at the idea of a blue stop, so I decided to make a go at swimming back to the reef. Breathing deeply and slowly kicking as forcefully as I could, I made it back and ducked beneath a large overhang of coral to get out of the current. There I rested with the other divers in view. I knelt down on a patch of sand, exhausted.

Blizzards of fish surrounded the little oasis I was tucked into. Everything was alive again. It was all overflowing, whirring and buzzing and darting and flashing. A group of shiny jacks circled me and shot off.

I felt like I'd just woke from a terrible nightmare. *Thank you, thank you, fish, so happy to see you!* I was back in the palatial overflow of insanely beautiful life.

As the fish swirled and darted, I asked myself, *What is this? This thriving?* It's thriving because it's an "us," not an "it." The "we" that we are is all about the "us"—that never-ending exchange of energy. Coral needs a specific type of algae, whales need krill, turtles need jellyfish and sponges, and parrotfish need coral. And us? We need fresh water. We need food and fresh air and sunlight.

An ecosystem is all about energy exchange: life force! And biodiversity is what makes it tick. It primes the pump. The food chain. The more biodiverse an ecosystem, the more robust it is.

But so what if some microbe or some itty-bitty insect in Timbuktu goes extinct? I mean really, why all the fuss?

Ah!

My travel companions: the organisms. Lactobacillus acidophilus, Bifidobacterium bifidum.

The probiotics had vanquished the heartburn and my feminine woes in the last two weeks. Like long-lost cousins from a distant branch of the Tree of Life, they'd moved in and put my house in order.

But me? An ecosystem? My body? Well, what's a mother's womb? *An ecosystem:* it provides food, water, oxygen, and yes, even probiotic microorganisms.

There are throngs of organisms in the world, some microscopic, others hidden from view, in treetops and tundra and in the ocean depths, all of which support the life we see around us. We don't know all the details of how that intricate web of life supports itself, but in many instances, the consequences of biodiversity loss are glaringly apparent.

With marine biodiversity, one of the greatest things at stake is food security. The erosion of biodiversity chips away at the resilience of marine ecosystems. In the worst cases, fisheries collapse. That means less food and a collapsed economic sector. It drives home a fundamental truth: the heart of life is interconnection. Biodiversity matters because we need each other to survive.

II

The River

The inlet was narrow. It was evening, and my kayak glided into a dream-like water forest filled with majestic mangrove trees. Mangroves in the Coral Triangle can grow ten times the height of those in the Caribbean, to over ninety feet tall.

We'd anchored along the southern part of the mountainous Batanta Island, a portion of which was the Batanta Barat Nature Reserve. The river undulated into some of the very last virgin forest in West Papua. For many years shipbuilders had come here to fell ironwood trees for the centerline of schooners.

The river was twenty or so feet wide and calm. I was so astounded by the height of the mangroves that it was a few minutes before I noticed a strange slime in the water. The roots were covered with silt. And there were no fish.

At the next bend, a bank of soil appeared, and amid the jungle brush were trees even taller than the mangroves, merbau trees. Known for their violet-magenta flowers, they can grow to 130 feet. Batanta Island was home to a wide variety of rare birds, including the red bird-of-paradise.

There was a guttural, mechanical whir in the distance—chainsaws. Before leaving home, I'd chatted with a colleague and mentioned I wanted to see some lumbering operations in Papua. I asked if he knew a good driver who could take me there.

"You must be kidding?"

"No, what's the big deal?"

"*You'll* be fine. They'll just deport you. But your driver? They'll kill him."

I had no idea that there was fresh blood on the iron thumb with which Indonesia ruled its acquired territories. I'd known of Indonesia's military atrocities in East Timor, but not that Indonesia had annexed half of the island of New Guinea in 1969 through a rigged election backed by military force and similar atrocities. And that the Free Papua movement had resisted the occupation ever since.

As I traveled, my conversations about human rights were hushed for fear of *being gone*—if you are foreigner, deported; a native, disappeared. While suppressing the local resistance movement in Papua, some military officials had brokered lucrative deals with companies in the so-called extraction industry.

At the next turn the sound of chainsaws grew louder. Yard-wide stumps of freshly felled trees littered the forest, and the air smelled of sawdust. The river grew thicker with mud.

Indonesia's decades-long crackdown in Papua—the massacres, mass detentions, sexual violence, and torture—was unquestionably a crime against humanity under international human-rights law. A Yale Law School study concluded that while intent could not be as readily inferred as it was in the Holocaust or the Rwandan genocide, the actions of the Indonesian government constituted genocide—the systematic attempt to eliminate a cultural or racial group.[55] If there were more Indonesians than Papuans in Papua, well, then Papua would be more amenable to becoming Indonesia territory. In response to international pressure, some efforts to address this had been made, including trials of military officials for human-rights violations, but abuses persisted.

Now men were visible in the distance, cutting through the base of trees with chainsaws. Others sliced the downed trunks lengthwise into planks and stacked them into piles. Sawdust coated the forest floor.

When it comes to damage to the ocean, it's unfair to point fingers only at big companies. We are all involved, as consumers. And local people had done much damage to marine ecosystems through dynamite fishing, damaging delicate coral with nets, and harvesting coral. But West Papua is an example of the many places around the world where indigenous peoples are stripped of the right to manage their natural resources and the economic benefits garnered from them.

Large-scale logging is one of the most salient examples. Corrupt government officials wheel-and-deal with companies to reap enormous wealth, little of which benefits the Papuans. West Papua has some of the most biodiverse rainforests in the world. Indonesia had earmarked over 27.6 million hectares (68.2 million acres) of them as "production forest" for logging.[56] Merbau shipments from Papua alone were worth over $600 million in Western retail prices *per month*.[57]

Another bend in the river. The banks were muddy from fresh rain. I thought I heard a metallic click. I swirled my kayak around. A man in fatigues, his boots caked with mud, stood at the edge of the river with an automatic rifle.

"*Kerajinan?*" I sputtered nervously. "Handicrafts?"

His brow furrowed.

"*Pasar?* Market?" I gestured with my hands as if tying a sarong around my waist. "*Sarung?* Sarongs? *Kerajinan pasar?* Handicrafts market?"

A pause.

Please, please! I'm a tourist! Right? All I want is a bunch of Papuan handicrafts?

It was truly a unique moment: for the first time in my life, I prayed a man would think I had not one single brain cell between my ears.

He cocked his head in the direction I'd come. I inhaled. As I paddled away, I did my best to wave goodbye, as if it were comforting to find a soldier in the jungle, like a security guard at the bank.

A long, woody crack filled the air and then the booming crash of another tree. Merbau is favored for flooring, because it's so durable and termite resistant. Most people who buy it don't realize that it may have come from a nature sanctuary and that at current harvesting rates, there will be no wild ones left in thirty-five years.

Indonesia still restricts access by foreign journalists to West Papua, and human-rights abuses continue. But five months after I was there in 2013, the government did bust the illegal loggers. They arrested a rogue police officer for lumber smuggling, including the felling of merbau trees from Batanta Island—$146 million in suspicious bank transactions were confiscated, and 115 containers of illegally logged merbau were seized.[58]

At the opening of the river, the seagrass and the coral were lifeless, covered with silt. When it rained, the sawdust and mud from the lumbering operation would fill the river, linger in the roots of the mangroves, and wash out into the sea. That "particulate matter" makes the water less habitable and vulnerable to oxygen depletion.[59]

Similar types of problems were caused in the northern part of West Papua by the Grasberg mine, the largest gold mine and the second largest copper mine in the world, owned by the American company Freeport-McMoRan Copper and Gold. According to Indonesian environmental ministry documents leaked to the New York Times, "nearly 90 square miles of wetlands, once one of the richest freshwater habitats in the world, are virtually buried in mine waste, called tailings, with levels of copper and sediment so high that almost all fish have disappeared."[60] A United Nations Environment Programme study of the Grasberg mine states that "elevated levels of metals, such as copper, lead, and arsenic, can cause direct acute and chronic toxicity, and bioaccumulation in fish tissues may pose risks to human health."[61]

The New York Times obtained Freeport's company records that documented that between 1998 and 2004, Freeport's payments to military personnel were nearly $20 million.[62] For many years Papuan workers at the Grasberg mine receive the equivalent of $1.50 a day in wages.[63] But at the time that I visited West Papua, the workers had unionized and were pressuring Freeport, through strikes and protests, to raise wages.

All of this was a harsh reminder that a sustainable world must also be a more just and peaceful world. Poverty, the struggle for equal rights, food security, the availability of fresh water, and political stability are inextricably linked.

It was getting dark. I pointed my kayak toward our boat. There was a shack next to a dock several hundred yards away emitting the sound of a generator. A small child came out of the shack, flashed a strange look at me, and then darted back into the jungle.

Around the world, runoff similar to that caused by mining or logging operations, including the runoff of fertilizers and other chemicals, is increasing oceanic dead zones, areas of water that do not have enough dissolved oxygen to support life.[64] Dead zones are reversible. The dead zones in the river I grew up along, the Hudson River, and the estuary I live next to now, the San Francisco Bay, have both been significantly reduced in my lifetime, thanks to the cleanup efforts of many dedicated people. But globally, dead zones are increasing dramatically. The largest dead zone covers 8,500 square miles in the Gulf of Mexico and is due to nutrients from Midwestern farms leaching into the Mississippi River, which drains into the Gulf.[65] It's roughly the size of the state of New Jersey. The largest estuary in the United States, the Chesapeake Bay, has a dead zone that averages 16 percent of the entire water volume of the bay.[66]

I'd traveled to one of the most remote places in the world to see so-called pristine seas. But what were these muddied, lifeless waters telling me? *No place in the world was untouched.*

Humanity is extracting so many resources that it is threatening the ability of the earth to renew itself. Deforestation accounts for 15 percent of the globe's carbon emissions. We are losing somewhere between 29 and 37 million acres of forest a year, thirty-six football fields worth per minute.[67] The Tree of Life, that magnificent, multibranched web of life, is being ravaged.

It is driven by greed, by indifference, and simply by not knowing what was happening. How many goods had I consumed through such means? The wood on the desk I write on? The battery in my flashlight? The thousands of fish I have eaten? It is also driven by *not knowing what to do.* How to lower our carbon emissions, change the way we live and what we consume. The first small steps forward are things like a solar flashlight or eating sustainable fish or buying sustainably harvested lumber.

But I wasn't thinking about it that way that night. My nerves were raw from the run-in with the gunman. I could only think of that Greek word from which *ocean* is derived, *okeanós:* a river circling the earth. This river through the jungle had so much to tell about what was happening to the seas. And as a global community, *the ocean is our river,* a life-giving source of nourishment, without which we cannot survive.

The bay that the river flowed into was littered with debris— food wrappers, nylon twine, plastic bottles, straws, cigarette packets, bottle tops, toothbrushes, chipped fragments of plastic and Styrofoam. The same currents that so much marine life rode into Raja Ampat also brought clusters of garbage, which piled up in inlets and bays.

I had been dealt a blow I wasn't prepared for, something I wasn't prepared to even think about, let alone deal with. *What happens to photosynthesis?* I asked myself. *If that's the basis of life, what happens when it's eroded? If the oxygen in every other breath comes from marine plants and algae, what happens to the atmosphere if there are bigger and bigger dead zones in the ocean? And smaller and smaller forests? Where will the oxygen come from?*

Paddling back to the boat, I kept asking myself, *How could I not know this was happening? Why didn't anyone tell me? Or did I read it somewhere, but I wasn't paying enough attention to stop and take notice?*

As I neared the boat, the sound of the generators and the chainsaws faded. But the stillness was strange. It was dusk, but no birds sang.

Through my binoculars, I saw planks of wood neatly stacked

on the dock by the generator shack. In the morning the wood would be gone, and there would be an eerie silence.

12

Blue Stop

My torso was trapped in the kayak. I couldn't hold my breath anymore. I opened my mouth and water burst into my throat.

My eyes bolted open. The sheets were soaked with sweat. A faint glow came through the porthole, the light of a quarter moon on the water.

Nightmare. Nightmare. It's just a nightmare. My hands trembled uncontrollably. I rolled over and imagined being curled up in bed with Charlie at home, our dog, Zack, nestled between us.

The next morning we were anchored in the Dampier Strait. On either side were islands with nothing but wild jungle. No boats, no buildings, just the sea and distant, green slivers of land. It was our last day on the water. That evening we would return to the port of Sorong, and I would fly to Sulawesi.

The reef below was a thin ridge of coral about fifty feet down, a raised platform surrounded on all sides by several miles of water that was thousands of feet deep. "If the current pulls you off," the divemaster reminded us, "do a blue stop."

As we descended, the divers ahead of me found coral knobs to settle behind to get out of the current. I kept my eye on a spot behind a cluster of coral where I could pause and get my bearings. But as I started kicking toward it, I realized it was exposed to the current, and I was being pulled off the reef.

I spotted another knob of coral that might be better and

kicked frantically to get behind it, but no matter how hard I tried, the current kept sucking me away. I tried and tried until I was totally out of breath.

Stop! Stop! Let it go ....

The current swept me away into open water. Within moments the reef was out of sight.

I was infuriated with myself, frazzled and out of breath. I'd screwed up. I wasn't strong enough to kick back onto the reef.

Get a grip here, would you? Blue stop!

I slowly headed up to fifteen feet and looked at my computer. It prompted me to do a six-minute safety stop—a mandatory decompression stop.

Six minutes? How far will I drift in that time? Will anyone see me? They may not even know I'm gone for an hour!

The computer must have calculated six minutes because of the buildup of gases in my bloodstream. It was our second dive of the day, and I'd been diving for almost two weeks.

It's a mandatory stop. You have to do it—it's too dangerous not too.

I pulled out my safety sausage and shot some puffs of air into it, so the boat crew would know I was doing a stop. But as it inflated, it tore straight off the cord. It flapped for a moment and then vanished in the current.

That's when it all came out, like oil seething from an errant gasket. All the sour machinations I'd been holding at bay, all the things I dreaded were true.

Big money, greed, genocide, corruption. You're no match for this! Look at you. You're weak, you're sickly. You're out of your league. Lioness firing on all pistons? Yeah, right.

I could feel the current sweeping me away. Nothing but blue water. No reefs. No sand channels. No bearings. Desperate to keep my focus, I locked my eyes on the dive computer, as if glaring through a straw: fifteen feet, six minutes. Everything else was a blur. My eyes welled up. *How could I have been so naïve?*

The stop was done. I looked up. Something was coming toward me with a yard-wide open mouth. It was the wide, ribbed throat of an oceanic manta. Its fins were so huge they could have draped over a car like a bedspread. The wingspan of an oceanic manta can reach twenty-five feet.

I froze. It came within a foot of me, eyed me, and then swished one of its cape-like fins a few inches over my head. There were large gill plates shaped like air vents on its smooth white underside. Then its tail came around with precision, close but not touching. Right behind it was another manta and then a third. They sashayed through the water in slow motion, like enormous prehistoric birds.

They seemed so calm and deliberate. They circled me for a few minutes and then descended and circled directly below me.

You should surface. Look for the boat. An island.

I slowly rotated 360 degrees, searching for some hint of shoreline—a rocky crest, the hint of brown or green one sees when approaching a reef. Nothing but blue sea.

I looked down again. They were still there, circling. I looked at my gauge. I still had plenty of air.

Surface! You may need that air for a surface swim.

Again I looked up and all around, then back down: still circling.

Fine, fine! Just, just …

I descended. They were at about forty feet when I came bobbing down with my air bubbles and shiny cylinder. The water temperature changed slightly. The current felt different. They circled me again.

I had the sensation that I was swimming with them, inside the arcs they made. We swam like this for a while. I checked my air gauge—down to half a tank of air.

You're gonna need to quit this soon.

A green-brown slope appeared. Platter-shaped coral. Air

bubbles. The divers! What? How? Had the mantas herded me back? Had their fins acted as buffers against the current? I ducked behind a big coral head and swirled around to look at the mantas, but all I could see were three faint black-and-white flapping shapes. Then they were gone.

13

It's Time

"*Selamat pagi.*" It was a man's voice on the phone. Then in English he enunciated slowly, "It is time now, Ibu. It is 4:30."

"*Terima kasih …*" I mumbled, "thank you."

I put down the phone. It was pitch black. I was alone. Chants wailed through scratchy loudspeakers from several mosques surrounding the hotel.

I rolled out of bed and groggily opened a thick set of drapes. Tall cranes and shipping containers carved a dim silhouette against sky. Dingy street lights illuminated concrete buildings as well as small huts cobbled together from scrap wood and corrugated metal. The streets were empty save for an old man wearing a cone-shaped straw hat pedaling a rickshaw barefoot.

Makassar is a large port city in South Sulawesi. A day and a half before, I'd flown in from Papua to wait for a flight that flew only twice a week to Wangi-Wangi, one of the Tukangbesi Islands, where the World Wide Fund for Nature (WWF), had an office.

When I settled into the hotel room, I lapsed into deep, heavy sleep. For over a day I barely stirred. It wasn't so much fatigue as that I was at a loss to absorb everything I'd experienced, let alone write about. So I began with what the psychologist Erich Fromm so aptly termed, "the forgotten language," the language of dreams.

Then the wake-up call and the dark, reverberant air. Muslims traditionally pray five times a day, the first before dawn. And the imam, the spiritual leader of a mosque, will chant at any time of day if he is inspired.

When the plane took off later that morning, it flew low over miles of urban slums—dilapidated metal roofs with muddy dirt roads and narrow passageways. Before lapsing into sleep in the hotel, I'd gone out to get some food. Drainage ditches were clogged with trash. The air was thick with car exhaust and smoke from burning garbage. I paused at a street cart selling barbequed fish: the charred bodies with motionless eyes were wild animals to me now, in terrible need of protection.

Some kids filled plastic bags with pieces of metal and plastic from a trash heap, scavenging for recyclable materials to sell to dealers. Their heads seemed oversized in proportion to their gangly limbs. In Indonesia, four out of ten children suffer from stunted growth because of malnutrition in early childhood, before age five.[68] I couldn't tell how old these kids were. Five years old? Maybe ten?

As the plane gained altitude, it flew over the water's edge, some stilt houses with wooden boats moored to them, some glitzy high rises and gigantic docks crowded with shipping containers. A man paddled a dugout canoe the size of a toothpick next to an oil tanker and a ship loaded with lumber.

The very first sailors and boat builders are believed to be the Austronesians whose origins date back to when there was a land bridge between Australia and New Guinea. They built the first boats—dugout canoes—some seven thousand to ten thousand years ago, around the time of the Agricultural Revolution. They predated the Polynesians. It was 3,300 years ago when Austronesians sailed east and settled in Fiji, marking the beginning of Polynesian culture, which flourished throughout the Pacific.

I felt like I was in the thick of a modern world infused with the remnants of a deeply ancient time, one long before our calendars clocked in. The plane leveled out over patches of lush farmland and steep, chiseled mountains. Then for a few minutes it traversed open ocean, making the short crossing to the Tukangbesi Islands.

Here I wanted to learn more about local fishing practices and about the Bajau sea nomads, who had lived for thousands of years in small wooden houseboats. Until the twentieth century, the Bajau's hunter-gatherer way of life differed little from that of the Austronesians some ten thousand years before. The Bajau were now transitioning to living in houses on stilts along the shore, but some still lived at sea. During monsoons, the nomads sheltered their houseboats in mangrove channels or erected portable stilt huts in protected coves.

A patch of beige and turquoise reef appeared, then a tiny, low-lying island—Wangi-Wangi. The open hull of a wooden boat sat tilted on a sand spit. A short landing strip came into view. The airplane landed and came to a halt with a screech.

"Before," Enci Wahab said, "the fish were right here." He pointed to the water in the channel beneath the porch. "But no more. Now we go a long way to fish."

We were sitting on a porch in a Bajau village called Mola Bahari on the island of Wangi-Wangi. Surrounding us were houses on stilts, some with woven bamboo walls and thatched roofs made from palm fronds and grass, others built from concrete and cinder blocks with metal roofs. Two WWF staff members, Sadar and Haji, had arranged for me to meet with a "fishermen's forum," a group of fishermen who had collectively agreed not to use destructive fishing practices. On the porch with us were nine other fishermen along with my translator, Rikardo Saliki. We sat cross-legged in a rough semicircle.

Next to Enci Wahab was a fisherman named Dorman. "Ten years ago, around 2000, was the worst," Dorman said, "Bomb-bomb everywhere."

"Bomb-bomb?" I asked.

"That's dynamite fishing," Rikardo said.

"You could hear the bombs going off all around you then,"

Dorman continued. "Now it is better, and there are a few more fish."

Just over a decade before, in 1996, the islands and surrounding water were designated the Wakatobi National Park in an effort to stem the destruction. Between industrial fishing and the local fishers, the coral reefs had been terribly depleted. The local fishermen worked with conservation organizations to create zoning regulations to protect them.

Enci Wahab started to say something and then paused as if to rephrase it. We waited. Words between us moved slowly, Indonesian to English and English to Indonesian. We often paused to digest in silence what had just been said or to phrase our words with great care, not wanting to damage the connection between us, like a fragile tether between two boats.

There was deep pride in the fishermen's faces, a keen, clear-eyed doggedness. Finally after a long silence, Enci Wahab asked, "You are married?"

"Yes."

"What does your husband do?"

"My husband works for a labor union. He helps make sure workers have health insurance and fair wages."

Enci Wahab nodded. "Okay," he said. "Here everyone is a fisherman. We eat fish every day. Every meal. If there are fewer fish, that is less food and less money."

Ronny in North Sulawesi had said the same thing: fewer fish, less to eat, less money. But they needed *more* money, because they had to buy gasoline for their boats to go farther to catch fish. And they needed to buy water, because the natural water sources had been contaminated, and to buy more rice, because there wasn't always enough fish to eat. What money was left went for tea, sugar, cigarettes, clothing, and their children's education. School in Indonesia is free, but parents have to buy school uniforms and textbooks.

"It is bad now, but we worry for our children," Dorman said. "What if this gets worse? Will they have food to eat?"

Millions of coastal people all over the world were asking the same frightening question. For them "a fish" was a unit of measurement comparable to "a potato" right before the Irish Potato Famine. It was the metric by which survival would be reckoned. In the Coral Triangle alone, 120 million people depended upon fisheries for their livelihood. Many fisheries had either collapsed or were on the verge of collapse. And the other staple of subsistence—rice—was threatened by an increase in droughts induced by climate change.[69] The United Nations, the World Bank, and food security experts were voicing the same eerie questions: there are fewer and fewer fish, and if there are even fewer in the future, how will people survive?

"In the past," Enci Wahab said, "the ancestors came together in times of great difficulty. So we all agree to come together. And we say no more bomb-bomb and no more cyanide." Cyanide fishing involves squirting sodium cyanide in reef crevices where fish hide. But the cyanide not only stuns the fish, it also kills other creatures and the coral itself. For every fish caught that way, one square yard of coral was devastated.

"And fishing nets damage the reef," Dorman continued, "so we use single lines now, and we make our own hooks."

"There are eighteen of us in this forum. We meet once a month," Enci Wahab added, making eye contact with all the other fishermen. "If someone uses the bomb or cyanide, we go to him and we talk. This is our reef, we say. If you do this, no one will have fish."

We talked for a long time. The fishermen showed me special hooks and fishing flies they had made by hand. Later, Haji, Rikardo, Sadar, and I wandered through the village, rows and rows of houses on stilts above the water, connected by narrow elevated walkways. Dried fish and clothing and brightly colored fabrics hung from porches. Below, old wooden boats were tied up, some with small diesel engines.

Rikardo and I chatted with two old women with mischievous smiles who were weaving cone-shaped hats from bamboo strips. Another woman pulled some clothing from a plastic tub and vigorously wrung the water out and hung it on a laundry line. Inside one of the bamboo huts, a young woman rocked a baby in a tiny hammock made of cloth.

There was something magical about this village, perched above the water, the houses linked by planks and little bridges, yet it was waist-deep in problems. In the past, all of the Bajau's refuse was biodegradable, but now the village was strewn with plastic debris. Vespas and motorcycles were driven awkwardly over the narrow walkways. And the population was so dense that sewage concentrated in the water between the stilt houses.

The government had wanted the sea nomads to settle on land—boats drifting in and out of Indonesian territory disrupted efforts to secure borders. But as the Bajau began living in stilt villages, they mined coral to fortify the foundations for their homes, gutting large areas of coral reef. Like the rest of humanity, their relationship with the sea was mired in destructive contradictions.

But protective actions by local fishermen are adding up. In the Coral Triangle in the past twenty years, there has been a 75 percent reduction in blast fishing. The biggest threats to coral reefs now are overfishing, nutrient runoff, and coral bleaching. The fishermen had begun to pierce the armor of that goliath of problems, the Tragedy of the Commons: the tragic loss of common resources because of an inability to forego narrow self-interest and agree how to preserve them.

Say you're a fisherman, and someone wants you to stop using fish bombs. You say, "If I stop, the other guy will do it, so what good is it if I stop?" Nation-states having been using this argument for years about remote offshore fisheries. The vast unmanaged commons of the open seas are still being ravaged because nations can't forge agreements to preserve them.

The Bajau fishermen had started to surmount that hurdle. They couldn't stop the industrial fishing boats, but they could stop the damage they themselves were doing. "We listen to the voices of the ancestors," Enci Wahab had told me. "They tell us to work together." Wisdom from long ago was starting to prevail over the Tragedy of Commons. The only way out of that vicious cycle was to come to a consensus as a community.

As we left the village, we walked over a concrete-fortified bridge to the mainland. I turned around and looked back at the village. A small child walked in the other direction, pulling a homemade toy—a long string with a stone tied to one end.

I settled in a small, clean-swept hotel with tile floors and high ceilings in Wanci, the main village on Wangi-Wangi. Light filtered into the hallway through windows carved with intricate Islamic patterns. The hotel sat at the edge of a large dock. Next to it were the gaping ribs of a rotting shipwreck and murky water filled with trash.

At the end of the dock there was a covered porch on stilts with a small restaurant. The first night I walked out there to get some food. The porch was empty except for a blond woman in her twenties, sipping tea and reading a book.

"*Hola!*" I blurted out.

She looked up and grinned.

She was the first Westerner I'd seen in several days.

"Have a seat. I've been in bed for days with a fever," she said, taking a sip from her tea. "This is the first time I've been out."

Her name was Lindsay Olsen. She was traveling the world, studying fisheries on a Watson Fellowship. She'd been in the islands for several weeks. We chatted for a while. I ordered some chicken and rice. The evening ocean air was sweet, and the smell of the chicken was pungent.

"Nobody really wants to talk about it," Lindsay said.

"About what?" I asked.

"What's going to happen to all these people if there are no more fish?"

"I know ...." I murmured.

Lindsay swallowed the last of her tea. "You should see the night market."

It was almost dark when we got there. Everyone was friendly, and it bustled with voices. There were stalls filled with fish and vegetables; small bins with water, kerosene, and petrol in small bottles; barrels full of nuts and rice. We stopped at a little cart, and I bought a deep-fried banana. Lindsay left a day and half later; she was the last white-bread Westerner I'd see.

⌇☙

"The idea for the forums came from the fishermen themselves," Sugi explained. "They discuss everything together. It's friendly. They become more connected. But WWF and The Nature Conservancy, we help them, we have special trainings for a member of each group. But the members talk among themselves without us." Sugi Sugiyanta headed the WWF office in Wanci. My translator, Rikardo, and I sat in his office in a small building that WWF shared with The Nature Conservancy.

The Wakatobi National Park encompasses an area of ocean sixty miles long, including four main islands, Binongko, Kaledupa, Tomia, and Wangi-Wangi. About one hundred thousand people live there. The fishermen's forums did more than help manage fisheries. They brought people together; they strengthened communities. And that would help them face new challenges.

Sugi was in his forties, lanky and calm. "We need more law enforcement. Boats still come from outside, fish bombers and boats with long lines. They will operate outside the preserve, but then they will sneak in. We need to keep the resources here for the local people so they can be sustained."

This was very similar to the goals of the MPAs in West Papua and what Helen Newman and Simon Day were doing with the Sea Sanctuaries Trust. And it was the opposite of what had transpired in Papua—resources being extracted with little of the profits staying with the Papuan people.

For several days Rikardo and I had been talking with fishermen. They told us they had returned to using traditional fishing methods that didn't damage reefs. They used *bubu,* large bamboo fish traps that could sit on a sandy bottom, and *huma,* small floating wooden platforms from which fishermen draped nets. They avoided areas where fish gathered to spawn.

Everywhere we heard the same words—less fish, less food. Poverty was not as acute as it was in Makassar, but the local people lived at the edge of subsistence. Our conversations were laced with polite desperation. It was obvious something was horribly wrong with the "great provider"—the ocean. I was hearing it from the people who were affected by it most: the ocean that once fed them was running dry, like a well.

Over and over again, the fishermen asked one thing of me. "Please tell people to eat sustainable fish." If people were not willing to pay a little more, the supply chain that supported these fishermen would never have a chance of prevailing.

Sugi helped connect these fishermen to supermarket chains through a sustainable-seafood program called Seafood Savers. WWF also worked with the Marine Stewardship Council (MSC). The blue MSC label on packaged fish tells consumers it had been sustainable harvested. Upon request, the MSC will send auditors to assess whether a fishery complies with their certification conditions.

It is the age-old tug-of-war between "what's possible" and the "inevitable status quo." The "inevitable" is "It's going to hell. People are so greedy and ignorant, they won't stop decimating the ocean." At the "what's possible" end was revamping supply chains to make them sustainable—everything from palm oil and fish to lumber and precious metals. How? Economic incentives, standards for best practices, trade management, consumer education.

In the fisheries industry, that means improving fisheries management and enforcement, establishing more MPAs, and certifying fisheries that meet sustainability standards. But re-vamping supply chains? Big business and environmentalists working together? Impossible? McDonald's Filet-O-Fish, made from Alaskan pollock and New Zealand hoki, is MSC certified.[70] McDonald's serves more than seventy million people in more than one hundred countries each day. It reminded me of Amdeep and the turtle fishers. Rather than demonize turtle fishers, the Marine Conservation Society had linked arms with them to manage the fishery.

"Little by little, change can come," Sugi told me. "People are no longer embarrassed to talk about conservation here. This is a big hope for the future. It's about awareness. And good policies and good implementation. But we must all get started. Then it becomes a new world, with a focus on the environment, not just capital."

A former fish bomber agreed to speak with me anonymously. He winced as he described blast fishing. "You throw the bomb from the bow. But you have to get the timing right."

Small-scale bombs were rickety concoctions of match heads, sand, and fertilizer stuffed inside soda bottles. "The fuse is short, so sometimes the bomb can go off by mistake in your arms. My friends—one was killed, another lost an arm, and another lost vision in one eye."

"Did you ..." I hesitated. It felt like my questions were twisting a knife in a wound. "Did you see the damage underwater?"

"Yes," he said with a grimace. "Then the reef is dead. No more fish from that place. That's when I start to understand this word—*ecosystem*—that if this is destroyed, there will be no fish."

There was silence. Then I said, "I didn't really understand what an ecosystem was either, until I saw one devastated."

Larger dynamite fishing operations used black-market dyna-mite that originated with a "big boss" in Singapore. The fish returned to the same boss through a chain of clandestine harbors and "little bosses"—the same organized-crime networks that ran narcotics.

The fish bomber had so many more excuses to turn a blind eye than I did, but he'd gotten to a place where he couldn't stand it anymore. It wasn't until I'd spoken with him that I really appreciated the proud and dignified tone of the fishermen's forum. Fish bombing paid far more than traditional methods. Sustainable fishing might reap $5 to $40 a day; fish bombing, between $85 and $170 a day.

They'd walked away from more money, and many of them, from organized crime. Even if those first steps forward didn't guarantee success, they were willing to change their ways and do what they could. They wanted to take care of each other, their families, and their communities. And that meant taking care of the ocean.

※

One day I asked Rikardo to take me to an old mosque in the hills. We rode his Vespa along narrow roads through small villages and lush grassland with coconut trees. Along the roads, women carried baskets of bananas on their heads. Everywhere people would wave to us.

Rikardo turned onto a long, steep pathway through the jungle, revving the engine to its limits to keep it from stalling. At the top of the hill, the Vespa chortled to a stop, and we got off.

The mosque was spacious and serene. It was built from wood and painted white with green trim. A few small homes nestled amid palm and banyan trees surrounded it. A soft rain started to fall. So we did what I had learned you do often here when you are stuck in the rain—you take shelter on a stranger's porch. A woman with her children waved to us, and we sat down on her porch.

Rikardo lit a cigarette. Despite my shyness, one of the children slipped into my lap—a little girl. I was awkwardly flattered. I didn't have kids and wasn't used to having kids sit on my lap.

"So what do you do the rest of the time?" I asked Rikardo. The little girl nestled her head into my chest. Her mother smiled.

"I teach school," he said quietly. "But soon I'll go to university."

"Where?"

"Kyoto. I have a scholarship to study Japanese literature."

"Really? That's wonderful!"

We paused and just sat quietly. The rain cooled the air. A cat slept on a pile of sandals on a shoe rack on the porch. I felt so deeply at peace. It was as if my heart had grown—the beats in my chest were sweeter, calmer, stronger.

After a while I asked Rikardo, "Do you know the haiku poet Bashō? He wrote *The Narrow Road to the Deep North.*"

"No," he said softly. "But I would like to read this book."

I bought a sarong. In the evening I wore it and wandered the night market. Women greeted me with wide-open eyes.

I'd shed my nervous Western skin. Kids raced up to me calling, "Hello Ibu!"

"*Apa kabar?*" I'd say. "What's up?" And I'd open my palm for them to give me a high-five.

As I walked through the market at dusk and shared greetings with strangers, words bobbed peacefully in my mind like buoys marking indescribable depths. "This is how it's going to be. It's going to be person to person and creature to creature. About the possibilities in each moment. It's going to be about taking care of each other."

The drones from the mosques began before sunrise, often amid steady rain. Then the soft clatter of old diesel engines in the distance—the fishermen heading out. Then the crowing of roosters and the first rays of light. Then the playful squeals of children echoing in the tile atrium outside my room.

One day Rikardo and I rode past miles of remote shoreline with empty stilt houses. At one point Rikardo pulled over, and we walked on the wet sand flats where the decaying buildings were.

The homes had been abandoned because of sea-level rise. I remembered a conversation I'd had with Ii Rosna Tarmidji, an environmental engineer who worked for Conservation International. She had told me that she interviewed coastal people in West Papua, and when she asked them where their homes had been twenty-five years earlier, they'd pointed out past the shoreline, into the ocean. They told her salt water was leeching into the drinking water in their wells. "That's when climate change really hit me," Ii said. "That's when I started to save energy, to change how I live."

Indonesia consists of over seventeen thousand islands, many of them low-lying.[71] Conservative scientific estimates have sea levels rising in Asia *at least* one meter by 2100. How many people would be displaced? Add to that droughts, crop disruptions, stronger typhoons and cyclones, contaminated water supplies, and declining and collapsed fisheries. If drastic international action is not taken to lower carbon emissions—binding international agreements to mitigate climate change—these problems will dwarf the humanitarian crises of the past.[72] They will trigger a humanitarian and ecological catastrophe that will render many parts of the Coral Triangle uninhabitable.

The houses on stilts were hollow, ghostly shells. No smiling faces, no friendly voices, no dried fish or bright fabrics hanging from the railings. No old women weaving bamboo hats. No colorfully painted boats. No children running to greet us. The hair on the back of my neck stood up.

＊

Sugi had arranged a crew for a visit to a very remote Bajau village called Mantigola, near the island of Kaledupa. When we left that morning, it was very windy, and the sky was full of dark storm clouds. The captain, Surpardin, steered the boat through large waves. The trip would take about an hour.

As we all huddled together in the back of the boat to get out of the spray, it was so clear I wasn't the same woman who'd arrived in Indonesia almost six weeks before. I was with three men I did not know well, whose language I barely spoke, motoring to a distant island in one of the most remote parts of the world, but we had so much in common: a concern for the life of the seas and the world around us.

＊

Mantigola was on a shoal north of the island of Kaledupa. It was truly a *kampong air,* a "water village." It was much more similar to the temporary stilt villages of the past. It was not built on land, but in shallow water. About a quarter mile of ocean separated it from the island of Kaledupa.

There was a main walkway through the village that was wide and sturdy. Some houses were connected to it by a few precarious loose planks. Many of the houses had wooden ladders down to the water, where boats were moored. Just outside the village in the open water I spotted a *kapal,* a traditional nomadic houseboat. One of the few remaining nomadic families had sought shelter from the monsoon for a few weeks in Mantigola.

Nowhere on earth is there a people whose lives are more deeply intertwined with the sea than the sea nomads of Southeast Asia—they eat, cook, hunt, sleep, and give birth at sea. In the past, they could be found everywhere from Australia to Burma to the Philippines. In Indonesia they are called the Bajau. In Thailand and Burma they are called the Moken; near the Philippines, the Orang Laut.

The village overflowed with the sound of voices, the high-pitched giggles of children, the clatter of cooking and hammering, the sound of ukuleles and singing. All of that mingled with the sound of the wind and waves. There were no car sounds, no Vespas or trains.

A man carefully descended a wooden ladder carrying his son, no older than two years old. While he balanced on the ladder, he carefully dipped his son waist deep into the sea for a bath. The Bajau are among the best free divers in the world—children start learning to swim when they learn to crawl.

The son of the village chief introduced me to a man named Lauda. He had the build of a competitive swimmer, lean with strong, wide shoulders. He was known in the village as an exceptionally good free diver. He showed me a pair of wooden diving goggles that he had carved himself. Two oblong pieces of glass were fitted inside them.

"Can I buy a pair of these from you?" I asked.

"Yes," he replied. He ran back to his house and brought me a pair.

"These," he pointed to his own goggles, "I keep them for myself, because I carved them to fit my face exactly."

We paused on a walkway where a group of kids were playing. One of them cast a single line with a hook in the water, holding the end of the line in his hand. I looked down and watched a school of fish swim beneath the wooden planks and wondered what this spot might have been like a hundred years before. While this village had fewer concrete pilings and less garbage than other villages I'd seen, the water beneath it was murky brown—it was full of sewage.

"How can one live like this?" I asked myself. But then I imagined how people a century from now might look back into our time with disgust at how we pumped carbon dioxide into the air—another "commons." We might view thousands of cars at rush hour with the same disbelief. New Delhi had recently exceeded Beijing as the world's top "killer city." Air pollution there was sixty times safe levels. Fourteen hundred cars were being added to New Delhi's streets *per day*.[73]

The village chief had invited us for tea. His son walked us to his house and introduced us. The chief, Arman, greeted us politely and gestured that we sit down. A lean young man wearing a sarong immediately came out with a tray of hot tea and a plate of teacakes. He knelt down adroitly and placed it in front of us and then silently vanished. The teacakes were carefully arranged on a round plate. I eyed them. My delicate Western gut had managed to get through nearly six weeks without getting sick.

Eat it! They've made this special for you.

Arman watched. I cautiously bit into a piece. It was delicious. Some kind of deep-fried green fruit. The crust was crumbly and laced with sugar. Arman smiled. I had no doubts he knew what had gone through my mind.

"When did you realize the oceans were in trouble?" I asked.

"Well, there were fewer fish," he said. "But it really began with questions."

I reached for another teacake. Rikardo reached for one as well. We were famished.

"Simple questions," Arman continued. "Why are there fewer fish? And I talk with scientists who come to study the ocean. They are worried that there are fewer fish too. Then I began to learn about the coral reef, about ecology, that the fish need the reef to live."

"But when did you know that you had to do something? That you had to change?"

"When we began to be hungry. When it became hard to get enough to eat. The elders know it best, because they have seen the difference between now and many years ago. And we are divers, we see the life in the sea with our own eyes." He pointed two fingers to his own eyes to stress the point. "In the past, fish were everywhere. We had special ceremonies of respect to the sea before we fished. We need to have that respect again, to care for the sea better."

Before I said goodbye to Arman, I asked him if there was anything he would like me to tell people in the United States. "Please tell them that we are a proud people. We are great sailors and great boat builders and great fishermen. We need to take care of the ocean, because we have no land. The sea is our home."

Walking back to where our boat was docked, I noticed a woman approaching the village in a dugout canoe with a triangular sail. She steered the tiny canoe through windy seas with an easy confidence.

The nautical historian Robert Hobman told me how, thirty years ago, a Bajau fisherman pointed an arm to the west and explained to him that "in the old days" they went to "the Red Island," which was very big. They stayed there for a long time, the fisherman said, and sometimes they came back. Bob thought the island might have been Madagascar, and the incident inspired his *Sarimanok* expedition. He and a team built an outrigger canoe to Neolithic specifications from a large hollowed-out log, without any nonorganic materials. Using a palm-woven sail, the canoe carried eight crew members thousands of miles across the Indian Ocean to demonstrate how Madagascar's first human settlers arrived around 500

BC. They navigated only by the stars and a crude, wooden sundial.

As we motored away, the village became fainter and fainter until it was only a line of gray and brown on the horizon. Rikardo sat on the opposite rail, lost in thought. The captain revved the engines as he steered through the swells.

The sun broke through clouds above us, but there was a wall of storm clouds on the horizon, so dense you couldn't see past it. The gray-black sky cut a searing edge against the light that still shined through the clouds where we were. Everything—boat, island, tree—was a bright shape bathed in the golden evening light against the dark storm front.

What was going to happen to that village when sea levels rose? What was going to happen to all the island people who subsisted on their catch from the seas? If fisheries collapsed, how would people eat?

People were already migrating in skyrocketing numbers from depleted rural areas to urban shantytowns. In the Dharavi slum in Mumbai, India, a million people lived in one square mile of land. It was built on a former mangrove swamp. Like many areas of Bangladesh, which are in the low-lying Ganges delta, the Dharavi slum is especially vulnerable to extreme weather and sea-level rise.

These millions and millions of displaced people—I did not know them, but they were no longer invisible to me. They weren't numbers with percent signs anymore. *They had faces and voices and names.* They were wise and brave, and they feared for themselves and for their children. If they were displaced to urban slums, they would lose nothing less that the very soul of their lives: the homes their families had lived in for generations, their communities and traditions that were so deeply interwoven with the life of the islands and the sea.

It was as if, collectively, we heard the alarm, but kept hitting the snooze button. Each time the alarm came back louder. In the Coral Triangle, if dramatic international action is not taken on climate change, there will be no coral reefs left by

2100, and the ability of coastal environments to feed people will decline by 80 percent. Forty percent of the coral reefs and the mangroves in the Coral Triangle have already been lost.[74]

The snooze button wasn't working anymore for me. The alarm wailed like a siren. I'd always had this idea that sometime in the future the damage to our planet would be so catastrophic it would trigger decisive action, the way World War II did. Everything from the food on our plates to geopolitics would need to change. Things would "come to a head," the "time would come." But that, in my mind, was "later."

Things had changed. No, I'd changed. *It was time now.*

In the distance was the harbor in Wanci. Just before we got to the dock, the rain came fast and furious. We docked next to a wooden building with a noisy compressor. I said goodbye to the crew and carried my gear to a porch on the other side. I stood there and hesitated.

I was so overwhelmed by everything the villagers had told me. And what wasn't said: the quiet desperation in their eyes. I'd arrived from a faraway continent with cameras and recording devices and nice clothes. They saw me as powerful, but I felt so powerless.

So many people were suffering, and now it was going to get worse? The hotel where I stayed was only fifty yards away, but the rain was torrential. I just stood there, frozen.

I can't stand this. This makes me totally crazy.

"Liz! Liz!" It was Rikardo. I ran back through the noisy compressor room and clambered back onto the boat.

The rain poured down on us in thick sheets. "Liz, is there anything you need to do?" Rikardo yelled over the deafening rattle of compressor.

"I need to do? What do you mean?" I screamed back so he could hear.

"Is there anything you need to do?" Rikardo shouted slowly, this time pointing to different places on the boat.

Need to do? I need to speak for these people! This place!

Rikardo's clothes were drenched. He looked exhausted. He wiped water from his brow and screamed even louder, "The boat is leaving!"

Oh, it was a language thing! He meant, "The boat is leaving. Do you have all your things?" But he was so spent that he was having trouble finding the right English words, so he had asked "Is there anything you need to do?"

"Yes!" I screamed.

I needed to write, to give voice to everything I'd seen and heard and known, to all the people I had met. The villagers were right: I had power. And they had power too, and they were starting to use it.

I put my hands on Rikardo's shoulders. "Yes!" I yelled, louder than I'd ever done in my life. "But I have everything I need!"

Rikardo smiled, and we both climbed out of the rain.

14

Ular Laut

"Bomb-bomb?"

"Yes."

"You want to dive a fish-bomb site?" Sugi looked a bit astonished, like he was thinking, "Haven't you seen enough already?"

"I'd like to take some photos."

"Okay ... Wednesday."

Wednesday was overcast and windy. Surpardin steered the boat north toward a dock that jutted out from a cluster of small houses. He hopped out at the dock and ran into the village. Each village has the rights to the water near it, so we were asking permission to dive that site.

We waited silently.

Had these villagers bombed the site, or had bombers come from elsewhere?

There was a thunk, and the boat rocked. Surpardin had hopped back in. I fingered the shutter button on my camera housing nervously. I dreaded seeing another dynamite-bombed site. We motored a few hundred yards away from the dock, put on our gear, and dropped in to the water. I clipped my camera to my gear and descended.

Just get your shots, and you'll be done with this.

Thousands of damselfish dotted the water, like stars in the sky. The reef was thick with anemones and clownfish and doctorfish and plate coral and sea fans.

What? This is no bomb site.

Sugi turned to look at me. His eyes sparkled through his mask.

Okay, buddy. I get it. We could just have … a little beauty.

Sugi had taken me to one of his favorite places to dive.

The current carried us swiftly though hundreds of butterfly-fish. Suddenly a banded sea snake passed right in front of me and vanished into a crevice in the coral wall. I swirled around to Sugi and pointed to where I last saw it.

We drifted upward toward the edge of a drop-off. The light brightened. "I should get some footage of Sugi," I mused.

I turned around. Sugi was right behind me, gently holding the snake. It was over a yard long. He cradled it softly in his hands, barely gripping it. At any time it could have slipped free. He positioned the snake with its head toward me.

My heart raced. But I was fascinated too. This creature: it was all spine and eyes and glistening skin. It looked at me with a penetrating gaze.

Sugi slowly turned, pointed its head away from us, and re-leased it as one might release a pigeon, with awe at its beauty, trusting it would take flight—hands fully outstretched.

We watched it swim away over the top of the reef, its black-and-white bands undulating in the light.

On my last afternoon in the islands, I sat alone at a large table on the second floor of the building the WWF office was in. The sound of the rain poured in through open wooden doors that looked out on the harbor. The rain was loud and envel-oping.

There were so many times now when I waited long periods for someone or for a boat, or simply waited out the rain. I'd started to like it. So I was there, just sitting, waiting out the rain.

Sugi came upstairs.

"So, Sugi …"

"Yes?" He sat down in a chair and crossed his legs.

"What do you call it—a sea snake—in Indonesian?"

"*Ular laut.*" Sugi smiled.

"You seemed comfortable with the snake."

"Yes."

"But I mean ... you seemed to know ..."

Sugi nodded and rotated his foot gently at the ankle joint.

"When I was in university, I took care of some snakes." He explained that his professor had studied cobras. In order to find out which muscle in a cobra's back allowed it to hold its head up, his professor had made small incisions in the back muscles of a group of cobras. "So," Sugi said, "I took care of the wounds."

"The cobras?"

"Well, the wounds needed to be cared for."

"With ointment?"

"Yes."

"How many?"

"A dozen. And when they were better, I released them into the wild."

"But how did you learn to touch them?"

"Well, first you have to establish a relationship. They can tell ..." He paused to find the right English words, "whether you mean well."

"The way a dog can sense your intentions, whether you are friendly?"

"Yes, like that. They have moods. You know, like people have moods."

There was a pause.

Maybe I can talk to Sugi about the mantas.

I told Sugi about being swept away in the current, the mantas circling me, swimming with them, returning to the group of divers.

"Well, I can't tell you what happened," Sugi said cautiously, "but I have heard stories like this, and I know of one time—a swimmer who was saved by a manta."

"Do you think they sensed that I was lost?"

"They are very smart. They can sense that you need help and that you are ..." He paused again for a moment and then continued, "that you are receptive. I have heard stories. One in particular—the manta helped a man stay afloat until he reached shore."

It had stopped raining. Sugi went downstairs to make some phone calls. I checked my email. I could hear Sugi chatting on the phone in Indonesian.

I thought about Sugi and the cobras. Me and the ocean. The rogue wave that almost killed me. It had taken a long time to learn to be underwater again, to trust that.

Nature. Ocean. One's environment: there is never absolute trust, and there shouldn't be. But does that mean it's some force to be conquered, consumed, warded off?

The snake embodies so well the contradictions in how we relate to the natural world. Is there any animal that can elicit a more visceral fright? And yet the symbol of the Hippocratic Oath taken by physicians is Asclepius's rod with a snake wrapped around it. In the ancient Greek myth, Asclepius had showed kindness to a snake, so it taught him the secret knowledge that enabled him to be a healer. In Greek mythology, a snake symbolized healing and wisdom.

It dawned on me that the snake was so much like what the ocean had been to me—object of terror and adoration, fascination and fear. I'd probably always have bouts of numbness from the accident, yet there was no place on earth I loved more. I had a lot in common with how humanity treated the ocean, and all of nature for that matter: we longed for it, but feared it, celebrated its beauty, but decimated it.

Maybe nature was neither a beautiful healer nor venomous enemy. Maybe it was time to establish a new relationship.

"We need to get started," Sugi had said. "Then it becomes a

new world, with a focus on the environment, not just capital."
So what would that new world look like?

At the top of the list for the oceans were: end overfishing, reduce nutrient pollution, curb carbon emissions, create more MPAs. The environment would have to be as core to our lives as capital had been the economic driver. The ideas were already there, and they were already starting to be implemented— mitigate climate change, expand renewable energy, migrate to zero-waste systems. And like the local fishermen, we could reach to the past for solutions. Charlie and I put up a clothes-line; the electric bill was lower. We put a garbage can outside our bathroom window—a primitive gray-water system. We emptied the bathtub with a bucket. We were saving 1,500 gallons of water a month, and our garden was bursting with life.

These solutions were like a wheel that had finally begun to turn, part of what was being called the "circular economy." It was based on the idea that the take-make-dispose model, which relied on large quantities of resources and energy, was "increasingly unfit for the reality in which it operates."[75]

So what would a circular economy be like? *More efficient.* The aim was a design that eliminated waste, relied on renewable energy, and eradicated the use of toxic chemicals. Products would be designed and manufactured so that materials like precious metals, polymers, and alloys could be reused.[76] And the enmity between industrialists (big, evil) and environmentalists (obstructive, unrealistic) need not prevail.

Care for the environment would be a matter of public health. In the mid-1800s an Austrian-Hungarian physician, Ignaz Semmelweis, discovered that the infection of female reproductive organs after childbirth—puerperal fever—was contagious and that higher rates of infection were due to medical staff handling corpses during autopsies before delivering babies. Semmelweis initiated an unprecedented practice: *hand washing.* The incidence of infection was dramatically reduced.

But most of the medical profession at the time was indifferent to his discovery. Like climate change or nutrient runoff today, they couldn't see it—or, rather, infectious diseases were not a recognized part of that era's worldview or "field of vision." It wasn't until a decade after his death, when Louis Pasteur's germ theory of disease explained his findings, that hand washing was widely adopted. Today Semmelweis is known as the pioneer of antiseptic procedures.[77] Hand washing is an accepted, necessary practice, even though we can't see the phenomena it counters.

In the future, might we regard a sustainable relationship with the earth with the same care that we wash our hands? Even though we don't necessarily see immediate results?

When my husband or I fill up the tank of one of our cars, we do it with a grimace, watching the dollar signs go up and up. Our friends Connie and Alan have solar panels on their roof, one electric car, and one hybrid. All of their electricity is generated at home, and it charges one of their cars. The other car, the hybrid, gets twice the mileage ours gets. Ergo, we are shopping for solar and more efficient cars. Will we see immediate results from that? Unlikely. But we know that, like washing our hands, it's needed.

Solar power is a low-cost energy solution for developing world nations as well. More than one-fifth of the world's population has no access to electricity. Kerosene lamps strain household budgets and produce toxic fumes. A simple solar lamp costs less than twenty dollars.[78]

It is a matter of implementing these ideas on an accelerated basis. The new bottom line will be a triple bottom line: capital, people, and the environment will get the same priority. Viewed through the long eye of time, this transformation might be as big as the Industrial Revolution or the Agricultural Revolution.

Sugi was off the phone. Silence. I gathered my gear, and we said goodbye. Then I walked out onto the street. It was bathed in dusty evening light.

At the front desk of the hotel, I pulled out a large bundle of Indonesia currency, *rupiah*. The rhythms of this place had seemed so slow, and now I felt that I was moving in even slower motion, wanting to make every minute last longer.

"Ibu Liz leaving?" the hotel owner asked softly.

"Yes." I suddenly felt terribly sad.

He slowly counted the *rupiah,* here and there flattening a crumpled bill methodically, as if he too wanted to stretch out the time.

I packed my things. I would leave early in the morning. I tried to take in as much as I could in the little time I had left, the high ceiling in my room, the ceramic floors, the rain that had suddenly begun again. I recited in my mind a list of things I would miss—the imams chanting; the gurgle of diesel engines at dawn; the glowing, lantern-lit faces of the villagers in the night market; giving the kids a high-five.

The last things I stowed were my passport and the wooden goggles from the Bajau village.

PART 4

The Mediterranean

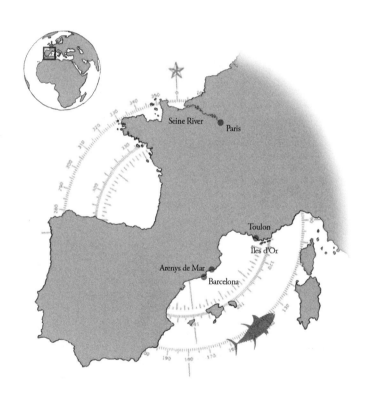

15

The Island

"*Rouge, s'il vous plaît,*" I said. "Red, please."

I was standing in what felt like a sleek, terrestrial submarine hurling itself north at over 180 miles per hour—Europe's ultramodern high-speed rail, the TGV. The bar in the restaurant car had an array of shrink-wrapped French food. I tucked a pack of brie cheese and French bread under my arm and walked with a small bottle of wine to the end of the car. With one push of a button, a glass door swished open to the next compartment.

My seat was spacious and warm. My phone and my iPad were plugged into an outlet below the armrest. The train was almost full, most everyone consumed in their own interior worlds, comfortably encapsulated in our carpeted, metallic tube as it roared through the countryside.

It had been several months since I'd been in the Coral Triangle, but the vividness of it had not faded. I poured the wine into a plastic cup and gazed out the window into the chilly northern light. Power lines flickered past like a deck of cards being shuffled. The plastic cup vibrated on the tray table. Everything was accelerated, as if the shutter speed of my senses had been suddenly thrust to 1/1000th of a second.

Riverbed. Bridge. A flock of birds.

I picked up the quivering cup and took a sip of wine. Every few minutes the train swooped into a tunnel, and for a few seconds I saw nothing but my reflection and the cabin's dim interior lights. Then the train zipped out of the tunnel with a shudder.

Village. Vineyard. Farmland. Patchworks of green and brown. Another tunnel for a few seconds. Then a burst of light. Freeway. Parking lot. Lumberyard. Gravel ditch. Silos, big-rig trucks, weighing stations. Everything taken, every inch of space, accounted for, consumed, cared for or carelessly ravaged. What wildness remained in that geometric reckoning was preserved because someone or some group of people has worked to save it.

I reached down into my backpack for a book and saw the wooden Bajau goggles. I'd brought them for free diving in the Mediterranean. I pulled them out.

Something more than the sum of any tears or grief or joy or elation happened when the wooden goggles met my hands: my heart welled up. Everything, all of it—Sugi, the mantas, the snake, Rikardo, the Bajau villagers, Marsha, the mangroves, the coral reef at the Northwest Point, Eiglys, the turtles, Jenny, the upwelling, Peter, the sea lions, the wind whistling through the whale skeleton. The voice of the man whose name I may never know at the Marine Mammal Center, with his New York accent, "You got to jump on the moments, you know, when the dots start to connect."

That word: gift. Something unexpected, beautiful. The beads of bonus minutes. The feeling had not faded since the accident. It was still so utterly miraculous to be alive. Every flicker of a millisecond.

The train whipped into another tunnel, shuddered side to side, and then bolted back out into the light.

Cows. Barn. Fences. An old farmhouse poised on a long, sloping hillside.

The goggles were carved perfectly to hug the side of one's brow. The last day in Sulawesi I'd put them on and went free diving just after sunrise. As I hovered, a school of blue-and-yellow fusiliers surrounded me with an uncanny ease.

Another train whisked by in the opposite direction. For a split second, our train rumbled almost violently, the electrical energy of those two opposed forces momentarily meeting.

Several hours before, the train had left Toulon, a small coastal city in southern France. There's a famous story there about a young man who was an accomplished athlete. He'd broken twelve bones in a terrible car crash, and his hopes to become a naval pilot were crushed. Both arms had been broken. One arm was paralyzed, and gangrene had set in, but he refused to let it be amputated. Slowly he regained the use of that arm, and the gangrene receded. He spent hours swimming in the harbor in a painstaking effort to regain his strength. One day a friend lent him a pair of goggles that he'd gotten from a pearl diver in the Philippines, just like the ones I held in my hand, made from soft wood and glass.

The young man put them on and went back into the water. The world below was no longer a blur. It was filled with dozens of fish. He looked back up and saw the pier in the harbor and cars passing along the coast.

Jacques Cousteau's life was never the same. "He wanted to live fully in each of these worlds, above and below all at once," his son Jean-Michel Cousteau wrote. "These two worlds were framed for him in such an impossibly beautiful way. The juxtaposition was a constant puzzle."[79] When Cousteau died, his legacy was not only as an explorer or a documentary filmmaker, but as the man who introduced millions upon millions of people to the wonders of the undersea world and inspired a generation of activists.

The train started to slow. My ears popped. We pitched downward slightly, as if we were entering a large basin. I unwrapped the cheese and bread and nibbled on it.

The words of the fishermen in Sulawesi were indelible: *please eat sustainable seafood.* The more people ate sustainable fish, the more the fishermen like the ones in Sulawesi, who had walked away from dynamite fishing, would be able to sell their fish through a sustainable supply chain.

So, who had a huge influence on how modernized world eats? Who could help convince people to eat sustainable fish? To care about it?

French chefs!

Some words on the intercom: *Gare de Lyon.* The train was pulling into the one of the main train stations in Paris. Everyone woke from his or her reverie. The compartment filled with the rustle of coats, the snap of briefcases and laptops closing.

For the next few days I'd speak with chefs and fishmongers and retailers about just exactly that—how do you transform a seafood supply chain so that it is sustainable? How do you put a piece of seafood in proximity to a fork and knife without pillaging of the ocean and needlessly contributing to the worsening living conditions in developing countries?

***

The hotel elevator was the size of a coffin. There was no way I was going to fit in it with my dive gear. "Don't worry," the concierge mumbled, "I send your bag up separately." He rolled my gear into the elevator and pushed a button—off it went.

I climbed a spiral staircase three flights and opened the hinged door to the elevator, and there was my gear. The building was over a hundred years old, and the door to my room was stuck. I called down with my cell phone to the concierge.

"*Poussez!*" he barked crabbily, "Push!" I turned the key and hurled my body at the door.

There was a wooden writing desk with ornate cubbyholes, a small bed, and casement windows that opened to a dark alley. I unpacked and then went out for a walk. I had time to explore before my meetings the next day.

It was drizzling and cold. There was a river a few blocks away. An almond-shaped island occupied a slipstream in the midst of the river's currents. A pair of old stone bridges led to it.

I walked over one of the bridges. A groundswell of sound filled the air—bells ringing. My head craned upward. In front of me was a massive stone edifice as high as the karst limestone islands in Raja Ampat. The bells were so loud it was as if the stone itself was singing. My chest vibrated.

It was the cathedral of Notre-Dame. The tiny island was the Île de la Cité in the heart of Paris. A huge rose window and archways layered with columns and carved figures adorned the entrance to the cathedral. The square was surrounded by clusters of centuries-old buildings and framed by a row of linden trees, whose leaves were turning yellow in the autumn air.

Some stairs wound down to an ancient crypt beneath the square in front of Notre-Dame. Housed there were the ruins of an ancient fishing village called Lutetia, occupied by a Gaulish tribe, the Parisii, during the reign of Augustus, from 27 BC to 14 AD. The Seine River then was surrounded by wetlands rich with carp, flounder, perch, pike, and trout. It originates in limestone highlands and flows north until it empties into the English Channel. Atlantic salmon and sturgeon migrate into the river to spawn.

A multimedia installation mimicked what it might have felt like to stand in that ancient village. Original slabs of stone were used to assemble a portion of a dock in front of a projected image of shelters with ceramic roof tiles and primitive boats floating on the river. A recording filled the air with the sound of water and seagulls.

Balsa-wood architectural models provided bird's-eye views of the transformation from tribal village to progressively more sophisticated municipalities, with aqueducts, bridges, and piers. In 308 AD the island town was fortified against barbarian invasions. In the late twelfth century, stonecutters began chiseling blocks of limestone from quarries. The construction of Notre-Dame had begun. What followed was a collective effort that spanned three centuries.

The long "eye of time" that had opened up when I saw Sugi and the snake, when I understood that civilization and nature had to be on a profoundly different footing and that we had to evolve toward a future that would reflect that—that eye had not snapped shut. Its vision persisted everywhere I went.

I climbed the stairway out of the crypt and walked toward Notre-Dame. Inside, the cathedral was filled with iridescent light and stony shadows. I remembered uttering to myself in the coral reefs in the Turks and Caicos, "This is my cathedral" as I reveled in that sensation that "everything is alive." Notre-Dame made me feel that way too. The rose windows, the cavernous archways, and the intimate apses filled me with awe.

Not just Christians, but also poets and philosophers and artists and architects, people from all walks of life came to Notre-Dame for inspiration. I arrived with my memory of the coral reefs in tow and a restless, searching feeling that my spiritual life and nature, especially the ocean, were inextricable. Other visitors have likened the atmosphere of the cathedral to the light of a primeval forest or the depths of a clear night sky or a sense of infinity.

There are physical parallels too. Just as the shipbuilders in Sulawesi used the tallest trees they could find for a keel, the builders of Notre-Dame used them as scaffolding for its towering armature. Throughout the cathedral you can see the roots of modern biomimicry—biologically inspired engineering. The flying buttresses are similar to tree roots or branches; the quatrefoil patterns, the spitting image of four-leaf clovers. Gargoyles? Fantastic animal creatures.

The vaulted ceilings recall an upside-down boat hull or the belly of a whale. Naval carpenters often doubled as cathedral craftsmen in the Middle Ages, the forces that supported cathedral vaults and boat hulls being so similar. Robert Hobman, the nautical historian who led the *Sarimanok* expedition, had said boat builders were likely inspired by whale ribs and the hydrodynamics of fish. Long ago, whale ribs were used as architectural framing for archways.[80]

The presence of biomimicry hearkened back to a time, not just in the Christian tradition, but in many religious traditions, when it was not an apocalypse or afterlife that was the focus, but our kinship with the animal kingdom and the earth: that our bond with the interconnected web of life was sacred and key to our sustenance. The hallowed cathedral, punctuated by towering columns, recalled a cavern with stalactites and stalagmites. I flashed back to diving in the cenotes of the Yucatan, underwater caves so calm that the water is described as "gin clear." One of those caverns was as long as a football field.

Biomimicry helped the cathedral architects and builders innovate, exceed themselves, and do the near-impossible. Now it was being employed in sustainability solutions, especially in the design of resilient, networked systems. Sometimes what seems impossible becomes less so when the right question is asked. In this case it was, "Who is the 'networker' par excellence? The queen bee of integrated life-support systems?"

You guessed it: mother nature. The biologist Janine Benyus coined *biomimicry* as "the conscious emulation of life's genius." The applications were so practical, there was no need for hype. Improve traffic flow patterns? Study neural networks. Brighter, longer-lasting LED lights? The jagged scales of fireflies. Benyus's exploration of biomimicry echoes Wendell Berry's notion of "solving for the pattern"—it's driven in part by the question "How might we consciously emulate life-sustaining patterns in nature to solve human problems?"[81]

It was no coincidence that the circular economy also drew on the study of living systems, the idea of "optimizing systems rather than components."[82] In the book *Cradle to Cradle,* Michael McDonough and William Braungart show how the flow of manufacturing materials can be optimized to preserve our earth. The shift would be from a cradle-to-grave model to a cradle-to-cradle one—the continuous, renewable use of materials.

I sat down in one of the wooden pews and looked up. I felt a twinge and some numbness in one hand. When I woke that morning, several fingers had been numb, but when I rolled over, feeling came back to them. I was still haunted by the fear that my back would go awry, and I'd lose sensation in my arms. The kayak accident had shown me how fast everything can be taken away. My life still felt like a long-distance telephone call that could be snapped off at any minute.

"Take advantage of that feeling," I told myself. "Don't waste the time you have." The arcs of the vaults overhead felt like a mythic sky that just kept going. "But would I really make any difference with my writing?" I felt so small.

When I left the cathedral, I paused at one of the large fluted columns and pressed my hand against the cool stone. Much of Notre-Dame is constructed from limestone. Take a magnifying glass to it, and you'll see coral fossils from the sea that filled the Paris basin forty-five million years ago.[83]

꧁

Outside, the wind was blowing. It felt like it was going to rain. I looked at my watch. I still had a little time. There was another place I wanted to visit, but I also dreaded going. A few hundred yards behind the cathedral was a memorial to the Jews, people with disabilities, gay men and lesbians, and anyone tagged as part of the resistance, who were deported from Vichy France to Nazi concentration camps. Stairs descended to a memorial chamber that included a dark, claustrophobic tunnel illuminated by two hundred thousand crystal lights. Each light symbolized one of the deportees whose life was lost.

The silence among the viewers was deafening. Being there was so halting, so almost completely unbearable, that it was an effort to breathe.

But the courage of that truth-making and the fact that it existed right next to Notre-Dame, that the moral bankruptcy of the church during World War II would not be forgotten— that was something. Another little-known fact that deserves remembrance is that the imam of the Grand Mosque in Paris hid Jewish children during the Nazi occupation.[84] History is rife with periods of genocide, some well recorded, but some disguised or indifferently dismissed, some almost to the point that they seem to vanish, as if they never happened. Engraved in stone at the exit of the Deportation Memorial were the words "Forgive, but never forget."

The Île de la Cité was layered with time like the rings of a gigantic tree: hominoids, the Agricultural Revolution, the Gauls, the Roman conquest, the Middle Ages, the French Revolution, the Industrial Revolution, World War I, World War II, cycles of pillaging and reconstruction, war and peace, stagnation and invention. North of Notre-Dame was the Palais de Justice, the highest jurisdiction in the French courts, and the Conciergie, where during the French Revolution, prisoners were executed by guillotine.

Edward Tufte, a Yale statistician and political scientist, writes that what science and art have in common is *"intense seeing, the wide-eyed observing that generates empirical information."*[85] When "seeing turns into showing" in a fashion that is both beautiful and true, when the credibility of the evidence also inspires a sense of wonder, it is what Tufte terms *beautiful evidence.*[86]

It was there, on that teardrop-shaped island. Beautiful evidence in layers upon layers of time: showing how human actions create our future. Cruelty. Beauty. Genocide. Justice. Tyranny. Truth. The vestiges of the past, some irretrievable in the silt of time, others reconstructed to inform a greater wisdom. And the light. The muted silver-gray light on the river. The effervescent light pouring through stained-glass windows. And the crystal light of each glass bead in the Deportation Memorial, which seemed to both howl and whisper at the same time.

I started back over a bridge toward the Latin Quarter, where my hotel was. Midway, I stopped and gazed down at the green-gray river. One of the ways archeologists were able to date the ancient fishing village was from coins recovered from the silt of the Seine, which showed the name of the original Gaulish tribe. Small, noisy drops of rain started to fall.

I was wearing the yellow rain jacket that I'd worn over a t-shirt in Indonesia. Now I had a sweater under it, but I was still shivering. I wiped a few cold beads of rain from my face.

Zoom out far enough, and look at the solar system as a whole, and you'll see that water is the game-changer—it's what makes life possible on this planet and not the others. Imagine for a moment the path of a raindrop—to soil, root, leaf, aquifer, reservoir, faucet, and then again piped to the sea or a lake or a river and then evaporating into the clouds to become a raindrop again. Then add *that number,* the one that is as persistent and perpetual as gravity, as the rotation of the planets: 97 percent of all the water on earth is in the ocean. Everywhere you go, dig deep enough, and you'll find that water is an essential part of every life form, even in one of the oldest cities in the world.

I looked back at the island. Then toward the city on the other side of the bridge. Cars and buses and trucks moved at a snail's pace, jammed tightly together. I had roamed onto the island exploring, now I was in the grips of something wholly unexpected.

Athletes often recount that at certain intense moments of focus, time seems to slow down or stand still. It was that kind of moment: the island had presented an invitation, sealed in an old-world envelope, to let the clock stop for a moment—in the midst of a century, a millennium, in the midst of millions of years—and situate myself in a wider stretch of time.

The cathedral builders, like the builders of other ancient monuments, seemed to have persistently exceeded their means to fulfill a goal that took several generations to achieve. In 1961, John F. Kennedy challenged Americans to put a man on the moon within a decade. Now another call was sounding in almost every corner of the world. This call had an unprecedented, halting gravity to it—so alarming that it was nearly unthinkable.

What was at stake was not the protection of a village against barbarians or a young nation against the technological prowess of a totalitarian superpower. It was the very means by which life regenerates itself after periods of destruction, *what allows life to come back*. What was at stake was what sustains us, what replenishes the air we breathe: a habitable earth.

It was a call to do the "near-impossible" and yet utterly necessary, swiftly and decisively: to stem the tide of destruction and forge a sustainable relationship with the earth, to work with all the vigor and intelligence and dedication we can summon, because otherwise we might fail. We are capable of it. And we're starting to do it. We just need to do it more—and faster.

Two mallards flew overhead, toward the island. To the astonishment of many, efforts to clean up the pollution-plagued Seine were showing signs of success. After vanishing for over a century, Atlantic salmon had returned to spawn.

I reached into my pocket for a coin, threw it into the river, and made a silent wish.

16

Plus Signs

"That was *the click!*" Michel spoke in English with a French accent. "I see the faces of students. This day I see that this," he cupped his hands together and put them down on the table as if clasping something precious, "is a *noble cause.*"

"When we say that word in French," Elisabeth said, "what is *noble* is good for humanity. It's a good cause for humanity, and a cause is something you fight for."

We sat around a circular table in a small conference room. To the left of us was a set of French doors adorned by ornate cast-iron railings. Elisabeth Vallet was the director of SeaWeb Europe, which supported sustainable seafood initiatives.[87] Michel Mouisel was head of international relations at one of the most prestigious culinary schools in France—Ferrandi-Paris.

It was the next day. A series of triangulated streets with baroque, balcony-laden buildings had led me to 51 rue Le Peletier, where SeaWeb Europe had its office.

"*Noble* in French, means respect," Michel continued. He was in his fifties and wore a blue-gray suit.

"It's a respectable subject to work on. It's not elitist," Elisabeth added. "It's an important, beautiful thing to work toward."

Michel was talking about a conference that SeaWeb had helped coordinate. "It was not only explaining the situation then that made me see the point," he said, "but that for children in the future, what fish will be left?" Michel was cheerful, but he didn't mince words. "What will you do when you have no more fish! No more fish? *Well, then you are not a big chef!*"

In the central fish market in Paris, there were once forty-five vendors. Now there were fifteen. The other stalls in the fish market were empty. Seventy-six percent of the world's fisheries were already fully exploited or overfished. The take of the global fishing fleet was over two times more than what the oceans could replenish over time.[88]

"At this conference there were representatives from every part of the seafood chain," Elisabeth added. The "seafood chain" meant every person involved from the moment a sea creature is plucked from the ocean to when it gets to a plate—fishermen, wholesalers, retailers, fishmongers, chefs, consumers. "Everybody along the chain now is speaking about this instability, because they realize that it is important to the stability of their business. But a lot still needs to be done."

"When customers buy some fish, you must inform and educate them," Michel added. "For instance, you can suggest, 'You can eat this fish; it's good and not expensive,' such as Atlantic sardines." Atlantic sardines were still considered sustainably harvested, whereas Mediterranean sardines were gravely over-exploited.[89]

"In the Ferrandi school," Michel continued, "we buy not bluefin tuna, but mackerel or sardines for the tests for chefs."

Atlantic and Mediterranean bluefin tuna stocks had been hunted nearly to the point of extinction. But sardines? Michel was referring to eating lower on the food chain. Sardines reproduce faster and reach maturity in around one year's time. A bluefin tuna takes four to six years to mature. Its lifespan is fifteen to thirty years. An orange roughy can live to over one hundred years. And the bigger the fish and the higher it is on the food chain, the more toxins, such as mercury, have accumulated in it.

Eating low on the food chain eases the burden on natural resources. Sounds heady, but it's like having a fuel-efficient car. Take beef—it has the staggeringly high energy-input to protein-output ratio of 54:1.[90] Fifty-four pounds of feed are required to reap one pound of meat. Chicken is dramatically more efficient, with a 4:1 ratio.

It was really starting to hit home that it wasn't just our cars that needed to be fuel-efficient: *it was our whole lifestyle.* Did we really need to eat foods flown in from far-flung locations? A tomato from Mexico traveled thousands of miles in a refrigerated truck packed in cardboard and Styrofoam. Charlie planted a vegetable garden and started saving seeds. His tomatoes traveled all of twenty yards to our kitchen. And his tomatoes were luscious.

The spigot of influence Michel had his hand on was big. Culinary institutes from all around the world approached Ferrandi for training. At any one time, there were fifteen hundred students and two thousand chefs in continuing education. Ferrandi-Paris and SeaWeb Europe co-funded the first national sustainable-seafood catering competition along with the Dinard catering school and the prestigious chefs' association Relais et Châteaux. Awards went for the best recipes using *poisson durable*—sustainable fish—showcasing that it could epitomize the best of French cuisine. Awards went not only for the best recipes but also to the candidate who could best explain what sustainability meant and which criteria he or she used to select fish for the competition.

"Okay, so say I'm a chef ..." I said to Elisabeth and Michel.

"And," Elisabeth picked up the thread playfully, "*your customers love cod!*" Cod, once a fisheries staple, was overfished.

"And whenever it's on the menu," I added, "it's the favorite dish!"

For five hundred years, the cod stocks in Newfoundland had seemed inexhaustible. Then in 1992 the Grand Banks fishery collapsed and forty thousand people lost their jobs.[91] But some cod from depleted stocks was still eaten.

"And if you don't serve cod," Elisabeth raised an eyebrow and flipped open a colorful, spiral-bound book, "and another restaurant does, maybe your customers will go there?" She thumbed through the pages until she got to *le caillaud*—cod. There was a photo of the oblong fish with rounded lips and a summary of the severely depleted stocks.

But you are not stuck between hell and a handbasket. You can make sure your cod comes from a sustainable stock, such as Norwegian cod, or you can choose a species other than cod. The book also had a recommendation for an alternative—pollock. And a culinary student at the time, Natacha Morin, had created an award-winning dish: *lieu noir rôti, sur une polenta crémeuse*—roast pollock with creamy polenta.

The book was *Le guide des espèces à l'usage des professionnels,* a species guide for seafood professionals. Elisabeth worked with fishmongers, chefs, wholesalers, and retailers to create a guide that reflected their thinking. "To make this work," Elisabeth explained, "people from all aspects of the chain of custody needed to engage."

Le guide was revised every year and sent to two thousand seafood professionals in France and Belgium. It was straightforward and handy, augmented with information on fishing practices, aquaculture, fisheries legislation, and sustainability certifications, such as the Marine Stewardship Council (MSC) blue label. It broke the "not knowing what to do" barrier. It gave the seafood professionals alternatives.

One of the tipping points in France was when Olivier Roellinger, the vice president of the chef's association, Relais et Châteaux, asked the five hundred member chefs—who came from all over the world—to sign a pledge to not cook endangered species anymore. All of them moved bluefin tuna off the menu in 2010.

"Other people started contacting us," Elisabeth continued excitedly. "They said, 'Wow! It's great what you have done with Relais et Châteaux, but we are just a grocery or a small restaurant in Paris. What can we do?' "

"Okay," Michel replied, cupping his hands on the table again. "That is the world. And you take a drop ..." With a self-deprecating grin, Michel raised one hand as if to mimic an eyedropper. "That makes ripples. And now," he pointed at me and my notebook and said, "You! We begin with you, too!"

Elisabeth grinned.

"But for me," Michel continued, "it's very important to inform all people, students, parents. All the time, not just during training at the school. For me this is a *noble cause,* because gastronomy is a *vecteur de paix.*"

"*Vecteur de paix?*" I asked.

Elisabeth translated, "A vector for peace."

"There is a respect and curiosity about each other," Michel continued.

"It contributes to peace," Elisabeth added.

"There is an exchange between friends."

"It's like an honor."

"A presentation."

"To connect."

"Okay, okay!" I interjected. "So what is gastronomy really?"

Michel grinned and paused. He had a thoughtful look on his face, like he was rubbing his hands together in his mind. "It's like a painting. You have the painting, the products are your paint." He gestured as if he were holding a paintbrush. "With this product you make some color, some harmony between the color and shapes. When you are a baby you drink milk, after that you must eat. That's not art! But you can transform a meal into a communication."

"A communication?"

"Yes!"

Arman—the Bajau chief. The delicious fried fruit and hot tea.

I told them about Arman. The water village. How Rikardo and I were adroitly served the tea and teacakes.

"So, Arman was telling me, as best he could, you are welcome here?" I asked. The question was obvious—food can equal hospitality, but Michel was digging deeper.

"Yes, yes!" Michel said. "The definition of art, for me, is to transform something very basic into something beautiful. *And good!*"

They had been the most beautiful tea and teacakes I'd ever had.

"The art of cooking," Michel continued, "began with the art of the table."

"There was an evolution...." Elisabeth piped in.

"But the meal wasn't so good."

They burst into rapid-fire French, so fast I couldn't follow. I caught a few words like *histoire* and *développement* like errant sparks. They were debating the history of gastronomy.

Could food lead the way to a new way of living? Well, the Eat Local movement certainly was propagating sustainability ideas. The number of farmers' markets had ballooned. Kitchen gardens were back. Urban gardening was flourishing—herbs and salad greens were growing in folding planters mounted on fire escapes.

Elisabeth and Michel were still debating. Laughter peppered the feverish exchange. Humor seemed built-in to this work, like calcium to bones. Got an intransigent problem to solve? Keep a sense of humor handy.

On that front, Elisabeth and I had gotten acquainted on an accelerated basis. On my way to our first meeting, I grabbed an espresso at a café. I spilled it on my pants. Then I got lost on the metro. When I had set my alarm the night before, I'd given myself two and half hours to have a leisurely breakfast and make the thirty-minute trip to her office. In my frenzied state, it took all of that to arrive smack dab on time.

Elisabeth greeted me with gracious calm, elegantly dressed in silky black slacks and a blouse. "It's so nice to meet you face to face," she said, shaking my hand. As I followed her down a hallway to the conference room, she asked, "Did you have any trouble getting here? You're right on time!"

Did she notice the espresso blotches?

I plopped my weathered knapsack down on a circular table. The room was pleasantly warm. I started to pull off my sweater. Something was tangled as I pulled it over my head. I pulled harder.

"Liz," Elisabeth inquired gently, "I think you are having a little trouble … *with your shirt?*"

I looked down. I was pulling up not only my sweater but also the shirt under it; my bra and money belt where in plain view.

"Don't worry," she said. "It breaks the ice."

Two guys who rented office space on the same floor as the

SeaWeb office came in. There was a espresso machine in the room. And of course, an espresso machine to the French is like a salt lick to deer. We would have frequent traffic.

"Olivier," the first fellow said, pointing a finger at his chest proudly.

The second fellow did the same with greater emphasis like a stand-up comic, "Olivier!" His name was Olivier too. We laughed.

"Elizabeth!" I said, tapping a finger to my sternum. I looked at Elisabeth.

Her eyes grew round with mischief. "Elisabeth!" she enunciated slowly as she tapped a finger to her chest.

Elisabeth and Michel had finished their debate. Switch: English! The short form of the developmental stages of *la gastronomie:* first a nice table setting, then a delicious meal, then the shape of the plate became important—rectangular plates, square plates. And now stage four: the food is going to reflect a sustainable relationship with the earth.

"You mean," I asked, "sustainability is the next stage of gastronomy?"

"Yes, to save the planet!" Michel said emphatically. "And the fish problem is an international problem." His voice grew even more serious in tone. "It is a similar problem with drinking water around the world."

"So it's parallel to how architecture is evolving?" I asked. "For the future, a building that is more energy efficient, that is better designed, is more beautiful?"

Yes, yes, yes. Elisabeth and Michel beamed at me: beauty was evolving.

"We need to hurry or we'll be late!" Elisabeth said, gathering her things. We'd said goodbye to Michel and were going to speak with a highly esteemed chef, François Pasteau, at his restaurant, L'Epi Dupin. We rushed down the hall and slipped into the elevator. Elisabeth pushed the button for the lobby. The doors closed.

Silence.

"You can write about your fear now," Elisabeth said, looking straight ahead.

My fear? Snakes. Drowning. Paralysis. Death. How could she know?

"Yes," she deadpanned, "Your fear that when you are in public, you will pull your shirt up by accident."

We walked to the metro at a quick clip. It was midday. The train platform was almost empty.

"Biology was fascinating to me," Elisabeth said. Her voice echoed in the hollow concrete tunnel. She was talking about when she was a child. "I was fascinated by how things were linked together. I still have a special fascination with the huge immensity of space, like ocean or desert."

A low rumble. The train was coming.

"It's seven years I've been here," she explained. Before coming to Paris she had worked in the agriculture sector. "I was fascinated with the sector. And then you think, wow, this is an emergency! And wow, that's a lot to do! And yes, I will try to help."

"It still overwhelms me. Some mornings I get up and I think, how is this going to all work out?" I told her.

The train arrived. The doors slid open with a screech.

It was full. There were no free seats. Elisabeth reached down to two tiny folding seats by the door. She sat down on one and gestured with a twinkle for me to sit next to her.

We sat squished together, knees high, as if sitting on two children's seats in a preschool. "But it's this …" Elisabeth said, "Everyone in the chain needs to be engaged. Everyone has a role to play!"

I dug into my knapsack for my notebook to write it down. "Say that again?"

"Everyone in the chain," Elisabeth repeated over the metallic squeal of the metro, "Everyone needs to be engaged; everyone has a role to play."

Maybe it wasn't about getting up in the morning and shouldering the worry of "how is all of this going to work out," maybe it was about rolling up your sleeves and getting to work—doing something you loved that played a role.

"Me then? My role?" I asked. "Writer—that's how I become a link in the chain?"

"Yes, of course."

The train rumbled and swished side to side irregularly.

Aromas of pastry and herbs surrounded us. "I was making a burger of red tuna—the bluefin," François Pasteau explained. "It's red like meat, so it was very nice looking. People loved it! It was one of my main dishes."

The staff was setting the tables for lunch in the restaurant. The walls had rustic wood paneling. Wine bottles were stowed in handsome wood racks.

"I saw a film on television about tuna fisheries, overexploitation in Japan. It was a shock to me." François was lean and had short brown hair. He wore a white chef's uniform.

Bluefin stocks had decreased 96 percent from preindustrial levels. In some parts of the world only 1 or 2 percent of the stock was left.[92]

"It was not easy to make the decision, because I had really nice recipes," François continued. "But I stopped it and after, when customers asked, I just tell them that if we carry on like that, tuna will be gone forever! And it was a bit silly. Afterward I realized I could make the burger with white tuna."

François stopped serving bluefin in 2007. But despite efforts to save the bluefin, the numbers continued to fall. The economic incentives to keep hunting it for sashimi and sushi were sky-high. One bluefin could fetch over a half million dollars at the time. Management efforts were especially complicated because bluefin migrated through international waters. The hunt had only got more efficient with high-tech harpoons and spotter helicopters. The black market was huge. Even the Mafia was in on it. As bluefin stocks plummeted, the corporate conglomerate Mitsubishi started freezing bluefin so they could be sold for astronomical sums after they "went extinct."[93]

Then in the fall of 2012, something happened—bluefin stocks ticked upward slightly.[94] How did that ice-ax arrest at the edge of extinction happen?

"We didn't give up," one the world's experts on bluefin, Sergi Tudela, had told me. For over a decade, the head of WWF Mediterranean had led a delegation to the International Commission for the Conservations of Atlantic Tunas (ICCAT). "The point," he emphasized, "is that joint efforts to drive change can save even the most hopeless of fisheries from collapse."

The ice-ax arrest was brought about by multiple ice axes, large, small, minute, and massive: decreases in fishing quotas, moratoriums, changes to "minimum landing sizes," reductions in fleet capacity, limited open seasons for fishing, position papers, petitions, awareness campaigns, documentary films, lectures, and books. Mega retailers like Carrefour in Europe and Costco and Whole Foods in the United States and Canada stopped buying bluefin. And yes, fishmongers and culinary schools and chefs said, "We do not sell or serve endangered species."

François said, "You don't wake up in the morning, and say, 'I want to make sustainable seafood!' For a long time I have been careful about what vegetables I bought, what meat I bought, what fish. I have been careful about how we work, even with staff, the energy."

Nestled amidst the wine bottles in the dining room was a placard with drawings of vegetables that said *Mangez Local*— Eat Local.

The day before, in the middle of a conversation, Elisabeth had said to me, "It's the beginning of the evolution of change." The movement toward sustainability was the beginning of a very, very big change. Had we been so narrow-minded as a civilization as to think our worldview might not undergo another dramatic shift? That the Industrial Revolution was the best we had to give?

With bluefin, no one knew if the efforts would succeed. It was impossible to do the math, to see whether all these efforts would add up. Take a simple arithmetic operation: $1 + 1 + 1 = 3$. The art of the possible is to get enough addends and plus signs to the left of that equal sign to give you the sum you need. But what if you don't know exactly how much is there? In the case of bluefin, how many efforts were occurring around the world? All the people who worked to save bluefin didn't know, but they just kept at it.

That's when the art of the *impossible* kicks in. Sometimes there are invisible actors to the left of the equal sign who make possible what seems impossible. The economic and cultural trappings hurtling bluefin toward extinction were not all-powerful. The runaway train was not unstoppable. "A billion right choices around the world," Jane Goodall has often said, "and we start moving to a new type of planet."[95]

"In the dressing rooms downstairs," François continued, "there is a poster with all the fish you can eat, all the fish you should not cook, based on the SeaWeb Europe guide. So every day when the staff changes, twice a day, they see it. I try to do my best."

Sergi had told me that just because bluefin stopped plummeting toward extinction, it didn't mean they weren't still in dire need of protection. "The message," he said, "is that we are able to put back something that seemed completely out of control. All we need is political will in order to go toward sustainability. And fish react to management. Sometimes quicker than we might think, and that's a good message!"

François was explaining that Paris's National Day against Food Waste was approaching and that he always worked to minimize waste. "I use the bones of the fish to make a *fumé* or a sauce," he explained, "I use everything, even with a vegetable. I make sure—the leeks, the greens of the leeks—you are making something with it too."

Sometimes the act of saving involves almost-innumerable specific acts. I scribbled in my notebook, "Don't discount invisible plus signs. Even if you can't do the math, don't quit."

Every day, we move through a world rife with veiled actions. We know so little of what really transpires. But as much as there was a veil over how much destruction was happening, there was also a veil over how many people were willing to take action, if they knew what to do and if they believed they could make a difference.

The day before, Elisabeth had explained that when she first came to Paris, she began working with fishmongers. She worked with Bruno Gauvin, director of the main fishmonger training center in France. "We approached fishmongers, face to face, sometimes three hours, talking in the evenings, because they are very busy." Five fishmongers signed a pledge to remove four items from their offerings—eel, bluefin tuna, shark, and deep-sea species. "But they were scared," Elisabeth said. "What if their customers go elsewhere?"

Elisabeth had introduced me to one of the fishmongers who took the pledge, Arnaud Vanhamme. Arnaud's choice was not easy—his fish shop was not in a chic part of town. He risked losing customers, and sales were already down because of a recession. So why did he take the pledge? "I have this job in my blood," Arnaud said. "I'm from four generations of fishmongers. I was born in this philosophy: you have to have good fish. So, what is good fish? A fish that is in danger—this is not a good fish, so we shouldn't sell it."

"When the fishmongers took the pledge," Elisabeth explained, "we made a press release. The main seafood-industry magazine devoted a whole page to it. It was on television, in important magazines. Six months later we all met, and the fishmongers tell me, 'I was congratulated by my clients!' "The fishmongers didn't realize how much support they'd get from their customers. The support that surfaced had been invisible.

⟨❧⟩

I said goodbye to Elisabeth that day in another metro station. "The people we work with," she told me, "it's them who make the change. We are nothing without them. They are the ones who decide to make the change." She went down one underground walkway, I another.

⟨❧⟩

The metro platform was crowded. The train came in, standing room only. A few last people squeezed into the car. As the train pulled away, our weight shifted into each other. Right next to me was an elderly woman dressed in an old wool coat. Her hair was pulled back in a bun. She carried a wicker basket and steadied herself by clutching the top of one of the seats. Tufts of carrots and lettuce bulged out of her basket. I wondered if she'd been a child in Paris during World War II.

"My grandfather went through the war in Paris," Arnaud had told me. "He was a fishmonger. Then there was one fish. Herring! They ate herring for five years. One of my grandmothers told me that when the Americans came, she discovered soap and chewing gum."

Arnaud had told me his great-grandparents started selling fish during the Great Depression. "Marie-Louise, my great-grandmother, she was born in Belgium in 1899. My great-grandfather and she came to Paris and started to sell fish in '33. She had *une charrette*—a cart with wheels—and she went by foot to the center of Paris and sold fish from it. She would walk twenty kilometers a day. Some of my customers still remember her."

The train halted in the tunnel. There was an announcement on the intercom. As we waited, everyone chatted in French.

After a few moments, the train resumed moving. But then it stopped again. There was another announcement, spoken so quickly that I couldn't make it out. Everyone fell silent.

"*Qu'est-ce qui se passe?* What's happening?" I asked the old woman in a whisper.

"*Il y a une alerte de sécurité.* There is a security alert," she murmured, her ears cocked for more from the intercom.

Accident? Terrorist attack? Bombing?

In the reflection of the metro car windows our fearful expressions melded together in the glass. We were all wedged together in warm clothing. Without the doors opening, it was getting oddly hot.

"Have you always lived in Paris?" I asked in French.

"Yes." She shifted her groceries to her other arm.

Still nothing. The train stood motionless in the dark tunnel.

"*Aux innocents les main pleins,*" the old woman murmured. "The innocent have their hands full."

Another announcement on the scratchy intercom. The car lurched forward. There had been a precautionary check. Someone had reported an odd-looking object on the tracks. Everyone started chatting. A few moments later we arrived at the metro station, and the doors slid open.

⚬᷒᷒᷒

"There's a saying here, 'You never went through the war.' There's a definite awareness—when everything is taken away in an instant—that nothing is forever." Cybèle was in her thirties. She had a friendly, no-nonsense demeanor and blond hair pulled back in a ponytail.

Cybèle Idelot was American but married to a Frenchman. She'd opened her Paris restaurant, La Table de Cybèle, just a year before. I'd told Cybèle how I felt the shadow of World War II so much more in Europe. Perhaps, I'd asked, Europeans understood more acutely what a cultural collapse was?

"I'm trying to think how to put it into words," she said. "That sense … it's more long term, maybe. They see a little farther into time, the impact things will have?"

She stood up and went to the bar. "For me, there was never any question. I mean, if you have a choice—to not deplete our resources—why not make the right choice?"

It was early evening; the doors of the restaurant would open soon. The black and white interior had a sleek, unpretentious look. The shelving behind the bar looked like a large bookshelf. Along with wine bottles and glasses, there were a few books with antique bindings and a playful figurine of a pig.

Cybèle brought back a freshly printed menu for that night. "We cite our producers on the menu," she said, running her finger down the offerings. "There are two different poultry farms I work with. The vegetables come from a farm about twenty minutes from here. I get up at 6:30 to go to the market. I love the fact that I'm in Paris, but when I come back from the market, I have dirt under my fingernails, that I stay close to nature."

"So where does the fish come from?"

"It's a group of gentlemen on the coast in Brittany; they are in direct contact with twelve boats. I select my fish by phone every morning. They asked me this morning, 'do you want monkfish? Bass?' And I said, 'No, those aren't the fish I work with.' They seem to offer them anyway, and I say no and just wait," she smiled, "until the bell goes off, until they offer what I want."

Every choice exacted a force on the supply chain, moving it toward or away from sustainability. The day before, Stéphanie Mathey, from the multinational retailer Carrefour, had explained to me that sustainability had become a part of their quality measures. She had adapted every quality-reporting tool—audit reports and specifications—to include sustainability. "We stopped selling bluefin, shark, orange roughy," she'd said proudly. "We decreased selling deep-sea fish caught through deep-sea trawling. We decided to have 100 percent responsible palm oil by 2015. We don't sell GMO products."

These things: choices. *Specific ones.* A beautiful, near-invisible entity existed adjacent to them now, that symbol first used by the fourteenth-century French philosopher and mathematician Nicolas Oresme: the plus sign.

The bell-ringer for Cybèle's menu that day was albacore tuna.

"But how do you know it's not illegally fished, not black-market fish?" I asked.

"They are small boats. It's all line fishing. The people I work with, I have confidence in them," she said firmly. "They know the name of every single boat that they work with; they are local fishermen."

For all of this to work, it had to work right at the source: the fishermen.

17

The Ring in the Fish

First Naima's iPhone alarm went off, then the church bells clanged, then my alarm clock beeped. It was six o'clock in the morning and pitch black. We were in a room with two twin beds and French doors that opened onto an alley across from a sixteenth-century church in one of the oldest fishing towns on the Catalonian coast of Spain, Arenys de Mar.

"I ... take a shower?" Naima asked.

"I'll do my yoga," I mumbled.

Naima Andrea Rodríguez was a WWF intern. She'd come with me to interview fishermen about an innovative approach to fisheries management—a co-management committee in which fishermen, scientists, NGOs, and government administrators were managing a fishery together on equal footing.

The day before, I was flummoxed by the excitement that burst from those who talked about it. In the WWF office in Barcelona, the Fisheries Advocacy officer, Susana Sainz-Trápaga, sparkled as if an especially stubborn piñata had finally broke open, and all the gifts had tumbled out. "You have to see it!" she exclaimed. "Tomorrow, you will see!" When do fisheries officers talk like that?

So we were there "to see," and Naima would be my translator. Naima was in her twenties. She'd just finished her master's degree, specializing in biodiversity studies.

We left the hotel before sunrise. The streets were quiet and so narrow it was as if the stucco buildings leaned inward over us. The ancient center of the village had crumbling walls and irregular sidewalks etched with medieval circular patterns.

The street opened onto a small plaza beneath a church with a spartan, clay-brown facade. Intricate carvings adorned two large wooden doors. Our footsteps echoed as we crossed in the dark. We made a pit stop at an espresso bar. Quietly we stirred sugar into our espressos. Naima's came in a little glass and was twice the size of mine.

"How do you say that?" I asked as she stirred her espresso.

"*Doble*," she said, knowing I was looking at her glass enviously, "*espresso doble*."

"Dough-blay," I sounded it out slowly.

I'd brushed up on my French, but I could not wrap my head around learning Spanish too. I got another espresso and paid. My change came in an empty sardine can. The other night in a restaurant, my bill had come on a wooden plate in the shape of a fish. In front of a tobacco store was one of those coin-operated children's rides—not on a horse, but on a dolphin.

We walked to the corner of the block and waited in the silent maze of narrow streets. It's often thought that the British have a monopoly on seamanship, but the Spanish seamen, the *marineros*—they were pretty plucky too. There's a monument in Barcelona dedicated to Christopher Columbus, who returned from his first westward voyage "off the edge of the map" to report to the king and queen of Spain. Columbus was Italian by birth, but his crew was Spanish.

A man in his fifties with speckled gray hair and sturdy features pulled up in a white van. It was Mauricio Pulido, one of the lead fishermen in the co-management committee. He wore a flannel shirt, jeans, and waterproof boots. We hopped into the van; it smelled faintly of fish.

Mauricio zipped through a short tunnel to the marina. A bunch of fishermen were prepping their boats. The co-management committee managed a sandeel fishery. Sandeel are bottom-dwelling fish that are only a few inches long, similar to anchovies. They are a valued local fish, suitable for school lunches, because the bones of the fish are tiny and can be eaten with no risk of choking. Kids eat them like french fries.

This fishery was "artisanal," which meant it used pre-1950s gear and the boats were small. It was very different from the industrial fisheries in the North Sea, where hundreds of thousands of tons of sandeel are harvested annually for fertilizer and livestock feed, food for farmed salmon, and health supplements such as fish oil.[96] This small Catalonian sandeel fishery brought in less than a thousand tons a year, and the sandeel stock was in good condition.

Mauricio introduced us to all the fishermen and to his boat's crew, Carlos and José. They loaded several hefty bags of ice onto Mauricio's boat, a thirty-five-foot blue-and-white *seiner*—a boat that employs a *seine,* a fishing net, that hangs vertically in the water. We quietly motored out of the dark harbor.

There was chilly sea breeze. Naima and I squeezed inside the small wheelhouse with Mauricio and watched as he steered; the only illumination Mauricio's navigational instruments as we skimmed through the water. Mauricio folded down two little wooden benches for us to sit on. It was warm and cozy; we chatted away merrily.

The night before, we'd had dinner with Mauricio and his wife, Emelina, at their house. Mauricio had caught me gawking at a large framed satellite photograph of the earth over their fireplace.

"I think of myself as a global citizen," he said. "I hung this here to remind me of that." As he spoke in Spanish, Naima translated. He explained that a decade or so after he started working as a fishermen, he'd learned to scuba dive.

"What was that like?" I asked.

"I could feel the fish around me with no fear. Very close." You could see it in Mauricio's eyes, the magic of it: the hunter and the hunted, meeting on equal ground. He paused and then continued, "In that moment, I felt the world was divided into two worlds. The world everybody knows and the deep world of the sea."

There were models of traditional boats and colorful glass bottles displayed on shelves. Framed watercolors of the Mediterranean landscape and dried sea fans were carefully mounted on the walls.

Emelina had grilled some small orange fish—red mullet. In the Mediterranean, fish is often grilled whole. She watched politely while I messily struggled to pick the meat from my fish.

"You would get used to it with time," she said with a wink. "It's just a matter of understanding the anatomy of the fish." She calmly pulled up the entire skeleton of a fish and laid it down at the edge of her plate.

Large doors were open to their yard. Two dogs sat peacefully just outside. Mauricio explained that, unlike many of the fishermen, he had not learned to fish through his family, but he had been fishing for thirty-three years.

"So how did you learn to fish?" I asked.

"When you have a need, you learn," he replied. He explained that he and Emelina had just gotten married and were starting a family. I chimed in with one of my boilerplate questions: "When did you realize there were problems with fisheries?"

"The first day!" Mauricio said. "One of the problems was that traditional fishermen wanted to catch all the fish they could. You can catch all the fish that you want until you sink the boat, until you sink the *Titanic.*"

Mauricio and Emelina explained how the co-management committee was formed. About a year and a half before, the sandeel fishery had been closed, not because the sandeel was endangered, but because the fishery failed to comply with European Union regulations regarding gear, such as the mesh size of the net, and the fishing location, the depth and the distance to the coast. Under the current law, a fishery needed to be regulated through a scientific management plan.[97] Inspectors came, and the next day the fishery was shut down—six ports, twenty-five vessels, over sixty families without income.

"It was terrifying," Mauricio said. "It felt like punishment."

There was silence. None of us needed to say what we all knew: the recession of 2008, the largest economic downturn since World War II had blindsided Spain. Five years had gone by, and there were no signs of recovery. The recession had morphed into what was called "the Crisis." One out of four adults in Spain was unemployed.

Mauricio had already had some contact with WWF through an association of artisanal fishermen. So when the fishery was closed, he contacted WWF's fisheries team, headed by Sergi Tudela, whom I had interviewed about bluefin. They both contacted Pilar Sánchez, a marine biologist at the Institute of Marine Sciences, and Mercè Santmartí and Itziar Segarra from the Catalan fisheries administration. Both were eager to help, but there were no funds for a scientific study, and budgets were being slashed.

At that same time, WWF was struggling to find new solutions. "We were crashing again and again against the same wall," Sergi had told me, when he described how the committee came into being. "For us it was very clear that the approach to go top-down—policy to change things—was not working, because of lack of adherence to rules and lack of enforcement. We were convinced that part of the solution was co-management, to have everyone involved and committed." So they started batting around the idea of a co-management committee for the sandeel fishery.

But even if they could get all the stakeholders together—the Spanish central government, the local Catalan authorities, NGOs, the scientists, and the fisherman—who was going to pay for the scientific study?

The fishermen. The fishermen? *The fishermen*. They would pay for it. Step by step they put together a "multi-stakeholder plan" through co-management, which in plain English means everyone has an equal vote. The result was a scientific fishery, a closely monitored pilot project that was due to become a full-fledged legal fishery just after I visited.

The lead fishermen, government officials, scientists, and WWF staff all met once a month. Each and every fisherman agreed to catch fewer fish and comply with the agreed-upon quotas. When the fishery reopened, the fish would sell for more money per kilo, so the fishermen would work less, spend less money on gas and supplies, and yet earn more.

Fewer fish caught, more money made. More fish in the sea. It was the reverse of the crisis that plagued the local fishermen in Sulawesi. "The committee proves that you can get more money catching fewer fish," Mauricio said. "This addresses a problem that affects fishermen all over the world. It's important to transmit this. We are not talking about change, we are making change, we're doing it."

"The most important thing," Emelina added, "is that the price of fish is higher when they auction off the fish, but not the market price. The middleman gets less money."

"Did it take the closure to create change?"

Mauricio nodded. "It was the only way to continue fishing. We are now in the beginning of co-management, the crisis of change. Only with a crisis do we think of our options, because we feel trapped. The crisis moved everything in a new direction."

〜

On the boat, there was a glow at the horizon where the sun would rise. Naima and Mauricio were chatting in Spanish. Mauricio pointed to vertical red streaks on the sonar. "These are the sandeel." Then he pointed to his navigational data, just above the sonar. "There are only certain sites where we fish for them."

Pilar, the committee's lead marine biologist, had explained that part of the new management plan was to generate maps of where the fishermen could operate. It was important that the fishermen did not damage the seagrass meadows, which were key to the stability of fish populations, because they harbored juvenile fish. The adult sandeel lived in sandy bottoms away from the seagrass, so it was just a matter of mapping where they were. "During the night, the sandeel burrow into small holes for protection," Pilar had told me, "and when the sun rises, they go out to find food in very big schools."

So Mauricio was looking for a sandy bottom and a big school of sandeel. Pilar's team of biologists also monitored the health of the stock. "We go out four times a month with them," she had told me, "and monitor the position of the fishing and the quantity of fish. We take fish samples to study their growth patterns." Every day the fishermen logged the exact locations where they fished and logged their catches for the scientists.

The dark sky glowed against the soft outlines of the coastal hills. In the distance a commuter train whizzed along, a tiny flickering band of lights. I shuddered for a moment. I felt strangely, deeply at home and wished Charlie were there. Charlie is what's called "Black Irish." He and his sister Michelle were the only ones in his family to sprout dark hair. Explanations abound, among them that Spaniards came to Ireland by ancient sea-trading routes and ever since the occasional dark-haired child peppered a blond-headed Celtic brood.

"So Mauricio," I said, "my husband, he loves to fish."

"What kind of fish?"

"Bass, line and rod."

Then I remembered the ring. I told Mauricio that Charlie's wedding ring slid off into the water on our honeymoon. We replaced it, but to me, it never felt the same. So before our first anniversary, I had another one made, with the same Celtic pattern. I bought a whole bass at a fish market and put the ring in its throat.

When I got home, I asked Charlie, "Would you make some fish?"

"Sure," he said. I leapt into the shower. "Next time," he shouted from kitchen, so I could hear him over the running water, "tell them to clean the fish!"

I fidgeted nervously under the showerhead. I imagined going into the kitchen, and Charlie would be nonchalantly flipping fillets, and that I'd end up rummaging through the trash searching for the ring.

A loud yelp burst from the kitchen. Charlie had sliced open the fish and for a millisecond—when he saw the Celtic pattern of the gold ring—he couldn't believe his eyes.

Mauricio laughed. He slowed the boat. The sun was rising, all around us the water was a hazy blue and orange. Carlos and José fed out the mesh net with floating buoys and lead weights through metal U-shaped guides. After a few minutes, they reeled in the net with metal winches. When the net was almost completely reeled in they hoisted fish into blue plastic barrels.

The sandeel were silver and brown. The light flickered off them as they struggled to breathe. Naima and I spotted a wrasse with turquoise stripes and two sea breams in their midst. They were classified under that mealy-mouthed term "bycatch"—unintended, unconsumed catches that often die.

If you want to lose your appetite for a certain type of seafood dish that's been dubbed "egregiously unsustainable," but your mouth is still watering for it, check out bycatch statistics. My favorite seafood was wild-caught shrimp. The bycatch ratio ran between 20:1 and 5:1 in weight.[98] Say I have a plate of shrimp scampi sautéed in olive oil and butter and herbs. For eight ounces of shrimp, there's about two pounds of fish or turtle or whale or dolphin that were killed and whose meat was completely wasted. That's the just the 5:1 ratio.

But the Catalonian sandeel fishery's bycatch ratio was very low, 1:100, which meant one kilo of bycatch for every one hundred kilos of sandeel. And most of those fish were returned to sea alive. Pilar's team monitored the bycatch, to show the size of the net mesh that the fishermen need to catch sandeel wasn't doing any substantial damage.

But I'd never seen bycatch with my own eyes. The wrasse and the breams had flinched their way to the top of the pile of sandeel, as if with one more effort they could hurl themselves out of the barrel. Their frantic eyes and wheezing gills were all the more evident because they were so much larger that the sandeel. Naima and I grabbed the wrasse and the breams and tossed them back. For a millisecond, the fish quaked in my hands, wildly alive, sputtering, desperate to get back into the water. They swam off with a flash.

José added ice to the barrel and a bucket of water. Then he combed through the fish with a rake with soft edges and grabbed the rest of the bycatch carefully by the tail and threw them back. Because the fish were out of the water for such a short period time, they had a decent chance at survival when they were returned.

They reset the net several times, until almost all the barrels were full. The barrels had black measurement marks—when the fish reach that level with one bucket of ice (to keep the fish cool) and one bucket of water (to keep the fish from being crushed), that's 140 kilos of fish.

Mauricio was hunched over his cell phone. After a few moments he called out loudly to his crew.

"What's happening?" I asked.

Mauricio had been comparing notes with the other boats on how much fish to bring in. He explained to me that he was going to give thirty kilos of fish to one of the other boats. He had exceeded his quota, so he was checking with the other vessels to see how much they needed to meet their quotas.

"You are giving the other fishermen some fish?" I asked in disbelief.

"Yes," Mauricio said. They were not competing against each other. They were working together.

Carlos sliced open another pack of ice and added it to a barrel of sandeel, occasionally tossing a larger fish back into the sea. Seagulls hovered overhead.

"Liz! Come here!" It was Naima. Mauricio would give thirty kilos to the other fishermen, but that left them still over the limit. So he would return about one hundred kilos of fish. We watched Carlos and José lower the net. As they opened it, the sandeel quivered free, re-formed their school, and swam away.

A small crane hoisted the blue barrels of fish into a large warehouse. There was flurry of activity at the dock. Other fishermen were coming in on other boats. Old fishermen, too frail to be out on the boats, shuffled through just to say hello.

The sandeel were sorted into rectangular plastic trays, weighed, and set on a conveyer belt. As they swished along, a camera generated an image of them on an LCD screen. We were at the fish auction. Potential buyers sat on bleachers and used handheld consoles to make a bid. As each tray came under the camera, it was announced with a bleep.

The fishermen greeted each other as they worked, their voices amplified in the tall building. Mauricio, Naima, and I settled in the bleachers to watch. The fishermen were calling out in boisterous, ebullient voices. "Many other fishermen," Susana had told me, "are not even breaking even, because of the price of fuel, and these small boats, they are the envy of everybody! They are the only ones making a real profit in the whole of Catalonia right now."

The joking and laughter got louder and louder. "And there's no black market anymore," Susana had added. "Before, more than half of the fish was sold without going to the official auction." Now, no side deals laced with shame. No hedging your bets, no distrust.

Sometimes when the "near-impossible" happens, it appears to be almost out of place, discordant with its surroundings. The grins on the faces of fishermen were not what I had expected to see at a fish auction on the coast of a much-devastated sea in a country mired in the worst economic downturn since the Great Depression. Their expressions were like the smiles of fathers holding their newborn children—that mix of awe and over-the-top cigar-lighting humor. As if they'd given birth to something, and they had! They had saved their fishery and given birth to a new way of running one.

It was beautiful.

Naima leaned over and pointed to a man in gray pants and a black shirt. "Mauricio wants you to know, that fellow over there is a buyer for Carrefour." Carrefour was the mega-retailer whose sustainability chief, Stéphanie Mathey, I had interviewed. The buyer followed the sustainability supply policy that Stéphanie had developed. There was another piece of the "seafood chain." I remembered what Elisabeth had said on the metro, "Everybody in the chain needs to be engaged, everybody has a role to play."

The day Charlie sliced open the bass and saw the ring—did he for moment flash on how it had gotten to our kitchen? One fish gobbling a shiny gold object, was eaten by another bigger fish, and then came the net, boat, fish auction, wholesaler, market, shopping bag, and plop, onto the wooden cutting board in our kitchen! The seafood chain.

Each of these sandeel had an invisible gem—something beautiful, golden—inside them: an invisible bond with the sea and the creatures of the sea that was less destructive and more reciprocal. What if more of our food had that same invisible gem? Could we get to a point where our bond with the sea was an integral part of who we are? Where a respectful, reciprocal relationship with it was crucial to our quality of life? And similarly with the earth, the soil, the air, the rivers, all of it? Could we begin to honor that source of sustenance as we would a wedding band?

Well, it was already happening! That was the circular economy. And there it was about transforming the seafood chain of custody. Charlie and I were just starting to catch on. We were changing what we bought. Chilean sea bass, which is actually Antarctic toothfish renamed to glamorize it for the gourmet market? No, thank you. Local blueberries in the summer? Yes! Blueberries flown in from Argentina in January? No!

I'd talked to Emily Howgate of Sustain, an alliance for better food and farming based in London. They'd had great success implementing a sustainable fish-sourcing program for the 2012 Olympic Games, so they thought, why not work to make London a "sustainable-fish city," in the same way that cities can now become fair-trade cities?

A sustainable chain of custody for every fish we eat? A ring in every fish? Too lofty? "Could London ever, realistically, be a fully sustainable-fish city?" I had asked Emily.

"Sustainability is a journey," she told me. And it's not perfect, she explained, but if all the government offices, hospitals, schools and a large share of major businesses in London sourced sustainable fish, why, that's a difference! The goal is no more lofty that the others we take pride in aspiring to: equal rights for each and every human being, freedom from slavery, from tyranny, and from oppression. However imperfect our fulfillment of them, we know these goals represent the best of us.

Mauricio came by after lunch on a motorcycle to take me to see the afternoon fish auction. Naima had gone back to Barcelona, so I was without a translator.

"Don't worry," Naima said when she left, "Mauricio said he's sure you will able communicate with each other."

Mauricio gesticulated wildly at the exhaust pipe on his motorcycle. I was wearing a pair of capris, and he was worried that I would burn my shins when getting on.

We went down to the marina. Mauricio introduced me to Ramón Tarridas, who was the president of the Mediterranean Platform of Artisanal Fishers (MedArtNet) and a spokesperson for the co-management committee. After a few awkward minutes, we giddily discovered we all spoke a little French. We chatted for a while, and then Mauricio and I went to the fish auction. This one was for fisheries other than the sandeel fishery.

A few buyers sat silently in the bleachers while different types of fish slid along the conveyer belt. There was no boisterous laughter, no slap-happy greetings. Just a bleep as a tray of fish came under the camera, a pause, another bleep, another pause. The magic was gone.

"*Allez?*" Mauricio asked in French after a few minutes, "Let's go?" No need to linger.

Mauricio had wanted to show me an old cemetery. We rode along the coast and then up a steep, narrow road with sharp switchbacks edged by tall grass to a bluff above the ocean. Almost all the graves were adorned with flowers. A row of trees carved a path from an ancient chapel to the sea like a compass heading.

Mauricio and I walked the arrow-straight path to the overlook. From there the full expanse of the coast was visible. "*El mar,*" he said in Spanish, waving one hand slowly across the radiant expanse of blue: the ocean. His proud posture, the joy, the sadness, the awe, the kinship with the sea—it was all there. He didn't need to say another word.

When we said goodbye, he gave me the look of a man who'd just entrusted you with his youngest child. That term *co-management committee*—it sounds so bureaucratic, but what was it really? A work of love, of community, of togetherness. There was one Spanish term he had used so often that I didn't need Naima to translate it. Just before we parted, he said it one more time: *confianza mutua*. Mutual trust.

18

La Semilla

"Con Mauricio?" Luís asked. "You went for a motorcycle ride with Mauricio?"

Luís sat back and grinned. He was holding a pair of aviator glasses. With his other hand, he flicked his wrist to mimic revving the engine of a motorcycle, as if Mauricio was a bit of a wild driver.

We were sitting in a café. Luís was probably talking about a younger Mauricio, many years back. Alright, alright—rather than stop and open the gate to the marina, Mauricio did weave through a set of narrow concrete barriers like it was a slalom course, and I remember thinking that he could probably do it in his sleep.

Luís Trias Martín had gray-black hair and a short beard. "The natural feeling of a fishermen is that of a hunter," he said. "Now it's totally different, because we share the fish. We are no longer hunters."

I was riveted. Here was this guy who exuded the vigorous brawn of a hunter-fisher saying, "We can't be hunters anymore." It was like Columbus announcing that the world isn't flat, like Galileo saying that the sun doesn't revolve around the earth. And now what? We can't be hunters anymore. We can't just take everything we can get our hands on.

It was the next morning. Naima was back. Luís and I turned to Naima simultaneously and start babbling excitedly at her, both of us gesticulating as we talked.

Naima put her hands up as if there were a mouse in her lap and burst out laughing. "Stop! I can't translate when you're talking to me at the same time."

Luís continued slowly, as if braced for another comedic interruption, "In the past, if you caught fewer fish, you were a loser. Now it's not just one person who wins; everyone wins. We catch less, we share, and we are all winners."

It was not lost on Luís that this was a tectonic shift. "My son is ten years old," he said. "He wants to be a fisherman. We have to recover respect for the ocean, return to that feeling of honoring it. If we don't, who will?"

Luís came from four generations of fishermen, and he described for us what life was like for the fishermen a century ago. His great-grandfather made his own nets and cast them from the beach. "They had a bond with the sea," Luís said as he gripped his hands together tightly. "All winter they borrowed money to live.[99] Then they'd pay that back when they sold the fish they caught in the summer. They had to catch the fish. It was a matter of survival."

This whole thing was like a puzzle, and each day Naima and I found another piece fitting into place. But the pieces were not policies or ideas, *they were people*—exchanging knowledge, working together. There was a feeling, an ease, a friendliness.

I got up to get some water from the espresso bar at the back of the café. While I waited, I looked out toward the ocean. Between us and the sea were the main highway and the railroad tracks. I imagined what this place might have looked like a century ago, as Luís had described, with no cars or motorized boats.

Sergi had explained that before fishing was industrialized, Spanish fisheries were managed by *cofradia*,[100] local fishermen's guilds whose history went back to the Middle Ages. In France they were called *prud'hommes*. "What remains of the *cofradia* is very important," Sergi said, "because these are the vestiges on which we can build something new, we can update them to modern times. This is the idea behind co-management."

I settled back at the table. A hundred years ago, Luís was explaining, a long net would be set from shore, and a little boat would take the other end of it out away from shore. You'd need at least twenty people to haul in the net.[101] So people would come from all over the village to help.

Could the things that infused the *cofradia*—the bonds of kinship and community, the elemental drive to survive—resurface in the form of co-management committees?

"Everything was based on trust," Luís told us. "We called all the fishermen, one by one; we sat and talked, explained everything. A lot of fishermen didn't understand the plan, but they agreed to do it because they trusted me and my family, because we had such a long history as fishermen." In the beginning, the committee met once a week, and at times those early meetings were rough at the edges, but bit by bit, barriers were broken down, and friends were made.

One day in the middle of a meeting, Luís had asked Susana, "So what do you get out of this?"

Susana looked him in the eye and said, "Conserve the sand-eel and fishing traditions."

"That was a click moment for me," Luís said. "There was a big gap between the ecologists and the fishermen, but when they started to talk, the gap narrowed."

I remembered sitting in Pilar's office at the Institute of Marine Sciences. It was adorned with posters of marine life. "We must think of the whole sea like a living being, and it's sick," Pilar said. "It's not dead, but it's sick." As a marine biologist, one of the things she brought to the committee was that focus—caring for the sea as a whole. "When we started," she explained, "some fishermen said, 'What? This is stupid! I fish in my own way, and you don't need to control me!' But now the fishermen, they are like angels, no?"

Angels? I thought. *Are you kidding?*

"They follow the rules," Pilar barreled ahead of my disbelief, "because they understand that those rules are there for them, and it's also better for the fish. The other thing is that now they are like a community, because before the other fishermen were the enemy—'If they catch lots of fish, I don't catch enough. My enemy!' Now they work together."

One of the biggest gaps to be bridged was the are-you-crazy? factor. "The high central government people," Luís told us, "they said, 'This is a joke. This isn't possible.' " Or, as Sergi had told me, "They were absolutely puzzled. They didn't expect this sort of request from fishermen! They're used to these patronizing situations where the fishermen ask for subsidies. And here the fishermen were asking, 'We need you—yes, you—to devolve your power to a multi-stakeholder body.' " Sergi mimed the reaction they'd gotten: "Huh? What?"

Another administrator came from Madrid. Similar astonishment. Fishermen, an NGO, and scientists all genuinely interacting? But then he invited the fishermen to go to another part of Spain to promote the model there. The committee was breaking down barriers between alienated groups—people were becoming friends, sharing knowledge. The scientists gave advice on when to fish and the best quantities. The fishermen explained things like "today there was a storm, so you'll find the fish over here," which gave the scientists access to what's called "traditional ecological knowledge."

Luís held up his hand, his phone was ringing. It was Mauricio. The final price at the fish auction that day was low, so the co-management committee had decreased the quota for the next day. This would make the price eventually go back up.

"When we saw that by fishing less, we were getting more money," Luís explained, "we changed our minds." Now the focus was to "fish for money." When you did that, you had an interest in limiting the supply in the market, and that often meant leaving more fish in the sea.

I told Luís how astonished I was by the exuberance of the sandeel fishermen at the fish auction. Did he notice it too? Luís nodded. "It's like a dream, we feel exultant." He scratched his beard and then continued. "It's a feeling that's hard to explain ... like gold."

"We felt handcuffed," Itziar said.

Naima and I had arrived at the last piece of the puzzle—Itziar Segarra, the Catalan fisheries administrator who had helped shepherd the proposal for the co-management committee through the organizational maze of EU fisheries management. She was explaining the political and economic lockjaw during the time the sandeel fishery was shut down, when the fishermen had called her office, pleading for help.

It was my last day in Spain. Naima and I had taken the metro and then walked to the administration offices in Barcelona. The streets bustled, but the stores were oddly empty. While we walked, Naima explained that "the Crisis" had hit her generation especially hard. They were being called "the lost generation." In late 2013, youth unemployment in Spain surged past 56 percent.

At the administration building, we ferried our backpacks through a security gate with armed guards and an x-ray machine. Itziar had greeted us when we arrived at her office.

"We felt handcuffed," Itziar repeated, "because the EU Commission said we'd need to present a management plan based on a scientific study. And that costs a lot of money. So there we were: we didn't have money, and we didn't have time."

There was no money because the economy had tanked, and there was no time because technically, Itziar couldn't devote energy to a fishery that had been closed. "And this kind of fishery," she continued, "only twenty-five boats, only fifty or seventy-five families? This is very far from the reality of Madrid."

"Madrid" meant the central Spanish government, which oversaw the Spanish fishing fleet, the largest in the European Union, which included supertrawlers and freezer boats. Itziar explained that any effort to save the sandeel fishery would have to be approved by both the Spanish government and the EU Commission. And the Catalonia independence movement was straining relations—Catalonia was organizing to break from Spain and become an independent European nation. "The political situation," Itziar added dryly, "was quite intense."

I cleared my throat and unwrapped a lozenge. I'd run a fever overnight and woke with a bad cough.

Itziar continued in an understated tone: "But if we could put a certain type of effort into this project, it could also benefit other fisheries." It was a bureaucratic plank to span the abyss: the time and energy allotted to develop the co-management committee could be justified, because they would not only re-open the sandeel fishery but also develop a pilot program that could be replicated all over the Mediterranean.

"But this is a big thing—for an administration to give up decision-making power to a committee," I said.

"It was the last chance for this fishery." Itziar was emphatic. "It was better to do that than to close the fishery. This is the reason the administration took the risk to lose control, to give it to other groups, like the fishermen and the NGOs. It was a real innovation."

"So the process of saying yes to this new way of doing things," I asked, "how did that happen?"

"It was person to person. Not paper!" Itziar spoke most-ly English, but sometimes broke into Spanish, which Naima would translate. "Face to face. It's very hard to work on this kind of project. It involved a lot of our personal time. It's im-possible to do this just on office time." There was a thick ma-nila folder in front of her that occasionally she'd rest both hands on. "Meetings, writing, reading," Itziar continued, "con-vincing the other administrations. We'd start the meeting at four in the afternoon, we'd finish at nine that night—hard, hard work! But one of the most important successes was that we became friends, we formed relationships."

It wasn't one yes. It was many of them. Over and over. Yes, I will come to a meeting and listen (even if I think this is a stark-raving crazy idea); yes, I will keep talking (even if we dis-agree); yes, I will be willing to think in new ways (even though at moments I can't stand the idea of it). The fact that it was a pilot program for artisanal fisheries throughout the Mediter-ranean energized them.

"So you could save a little," I asked, "and create a tool that would save a lot?"

"Exactly!" Itziar replied. "Today this plan," she placed both hands on the folder again, "*this* is with the European Commission for evaluation. If this is approved, it will be made into law, and co-management will be the adaptive management approach to follow." On that very day, a year and a half's intense work had culminated. If approved, the program would become a legal option for any artisanal fishery in the entire European Union.

Mauricio's quip about being a global citizen? He wasn't kidding. A month later, the committee would present the model at the first regional symposium on small-scale fisheries in the Mediterranean organized by the General Fisheries Commission for the Mediterranean (GFCM) in Malta. Three months later Mauricio would go to Mexico to do the same at an annual meeting of fishermen. Sergi had just returned from Tunisia. "They are ready in North Africa," he'd told me excitedly. "Different people, but similar fisheries. Once you have a success in place, it self-replicates almost automatically. Good ideas get picked up."[102]

It was viable economically, it strengthened communities, it helped people bridge political and cultural barriers, and natural resources were shared and preserved. Because the scientific monitoring was paid for by the fishermen, the future of the program was built-in. More and more, I'd noticed, people were talking about initiatives like these—adaptive, community-based, networked, task-specific—because they not only made the shift to more sustainable operations but also honored individuals and communities. And the kicker was that they worked so well that they rendered the previous models obsolete.

But there was one last thing, which in reality was likely the first, and as crucial as oxygen: kindness! It was so pervasive over the last four days, so fused with the trust and pride and warmth I experienced, that I might have shaken it off as peripheral. But almost everyone told me that it was the "hearing out," the countless hours of listening and discussion—a respectful kindness—that provided the "breathing room" that enabled them to work together. If the co-management committee had managed to break through the Byzantine, corruption-ridden world of EU fisheries, who's to say similar models like this couldn't work elsewhere?

"It's *la semilla,*" Itziar said, mixing English and Spanish. She held her thumb and forefinger close together, as if holding something the size of a pearl.

Naima's eyes widened. Itziar turned to her and said something in Spanish.

"It's the seed," Naima translated. "The co-management plan is the seed that can become a tree in fisheries management."

It was getting late. I told Itziar that I hadn't expected to have such an upbeat interview with a fisheries administrator.

"Okay," she chuckled at the happy irony. "I give you some hope."

"Yes," I said. "All these different people. They are making a living, and they feel more connected. They feel better, proud. Like it's fixing other problems."

"Yes, it is like this ..." Itziar said softly. She paused. Naima and I exchanged glances. Sounds from the street filled the room: muffled voices, cars, the growl of a large truck, and a long, metallic squeal and a burst of air—the brakes of a bus. It was growing dark.

"I think that we have time to change the situation," Itziar said, slowly and clearly in English. Each word, it seemed, she gave a special effort, "We have time *if we want.*" She enunciated each word deliberately. "This is a good opportunity to demonstrate that if you want, you can do it. There are other fisheries that don't have the same economic value, so any change is difficult, but we need to work in this way. The fishermen, they don't have any other chance. And we? The administration? We don't have any other chance. We can't wait another ten years. We need to work hard, just now."

That evening Naima took me to a little café. We shared a piece of pizza laced with spinach and cheese and olive oil. "This is where I used to come when I was in university," she told me.

She walked me to the railroad station to help me find the right train. It was the main Barcelona station, an electronic beehive the size of a city block. We'd had such a good time together. On the way into the station, we put our arms around each other's shoulders.

"We're going to know each other when I'm eighty, right?" I said, straining my voice over the noisy crowd.

Naima smiled and then blurted out, "You have to understand," looking straight ahead as we walked, "I love biodiversity. I love every little creature."

"I know …." I said hoarsely. I was starting to lose my voice. My back hurt. At the ticket kiosk, I fed a Euro bill into the slot. A ripple of fear ran through me. One hand had gone numb, as if it were in a frozen mitten.

The cough is messing with your back. It'll mend.

A ticket dropped down into a bin. I reached for it with the other hand.

"Okay!" Naima said hurriedly. "See that?" She pointed to a descending escalator with the numbers 7 and 8 above it.

"You are track 8. You have five minutes," Naima said. She handed me a red fish talisman. "Liz, I want you to have this."

I choked up. I clumsily yanked my rain jacket from my backpack and wrapped it around her neck. "I've traveled all over the world with this."

"No." Naima said, "you can't …."

"There's no time for no," I croaked. I slipped through the entry and leapt onto the escalator. As I put my hand on the escalator railing, the numbness subsided.

We waved until we couldn't see each other any more.

19

Thousands of Selves

Something glittered as if a basket of sewing needles had been tossed into the water. But the needles weren't sinking; they were rising. The slender metallic shapes grew larger. A school of several hundred barracuda was rising out of the blue depths.

They made a long, wide arc and then formed a sparkling merry-go-round, circling me. Their skin was shiny like crumpled aluminum foil. I remembered the photo of a sea lion surrounded by the "mill formation" of sardines. Now I was inside the mill, seeing it from the inside out.

For a moment, a veil lifted—a glimpse of a mystery. But then the barracuda dispersed, and the feeling slipped away.

Pilar had explained that scientists mapped the seafloor to make sure the fishermen weren't damaging the seagrass beds in Catalonia. Before I left Europe, I wanted to get a look at the seagrass myself and understand more of why they were so important. Just a few miles southwest of Marseilles there were some tiny islands surrounded by seagrass, the Îles d'Or—the Golden Isles. A large share of their territory and the water surrounding them was protected as part of the Port-Cros National Park.

A divemaster led a group of us along what looked like an alpine rock face—the seascape beneath a rocky island called La Gabinière. Clumps of seagrass grew in the crevices between the gigantic boulders. Schools of slivery sea breams chomped on the seagrass like little cows.

The water had an unusual sparkle to it. The last time I'd donned my dive gear was in the Coral Triangle, and it had been at almost exactly latitude 0. Now I was at latitude 43. The northern light was so angular that when one of the breams yanked on a piece of grass at a certain angle, its scales emitted a flash like a signal mirror.

Now I could see what Marsha had told me about in the Turks and Caicos, that seagrass meadows had an abundance of life parallel to that of mangroves. They were filled with juvenile fish and crustaceans and anemones. The seagrass in the Mediterranean was over a yard tall, with stocky, dark-green strands.

"This type of seagrass is called Posidonia, after its Latin name, *Posidonia oceanica*," the Port-Cros park operations director, Nicolas Gérardin, had told me. "We call it a keystone species; the whole marine ecosystem balance relies on this species. Over 70 percent of all fish in the Mediterranean take shelter in the Posidonia at some point in their life cycle."

A slender, inch-long fish peered out from between two blades of grass, a very young barracuda. As soon as it was more than a foot long, it would depart for deeper waters, where the barracuda congregate in large schools. La Gabinière is at the southernmost end of the islands, where the shallow coastal waters drop off into the deep pelagic waters of the Gulf du Lion, which drops to over seven thousand feet.[103]

There was a tap on my shoulder. It was the divemaster, Pierre. He waved at me to follow him. The current was light enough to make a go at swimming to Le Sec de la Gabinière, a seamount—a kind of tiny underwater island—just to the southwest. We swam after Pierre. Soon the rocky edge of the island vanished and we were swimming in open water. A few minutes later, he turned around and pointed downward. Forty feet below, in the open sea, was an outcropping covered with seagrass and purple-and-yellow sea fans.

As we descended, two enormous grouper, each over a yard long, came into view. They hovered in a cut between two knobs of stone. Their lumbering bodies barely moved. Grouper usually have one cave or crevice they consider home and several others close by they circulate to and from. These groupers may have lived there all their lives, perhaps over thirty years.

Large fish like this play an important role in healthy fisheries. They have been shown to have exponentially more young than small fish, because more of their energy can be allocated to reproduction. The research of Steven Berkeley, a biologist at the Long Marine Lab, has also revealed that large females produce higher quality, more resilient larvae.[104]

It had been two decades since I'd seen grouper that big. The Nassau grouper in the Caribbean were now on the International Union for Conservation of Nature's dreaded Red List of species at high risk for extinction. But the grouper at Le Sec de la Gabinière had been given a chance to grow old. And they hadn't done it in some far-flung location, but in close proximity to one of the most populated areas of the Mediterranean. It was possible because they lived in a marine preserve whose boundaries were respected.

Before I'd left Paris, I visited the Museum of Natural History, whose exhibits highlighted biodiversity and species preservation. On the main floor was a life-sized procession of African wildlife that recalled the march of animals onto Noah's ark. An elephant, a rhinoceros, and a hippopotamus led the way, dwarfing the museum visitors. Lined up behind them was a caravan stretching over thirty yards—antelope, armadillos, a cheetah, gazelles, a lion, water buffalos, zebras.

In the dimly lit atrium, the procession was arrestingly somber. The caravan of glass-eyed animals rang out like a bell to visitors, calling on them to turn the tide of the greatest destruction ever wrought by humankind: the sixth mass extinction.

Could humanity come together on this? We had started. The zeitgeist of our times was shifting—terms like *biosphere, carbon neutral,* and *zero waste* were coming into prominence, signaling a shift in worldview.

"It's now a matter," Elisabeth had told me in Paris, "of accelerating the change." If the sixth mass extinction were a burning building, the sirens were wailing, and the bucket chain was forming—people were refusing to eat endangered species and petitioning politicians. Heeding pressure from student activists, universities were divesting their endowments from investments in the fossil-fuel industry. It was matter of lengthening that chain, longer and longer. And faster.

People don't join a bucket chain because it's a safe bet—the passion for rescue doesn't calculate odds. Its risks are the ones that make life all the more worth living, *risks with heart*. The passion for rescue is a lived, breathing hope.

One of the great champions of ocean conservation, Sylvia Earle, founded Mission Blue to ignite more support for marine protected areas, which she called "Hope Spots." These areas are like Noah's arks for sea creatures, large enough to save and restore the oceans. The "passenger manifests" for these arks had to include keystone species like seagrass and coral and microorganisms. MPAs had to be established in places where those species lived.

La Sec de la Gabinière was in the middle of such a protected area. One of the groupers nudged in my direction and set its gaze on me. Its jowls were paunchy, its skin scuffed up. I reached down and stroked one of its fan-shaped fins as if it were the ear of a dog. Pierre signaled it was time to leave. We turned around and began the short crossing through the open water, back to La Gabinière.

"We don't know it, but we have thousands of selves," Naima had told me when we were talking about biodiversity. She meant that it wasn't just the organisms in our guts that keep us healthy, there are microorganisms in our nasal passages, mouth, and skin, and all of them keep us healthy—the "human microbiome."

Each of us hums with life; each of us is a busy orchestration of many creatures. The passenger manifest for the ark has been updated: to save lives, we must save the thousands of lives that make each one possible—from a blue whale to a speck of plankton.

⌒

There are three major islands in the Îles d'Or—Levant, Port-Cros, and Porquerolles. La Gabinière is just southwest of Port-Cros. When we finished the dive, the boat crossed to Porquerolles, where I was staying. Portions of the rocky islands thrust up out of the ocean like alpine peaks.

Two years before, I had spoken with Nicolas Gérardin, the park's operations director. He was the one who'd put the bug in my ear to visit the Coral Triangle. Thirty years before, he'd bought an old sailboat and sailed halfway around the world. "I sailed along the Eastern coast of Papua New Guinea. I saw people who lived totally in fusion with their natural environment; they depended on it every day. It showed to me how wide the distance is between the people who live in the cities and in nature, and that moving to the city cuts them from their roots."

When he returned to France, he had been away for ten years. "It was quite tough to reinstall myself into an organized life or a structured sort of society." He was offered a job in the Port-Cros National Park. He would live on the island of Port-Cros, which had only thirty-five inhabitants. He'd be in France, but surrounded by nature. "It was for me the opportunity to work in the field of the environment and devote myself to its protection. It was sort of a passage for me from a free life to an organized life."

Now, two years later, my journey was almost over. And I knew I hadn't come to these islands just to see the seagrass. I'd come begging for some kind of integration myself—something that would tell me how to live, how to make the passage from this journey to a more "organized life."

There were over six miles of open water between the two islands, but halfway across, white butterflies fluttered over the waves. As we got closer to Porquerolles, the scent of pine trees filled the air.

In the summer, tourists flock to Porquerolles and take in the rocky vistas and wander trails through the forest and the olive and fig groves maintained by the Conservatoire Botanique National, the national botanical conservatory, which safeguards threatened plant species. Then, in the fall, like an exhausted snail, the island coils into its shell for the winter, and the two hundred or so inhabitants savor the quiet.

When I arrived, in early October, things had already settled into a hushed peace. I stayed in an old villa retrofitted into a hotel next to a small nineteenth-century church with plain windows, a clock, and a prominent bell tower. In front of it was a dusty square with a flock of white pigeons. The brass key to my room had a hollow ring at one end, like the key to an antique trunk.

A young couple, Sébastien and Stéphanie, ran the hotel. When I came back from diving, Stéphanie was sitting with her kids in front of the hotel.

"You live here all year round?" I asked.

"Yes, it's nice for our children. The school is just here." She pointed to a narrow street off the square. She was slender, with delicate features and long dark hair.

"Do you like it here, when it's not summer?"

"It can be very stormy. The mistral winds can be ninety kilometers. But when it is calm, *il fait magnifique*. It is magnificent."

There was a little gelato stand on the square. Later that day, I got a chocolate cone and wandered back to the docks. In front of the dive operation, one of the staff, Vivienne, was working.

"*Allô*," she called out. "Hello!"

I offered her some of my gelato.

She beamed and leaped into a kitchenette to get a spoon. We stood for a few minutes in the warm sun while she gingerly extracted spoonfuls of gelato from the cone.

I felt like I was in Sulawesi—that openness and warmth. What was that? I'd felt that way in Paris, too. And in Spain. It wasn't just about generosity. *It was how it felt.* Well, my heart had cracked wide open in Sulawesi.

***

The next morning the dive boat motored to the rocky point of Porquerolles called the Médes. It was sunny, and the water was almost as smooth as a glass mirror. It was late autumn, and there had been several weeks of unusually calm, windless weather. As I sank into the sea, I was startled by how clear the water was. It reminded me of the gin-clear water in the underwater caves of the Yucatán.

The rocky terrain was covered with bright orange sponges and sea lettuce, a type of algae that grows in flowery swirls. I hovered in a sand channel and peered sideways into the tall seagrass. There was an ultrafine fizz, tiny bubbles on the surface of the seagrass blades and in the water.[105]

"No," I mused. "It couldn't be!"

But it was: *oxygen*.

If you'd asked me the day before if I understood photosynthesis, I'd have said, "Sure. Carbon dioxide in, oxygen out. What's not to get?"

But now that truth came fully alive. I could hear my noisy breath through my regulator. I had thought of breath as inhale and exhale, but now I was vividly experiencing another dimension of it, a key and rather large-scale one: the biosphere.

I turned slowly in the water with my fins; all I could see were the seagrass meadows. I recalled seeing NASA images of them taken from satellites. One spanned 770 miles along the coast of Australia. Another, just below the Everglades, covered over five thousand square miles. There were miles and miles of seagrass, from the Mediterranean to Mexico to New Guinea to Zanzibar. And mangroves and plankton and forests and rainforests—all pumping out oxygen. We might go without food for months, water for days. But air? Minutes.

A houseplant would never look the same. Photosynthetic organisms are the Teddy Roosevelts of all life—they speak softly, but carry a big stick. They pump out oxygen and sequester carbon. "A square meter of Posidonia," Nicolas had told me, "produces twice the volume of oxygen in twenty-four hours than a square meter of tropical forest, up to 14 liters of oxygen per day." One acre of seagrass absorbs over seven thousand pounds of carbon a year, the equivalent of the emissions of an average car traveling over three thousand miles.

In some areas of the Mediterranean, scientists have estimated as much as a 30 percent loss of seagrass beds in the last fifty years due to damage by fishing gear, dredging, pollution, and poor anchoring techniques.[106] That's why it was such a big fuss to map where the co-management committee used their nets to fish for sandeel.

I recalled Marsha telling me that over 50 percent of the oxygen in our lungs came from plants and algae in the ocean. The oxygen in every other breath we take comes from organisms in the sea. Nicolas had told me that scientists call Posidonia "the lungs of the Mediterranean."

⁐

After sundown I went for a walk. A dirt road led past an ornate wrought-iron gate and wound up a steep hill through a dark canopy of pine trees. Some bushes with white flowers emitted a fragrant scent. The air was silky warm. At the top of the hill, the harbor came into view. The water was calm and wind-less. The road led inland to an eighteenth-century windmill perched on an overlook. Below, the moonlight illuminated olive and fig groves and the forest. From across the island, a lighthouse flashed.

Everything felt so vivid. I remembered the French woman I dove with when I first returned to the Turks and Caicos after over a decade—how she said, "I must recover my sensations" when she explained she'd need to get used to being underwater again. And I remembered that "everything is alive" sensation I'd felt diving in the reef. Now it wasn't just in the ocean that I felt it. Sea, sky, land: the world was more alive. Some recovery beyond my own imagining had occurred. I wondered if that intense sensation of aliveness—that "hum" of life—might be the thousands of selves that Naima talked about.

But the price for that openness had been high. The world was so much more cruel and greedy than I'd ever fathomed. It felt like what last shreds of innocence I'd retained had been stripped off. But a second innocence was slowly growing in its place. Like an offshoot sprouting from a felled tree, its roots were sturdier and less easily vanquished: the willingness to say yes, to begin again, to trust, to risk.

I retraced my steps to the hotel. In the middle of the night, a warm wind stirred. The lace curtains over the windows billowed like the sails of a boat.

Just before sunrise, the windows in my room slammed wide open, and rain blew in. Bolts of lighting illuminated the court-yard and the church. I latched the windows shut and got a towel to mop up the water. A few minutes later, the rain halted, but not the wind. It shook the trees and rattled the windows—long gale-force gusts.

The wind howled all day and persisted at nightfall. There was no going out on the water in that. Late at night, as I was dozing off, the phone rang. It was Pierre, the divemaster.

"Hello, Liz," he said with a French accent. The connection was scratchy. "I just tell you, we dive tomorrow."

"Really?" There was a large clank and a scraping sound as the wind blew over another metal chair in the courtyard.

"Yes, yes. It will be calm. The mistral, it just lasts a day or so."

Jean-Luc, the other divemaster, drove the boat toward a site just off the Médes. And it was calm. A friend of Pierre's would dive with me. On the way, he told me he played the bass. I told him I was taking singing lessons and that I'd never really sung before in my life.

As we got our gear ready, I said, "It's such a trip to think of my vocal chords—my body—as a musical instrument."

"Yeah, when I play the bass," he said, "I feel the sound in my body. It's like a big heartbeat." He was all geared up, sitting at the edge of the boat, ready to roll back into the water.

"Heartbeat? You mean you feel the rhythm in your blood?"

"Yes."

I snapped the last buckles on my gear shut and sat next to him, ready to roll backward into the water with him.

He smiled. "Maybe someday, you can feel your voice in your veins."

We sank to about seventy feet and knelt on a sand patch. Out of the corner of my eye, I saw a large school of yellowfin jacks approaching. They made figure eights around us, over and over, almost touching. Did they sense our gentleness? I knew too much now to believe otherwise.

"Give Sabine a *bise!*" Stéphanie called after me as I left the hotel. *Bise* means "a kiss on the cheek"—the French equivalent of a hug. Stéphanie had plied me with espressos and butter cookies, and now I was off to chat with an artist, Sabine Chautard. Everyone had been telling me, "You must meet Sabine." She was a painter and had done illustrations of the seagrass meadows for the park.

I walked down a narrow path just wide enough for a bicycle. Low-lying stucco farmhouses had deeply recessed windows with thick shutters reinforced with horizontal slats of wood and large, sturdy hinges. The island was like a boat whose hatches could be battened in a flash.

The parkland on the island dwarfed the village. A car was an anomaly. It didn't feel like the rest of Provence. The colors of the buildings were brighter, recalling the brilliant yellows and blues of Tunisia or Algeria. Only a few hundred miles of open ocean separated them from Porquerolles.

But there was more to it than that. Annie Aboucaya, a park botanist, had explained to me that thirty million years ago, the Îles d'Or, Corsica, Sardinia, and the Balearic Islands were a part of a huge mountain range—the Maures Massif. The islands share unique native plants and a specific type of stone that is different from that found in the mountains in the main part of Provence. So even if you couldn't put your finger on it, something about the landscape felt different.

Sabine's studio was in a little stucco building with blue French doors covered with bougainvillea. The doors were open, but Sabine wasn't there. I hesitated and then stepped into the small studio. The lights were not on, but enough light streamed in through the doors to illuminate wooden racks with postcards of her illustrations of islands, seascapes, harbors, fishermen, forests, plants, fish.

Another wall was covered with framed watercolors, including a landscape that had been painted on a nautical chart. The latitude and longitude lines, the compass rose, and the contours of the island, which for so many invoke the sea's mystique, had been incorporated into a painting of an island—trees, rocky coast, undulating hues of blue water, a seagull. The chart wasn't a blank canvas. The painting had evolved with its shapes, taken its magical aura up another notch.

I felt like an intruder, like I was reading a diary of the outpourings of a love affair with the islands—the beauty, the joy, wildness, peace, profundity, mystery.

Still no sign of Sabine. There was a courtyard behind the studio. An old woman was visible through the back door.

"*Allô! Je suis un présent pour Sabine.*" I said, struggling to tell her, "I am here for Sabine," but the mangled words actually meant, "I am a present for Sabine."

The old woman looked at me curiously. "*Vraiment? Vous êtes un cadeau?* Really? You are a gift?"

"No, no …"

"*Vous avez un cadeau pour Sabine?* You *have* a gift for Sabine?"

"No …" I sputtered.

She shook her head and called out loudly, elongating the vowels, "Sabine!"

A moment later Sabine came down a stairway. She was in her early forties and had long dark-brown hair. She eyed me warily. "Yes, yes, just ask your questions," she said perfunctorily.

But as we chatted, the world behind the eyes of the woman whose paintings I saw unfolded. She was the daughter of architects and said she had grown up "always looking with the eyes, always drawing. And I always wanted to paint on different materials: a map, fabric, a piece of driftwood."

On one wall there was a long piece of driftwood with a barracuda painted on it. The porous wood gave texture to the hues of the barracuda's scales and the varied light of the blue water.

She led me back into the courtyard and pointed to some slabs of driftwood leaned against a wall. She picked up one piece. "I bring these home. This one ... I don't know yet what I will do. Sometimes it is two, three years before I know. But I know I will have an idea for it."

Back inside the studio, I opened a book she'd written and illustrated, *Carnet de Mouillages,* a guide to anchorage sites in the Îles d'Or. "One of the main threats to the Posidonia is anchoring, mainly of leisure boats," Nicolas had explained. Instead of tying up to a buoy, people dropped anchor in the seagrass, unwittingly uprooting them and breaking their stems. It was a "plus signs" phenomenon. What's the harm of one boater dropping anchor in the seagrass? In the forty or so miles of coastline opposite the Îles d'Or, there were over 130,000 active leisure boats using anchors.

Sabine's book showed where the safe anchorages were with illustrated maps, including the precise latitude and longitude of the buoys. Each description was embedded in a collage of watercolors of the surrounding landscape. The pages for La Gabinière had a grouper next to a pastiche of images from her sketchbook—the island from the open sea, the seagrass underwater, and an aerial view of the island.

"I am twenty years here," she said, "but it is always new, the landscape." I flipped through page after page. Almost fifty locations were illustrated, hundreds of anchorage sites, hundreds of watercolors. "It is always infinite for me. It's always changing, the light, the colors. I paint a certain place, the rocks, the water, then I come back, another time of day, in different weather, different season. It is always new."

The book also illustrated what to do if you can't find a buoy to anchor on—the techniques for locating a sandy bottom and making sure your anchor lands on it and not the seagrass. There were maps explaining the regulated zones for fishing and diving and anchoring.

On the first page of the book was a lighthouse painted onto the compass rose of a chart. A few pages later, there was a watercolor of the seagrass and forty-some detailed drawings of some of the many inhabitants of the Posidonia. They were fragile, they were endangered, and in Sabine's drawings, they were honored: blennies, breams, crabs, damselfish, octopus, starfish, wrasses.

Sabine's painting transmitted it loud and clear: the seagrass was their home. One of the most fundamental human desires is to feel that we matter, that our lives matter. But can we have any genuine sense of value if we don't acknowledge that other creatures matter too? Perhaps they too have a right not to be rendered extinct?

"The environment, the creatures who live there," Sabine said to me, "this is for me important. We live here in something very sacred."

There was a narrow dirt road that went south, to the other side of the island, a little less than an hour's stroll. It was close to dusk, and I wanted to go see the sunset. There was no one to be seen on the road. Pine trees formed an arc over it. On either side were the fig and olive groves maintained by the botanical conservatory. The rows of scraggly trees converged into the hilly distance.

The island is a "garden island"—sea and land are both cared for. This is true of many coastal parks around the world. The Point Reyes National Seashore, where Jenny Stock worked, is on a peninsula surrounded by a marine protected area. "Wildness"—wilderness—will need to enter its second innocence. The first was not chosen; the second will have to be. And it will be our choice.

Another dirt road appeared, veering off to the right. It too was lined with a rhythmic row of evenly spaced trees. The evening's angular light had grown rosy and golden. A hundred or so yards away I saw a woman standing still. She looked transfixed. I didn't dare disturb her. I imagined for a moment she might have been a botanist at the conservatory, lingering in the last glimmers of evening light before walking home.

I kept walking toward the south side of the island. I remembered asking Annie, one of the park botanists, when she had really known she wanted to become a botanist.

"You mean the big *flash*?" she joked with a self-deprecating smile. The term *flash* is slang for a revelation in French.

"Yes," I grinned, "the big *flash*."

"If there was one, it was when I began to work with the botanical conservatory on Porquerolles."

The conservatory saved seeds of endangered plant species in a "seed bank" that had the seeds for over seventeen hundred species. Annie told me that they had germinated some seeds of threatened plants and cared for them until they had grown into small plants.

"There was a day we went into the wild to replant them," she gestured with her hands, as if carefully putting a plant into the ground. "That was the big *flash*." She grinned, adding, with emphasis, "Because we gave these endangered species a second chance."

I kept walking. But a few moments later I glanced back; the woman was still there, lingering. I wouldn't see another soul that night until I returned to the village. Annie and Sabine, they'd found their place in the bucket chain—the growing linkage of people at work to preserve the earth. They'd found something they loved to do that contributed to making the world a better place.

And I had too.

I'd published some articles. I did my first radio interview in over ten years. All the skills I'd honed from my first book, they came back—like riding a bicycle. But the wheels turned in a new direction. Now it was to help preserve the life of the seas. And I was starting to understand something: one of the world's most belligerent lies is delivered in the guise of the seemingly innocuous words: "Don't bother, your voice won't matter."

How many times had I thought that myself? But the day after I'd resolved in JFK Airport to find a way to be a part of ocean conservation efforts, I watched a TED talk by Sylvia Earle, the founder of Mission Blue. Her words caught my attention: "I wish you would use all means at your disposal—films, expeditions, the web, new submarines—and campaign to ignite public support for a global network of marine protected areas, hope spots large enough to save and restore the ocean, the blue heart of the planet."[107]

She'd sent out a call—strong and clear. And just like that Charlie Parker tune, with its understated profundity, she ended her speech with four words: "Now is the time."

I heard that voice, her words. I felt needed. Truthfully.

Walking down the dirt road from Sabine's, I asked myself something so simple I felt embarrassed that I'd never *really* asked myself this before: "What if I really lived as if my voice mattered?"

Close to the southern edge of the island I followed a narrow trail through the woods. It brought me to a bluff overlooking the ocean. I found a perch on which to sit and watch the sunset. The stone was still warm from the day's heat. I remembered what Annie had told me about the Maures Massif. I was sitting at the top of an ancient mountain range.

The sea turned blue-violet and a slice of moon rose. There was nothing but open ocean until Africa. What is it about distances? Mountaintops, great expanses of water—they bring something out in us. To the south and west and east there was nothing but the open waters of the Med.

Just before I left for Europe I'd read the book *Blessed Unrest* by Paul Hawken. He described how he'd begun to wonder if we really knew how many people around the globe had joined the effort to preserve the earth and protect human rights. He searched the government records and tax census data of many countries to see how many organizations were devoted to these causes.

"In trying to pick up a stone," Hawken writes, "I found the exposed tip of a much larger geological formation."[108] His calculations led him to believe that there are over a million organizations devoted to sustainability and social justice, the largest social movement in history. Social psychologists Paul Ray and Sherry Ruth Anderson had documented a similar cultural upwelling through focus groups and social surveys. Beneath their overturned stones were millions of people.[109]

"Could it be," Hawken writes, "an instinctive, collective response to a threat?" The threat that the earth has a "life-threatening disease, marked by massive ecological degradation and rapid climate change?"[110] But a movement? Where's the figurehead? The manifesto? Might it be like the co-management committee—bottom-up, community-based, decentralized?

I'd seen it!

My entire journey had been like donning a pair of wooden goggles and seeing underwater clearly for the first time. But it wasn't the undersea world that they revealed. It was this: Amdeep, Eiglys, Enci Wahab, Helen, Jenny, Joanna, Luís, Marsha, Mauricio, Michel, Naima, Peter, Sergi, Sugi, Susana. The list went on and on: all the people all around the world who worked to make change, thousands upon thousands upon thousands of "selves." The Ellen MacArthur Foundation had started Circular Economy 100, a global network of leading companies and innovators, to accelerate the transition—companies like Cisco, Coca-Cola, Hewlett-Packard, Renault, and Unilever.

But powerful enough to change the course of civilization? The runaway industrial locomotive? I remembered seeing the homes abandoned because of sea-level rise in Sulawesi, how the hair on the back of my neck stood up. This time it was an opposite sensation—a gigantic, beautiful force afoot in the world. Something deep inside me shuddered, bolted awake. *Don't discount the invisible plus signs. Even if you can't do the math, don't quit.*

⟡

I'd lingered too long. The trail back to the road was pitch dark. But soon the moonlight illuminated my path. The road was now a soft tunnel of trees and singing crickets.

Suddenly there was a bolt of light. I stopped. Fear rippled through my chest. Then it was dark again. I resumed walking.

Another flash.

"Who's there?" I squawked, and swirled around.

It was the broad sweep of the lighthouse's beam, which had just been turned on. It moved swiftly and then vanished, leaving a fleeting paths of light and long shadows that flickered through the trees and the olive groves and out onto the jagged coast and the wide, southern expanse of sea.

PART 5

The Silver Bank

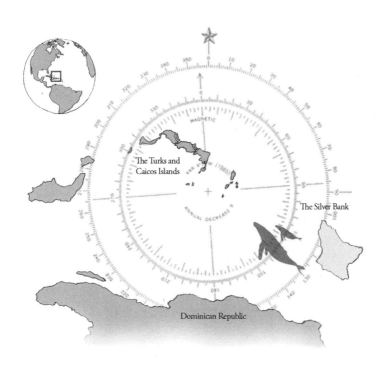

The Turks and
Caicos Islands

The Silver Bank

Dominican Republic

20

Song

I woke suddenly and lunged for the bathroom. The vomit came out so fast it was if a pressurized jar had burst open. When I came out, Charlie was up, vomiting on a rolled-up sheet in our cabin.

We went outside to get some air. The boat lurched in swells the size of small hillsides. It was early morning, and we were on a boat eighty miles southeast of the Turks and Caicos Islands. Overnight, the boat had crossed from the Dominican Republic over a fourteen-thousand-foot oceanic trench to a seamount just fifty to ninety feet below the surface—the Silver Bank.

Normally the passage is quite calm. Just our luck: it was the roughest crossing they'd had in two years. I'd wanted to come to the Silver Bank because every winter, some three thousand to five thousand humpback whales go there to mate and give birth and nurse their young. Many of these whales skirt the Northwest Point in the Turks and Caicos when they migrate to and from their northern feeding grounds, which stretch from Stellwagen Bank, just off of Cape Cod, to Newfoundland. Lizzie, at the School for Field Studies in South Caicos, had told me that the whales came through the cut between South Caicos and Grand Turk Island.

It was early spring, and some of the humpbacks had already started to migrate north. About a half hour later, we crossed onto the Silver Bank. The seas settled dramatically in the shallow waters. We motored smoothly toward a mooring on the northern side of the bank. For as far as I could see, there was only ocean, and the windy seas did indeed have a silvery sparkle.

The humpbacks come to the Silver Bank because the shallow, calmer waters are an easier place for a mother whale to give birth and for a calf to take its first breath and build its strength before undertaking the long migration north through open water. And because the bank is so shallow, there are fewer opportunities for predators, such as orcas, to attack calves from below.

Soon the air filled with the loud rattling of a mooring chain, and the engine stopped. We went upstairs for a briefing in the galley. "Okay, little bit of rough ride, but we're all here," Gene Flipse, our captain, said. He was tall and lanky, and curly brown hair graced his forehead. I bit off a piece of toast, cautiously chewed, and swallowed it as if I had a goiter in my throat.

"So, we go out," Gene said enthusiastically, "and we cruise around and look for whales." There were two small boats, called "tenders," which we'd use to go out and search for whales.

The ideal situation would be a mother and calf that are resting. "The mothers and calves have very, very close relationships with each other," Gene explained. "They are almost always in direct physical contact, except when they are separated to breathe. So if you see a calf on the surface circling, that means 'mom's just below,' and the calf will go down."

Gene held up two small plastic replicas of humpbacks, a mother and a calf. As he talked, he simulated the diving and surfacing behavior. The mother breathes every twenty minutes or so, but a newborn calf needs to breathe every three to five minutes. So a mother will rest below while the calf comes up, takes a breath, and then, Gene said, moving the calf model back down to the bigger one, "after it is finished breathing, it's going to dive back down and nestle up next to mom."

Gene explained a phenomenon called "whale time"—of patiently following the whales' breath cycles and reading their behavior to see if it's a good opportunity to get in the water with them. If the whales are deemed suitable for a "visit," Gene explained, then he or our other guide, Elisa Buller, would prompt us to quietly slip into the water and float "like harmless seaweed or jellyfish," and "present ourselves" for an encounter. "The whales use their hearing as their primary sense out here," Gene said. "They are very highly attuned, and they hear us coming."

We wouldn't position ourselves any closer than thirty to fifty feet from a whale. That was the "stop point" for our approach. The Silver Bank was part of the Dominican Republic's Sanctuary for the Marine Mammals, in which whales were protected by law against aggression. The sanctuary had, Gene told us, "a very conservative definition of *aggression,* which is that if you are moving toward the whale closer than that stop point, that's considered an act of aggression."

But, should the whales come closer to us, well then, by all means, "Come say hello!" "You just have to stop and stay in position," Gene told us, "and wait for the natural curiosity of the animals to bring them to you." So in terms of the tone of the interaction, our little expedition could be termed a "swim with humans" encounter for whales.

We went down to the main deck to put our gear in order. My fins suddenly seemed so small. The scale of the creatures we were about to encounter had finally registered. I remembered Ms. Blue, the blue-whale skeleton at Long Marine Lab that was almost ninety feet long. Okay, a full-grown humpback whale is smaller—only forty-five feet long, just a little longer than a school bus, and, shall we say, one of the "lightweights" of the family, maxing out at fifty tons.

There were dark clouds on the horizon. A storm was blowing in. It was too rough to go out. Charlie went up to the galley in search of some sea-sickness medication. Exhausted and queasy, I lay down in our cabin and closed my eyes.

My innards were dizzy. For the last stretch of my research, I'd wanted to go to three regions of the world in the course of one year, immerse myself. Well, I'd done it, but something was missing, some nugget. Some understanding I was searching for still eluded me.

Ever had a conversation in which someone said to you, "I had this feeling ..."? You know, about a man or a woman or a house or a job? Well, I had this feeling that my journey would bring me to a certain "place." But that place? I hadn't gotten there.

Our cabin had a big picture window. Rain started to pelt against it. *Maybe it will just be that way,* I mused. *Maybe it's a mystery you accept. Maybe that's part of the magic, it lures you forward.* We would have just five days on the bank. I tried to resist wondering how long the stormy weather would last.

I was so tired, *long-term tired.* The fatigue had been building for months. I thought it'd be great to come full circle, back to seas that were just a day's sail from the Turks and Caicos. But I didn't realize that no matter how strongly anchored you are in a sense of purpose, it doesn't insulate you from grief. Our flight to the Dominican Republic passed through the same airport gate I'd taken to fly to the Turks and Caicos. The sense of déjà vu was so strong, the sadness I'd felt when I witnessed the coral reef bleach. When we boarded the plane, I burst into tears.

I'd urged Charlie to come with me. This was the last stage of the journey, and I wanted to share this experience with him. Now we were both seasick, and I was exhausted.

I rolled over on my side and looked out onto the surging seas and thought, "Did we really need to come here? Couldn't it have been enough to write about the whales?"

No.

No, no, no!

The whale thing was too much about the ocean not to do it. The story of men and whales is the story of the civilization and the ocean writ large. From the ancient Babylonian myth in which the god Marduk slays the sea-monster Tiamat to Melville's *Moby Dick* to the ultramodern, explosive-laced harpoons launched from factory ships, whale hunting is symbolic of epic battles with nature—slaughter for survival.

Whale oil literally greased the wheels of the Industrial Revolution. The steam engine? Whale oil. Watches? Whale oil. Sewing machines, railroad signal lamps, altimeters, microscopes, textile factory looms. Whale oil. Known for its exceptional stability and low viscosity, it was the preferred lubricant for everything from the gears of trains to fine mechanical instruments. By the mid-1960s, the global population of humpbacks, that some estimate was once over a million before commercial whaling, had been whittled down to about 1,500. So what happened? Why weren't they hunted to extinction?

The environmental movement. All that public outrage and uproar, all the demonstrations, sit-ins and petitions and legal actions worked. Despite that victory, whales need increased protection today. As of 2014, Iceland, Japan, and Norway still hunt whales with industrial-age equipment, defending their practices with thinly veiled assertions that they hunt a limited number for "scientific purposes." Whales are also greatly at risk from collisions with large ships, entanglement in fishing gear, and chemical contamination. Still, humpback whale populations are now coming back, increasing by about 5 percent a year. And humpbacks, in particular, became the poster child of the environmental movement in the 1960s and 1970s and the push for a worldwide moratorium on whale hunting in 1986, in large part because of one trait: *they sing.*

In 1967, biologists Roger Payne and Scott McVay discovered that humpback whale songs have a complex syntax, with phrases that repeat in patterns known as "themes." Each song has two to nine themes, which are sung in a specific order. It's still debated why humpbacks sing, but it is generally the males that do the singing. And they usually sing at night.

Payne released a recording, *Song of the Humpback Whale,* with his then-wife, Katherine Payne, and his colleague Frank Watlington. It sold over thirty million copies. The rhythmic sequences gleaned from nighttime recordings made from a small boat in the North Atlantic galvanized the Save the Whales movement and the environmental movement as a whole. Some unexpected, emotional connection was forged.

So I wanted to see these inspiring creatures with my own eyes. *Get some rest,* I told myself. I dozed off.

A bell rang. Loud. "Okay, everybody." It was Gene's voice. "Weather's better. Let's go!"

It was still windy. The tender bobbed as we loaded our gear. We motored away, eyes glued to the horizon. Gene stood in the stern of the boat, mask on his forehead, alert, searching.

A half hour later we spotted a mother and calf resting. Gene started timing their breath cycles. After about twenty minutes, the driver brought the boat close to where the mother had last descended.

"Okay, I think we might have an opportunity here. Let's get geared up," Gene bellowed over the wind and surging seas. He stood balanced on the handrail in extra-long fins, one hand gingerly holding one of the support poles for the sun tarp, as the boat rocked back and forth. He was the corollary to the British term "proper sailor"—a proper man-fish. He was filled to the brim with excitement and energy, like a conductor leading an orchestra through a favorite symphony. He knew the routine so well—time breaths, fins on, mask on, into the water, approach gently, signal to the driver.

Gene slipped into the water, moving his fins so they did not break the water's surface. Every few moments, the sun burst through the dark clouds and the waves glittered. A moment later, he signaled to the driver, and we got the go-ahead to slip into the water.

I didn't see anything. Then I realized I didn't see it because it was so big. A dark bluish shape so fully filled the field of my vision that I couldn't comprehend what I was looking at. Even at forty or so feet away, I wasn't looking at a whale. I was looking at … part of a whale.

It was motionless. Excuse me, *she* was motionless. Just above her, nestled in the crescent of her back, was her calf. The mother turned and circled us three times in slow motion. Her calf swam with her in synchrony, always staying just a few inches from that snug arc in her mother's back.

I didn't touch my journal that evening. The beauty of the whales so exuberantly defied what I thought was possible, their gentle grandeur, that I was dumbstruck, beauty-struck.

We spent four more days like that, looking for whales, watching them on the surface, and getting into the water with them. The stormy seas passed, and the waters calmed. Humpbacks are notorious for their playful acrobatics. We saw them breach and extend their heads out of the water to have a look at us ("spyhop"), and slap the surface of the water with their flukes ("peduncle throw"). A peduncle throw can mean many things. It can mean "bug off, fella," if a female is tired of a male's advances. Or a male that has established himself as a female's "escort" might use it to discourage another male's advances.

"Sometimes the calves," Gene told us, "when they get playful, will get a little wound up and wander off and get a little bit too far from mom. They can get separated quite quickly and then mom will fire off a peduncle throw like, 'Hey, Junior! Get back here!'"

Once when we were in the water with a mother and calf, the mother rose vertically in the water to breathe. Straight ahead of us, forty-five feet of whale vertical beneath the surface. A gentle, living, breathing creature over four stories tall.

And well, I haven't told you about all of us in the tender. The gear stowed at the center of the boat included small fins and masks and wet suits a third the size of ours. Gene's partner, Cloe, had come with her daughter, Lucaya, who was six years old. And Dave, a friend of Gene's since high school, was there with his wife, Suzanne, and their daughter, Eva.

There was a contagious mirth that we couldn't have replicated without our younger boat-mates. When the humpbacks were "pec slapping," slapping their pectoral fins on the surface to signal to each other, Lucaya and Eva leaned over the railing and squealed, "The whales are waving! The whales are waving!" (They were right. The whales *were* waving.)

There was an alcove in the front of the tender, above the bow, that mariners call a dodger. Eva and Lucaya made it into a clubhouse, draping a sarong across the small opening to make a curtain. They filled a bucket with water and made a mini-aquarium with seaweed and baby crabs and shrimp.

And there was "whale time," when our banter ceased, and we'd silently scan the surface for a breach or a fluke or a blow-hole. One afternoon Lucaya slept on one of the benches, her head nestled on a rolled-up windbreaker. As the boat rocked gently, small waves made lapping sounds. Cloe sat with her, seeming to doze a bit too. But even when her eyes shut momentarily, her hand stayed on her daughter's shoulder, should the boat lurch and Lucaya be in danger of rolling off the bench.

Down below, the whale calves had their own way of settling in with their mothers. Charlie told me he'd seen a calf hover just below the mother's belly and the mother wrap her pectoral fins around her calf to tuck it into position. The hump-back's long gray-and-white fins are not stiff like oars. They're like our arms, with highly mobile shoulders, elbows, wrists, and long finger bones.

Occasionally we'd see the other tender from our boat. It was being used by a film crew from Brazil. Why were they on the Silver Bank? Because the whales in Brazil wouldn't let photographers near them underwater, due to the long history of whale hunting there. It was only in 2008 that Brazil declared all Brazilian waters a safe sanctuary for whales and dolphins.

The sanctuary encompassing the Silver Bank had been in effect for almost thirty years. Established in 1986, it was the first humpback whale sanctuary in the world. Like some whale Shangri-La, it had eluded the harpoons. This breeding ground, "delivery room," and cradle had remained a safe haven.

Whales sleep, but they can't do it for long, otherwise they'd drown. It's believed that, like dolphins, only one hemisphere of the whale's brain sleeps. So they rest, but they're never completely asleep the way we are. We breathe automatically, but whales are conscious breathers, slipping to the surface intermittently, even as they rest. Inspired by that, Gene had named his operation Conscious Breath Adventures.

The mother, Gene told us, "nurses her calf to the tune of fifty gallons of milk a day, which is very, very thick, very rich milk. The whole time that the females are down on the Silver Bank—and the males, for that matter—they are not feeding, they are fasting." By time the mother reaches the northern latitudes to feed with her calf, she'll have lost a third of her body weight.

One more thing—subtle, but unmistakable. Having kids on the boat changed our behavior. Somehow we were more polite, generous, and positive. The girls brought out the best in us. It was as if we'd shined up the chrome bumpers of our personalities because there were kids on board. There was more patience, more kindness, more sharing. More "best."

We all think we do our best. But children bring out an even "better best" in us. They push the seesaw in the direction of hope, encourage us to take responsibility not just for our lives but also for the future. And no matter how many times a pandering politician utters the same words disingenuously, the bottom line is it's true. Truth never wears out. It's inextinguishable.

⟨≋⟩

One of the best spots to sit was on top of the dodger, just above the bow. It had a great view. Eva was sitting up there one day, and I scrambled up to join her. She was wearing my red fleece jacket to stay warm. The oversized sleeves squished into a thick, cozy wrap around her small arms; the collar rose up above her ears.

"How old are you?" I asked.

"Seven," she said with a precocious glance, like, *Couldn't you make more interesting small talk?*

We quietly looked out at the horizon, searching for whales. Charlie leaned his forearms against the top of the dodger behind us, his camera poised, should a whale suddenly breach. We were all lost in silent, ripe waiting.

There are questions in life you don't answer with words. You answer them with how you live. For me, the biggest one had always been, "What truly is love?" Now I had another to guide me: "What if I lived as if my voice mattered?"

The horizon was ultramarine blue, speckled with light. I looked back at Charlie. The wind blew his thick black hair up and away from his forehead. He looked up at me and winked.

Remember the garage? When I wanted to quit the book? And I'd swung this deal with myself that it'd be like some wild motorcycle ride, and that I could ease up on the throttle when the journey came to an end?

I sighed. *The book's finishing, but this journey, this love of ocean, this deepened love of life, I've barely begun ....*

"B-r-e-a-c-h!" Eva squealed, pointing to the horizon. The burst of water looked like a depth charge. Forty tons of whale leaping completely out of the water and plunging back certainly would mimic that.

"It's a rowdy group," Gene called out. It was a group of male whales competing for the attention of a female. As we got closer, the water seemed to boil with energy. At least nine or ten whales swiftly crosscut each other. Looking downward, I noticed elongated slivers of turquoise moving underneath our boat.

"Gene," I asked, "what's that?"

"The fins."

They were the bright white of the sixteen-foot fins seen through the tinting of the bank's water. It was actually more than twenty whales that had gathered. At any one time, only half of them came to the surface to breathe.

Whales in a rowdy group will breach on top of each other and rub the tubercles—the knobby protrusions on their chins—raw. We could see scuffs and cuts on their dorsal fins and skin from their oceanic barroom brawl. And while it was all rough-and-tumble, they were very precise about whom to push around. The lady they were competing for was off-limits, easy to identify because of her unblemished torso. And not once did a whale bang up against the side of our tender.

"They don't have arms to throw punches, but they have pec fins and their big tail flukes," Gene said. "They also have what's called the anvil, that bony knob on the bottom of their chin. They hit each other with that."

The energy whipped up, higher and higher, whales swirling and banging into each other and breaching and diving beneath our boat. "Just think of it," Gene called out ebulliently. "There's hundreds of thousands of pounds of raging humpback whale all around us!"

They were hot on the trail of that millennia-old tradition that never runs dry: mating. The unit of measure for testosterone levels would not have been milligrams—more like gallon jugs. It was late spring, and many of the females had already mated and left for the northern feeding grounds. The mothers will often be the last the leave, lingering until they deem their calves fit to make the journey north.

But single females? Fewer and fewer as you get later into spring. "The competition," Gene said, "can be fierce." There was a computer programmer from Texas, Bryan Hager, on the boat. He leaned back, stroked his thick beard, and chuckled with a self-deprecating, mock-Texas drawl, "Da girls ... dey all get purdier at closin' time."

The last night on the Silver Bank I slept fitfully. My throat felt tight when I woke. I climbed up to the top deck. The night before, a group of us had lingered there and gazed up at the sky. Freed from the glare of urban sprawl or even buoys or lighthouses, the sky lay naked above us. I'd never seen stars so bright.

Sometimes change happens so fast you don't see it, and then suddenly it hits you all at once. In the morning light, all I could see in all directions was the steel-blue horizon. But it was no longer flat. It wasn't the straight edge that so many thought Columbus would sail right off of when he sailed west from Spain.

It was curved.

If my travels had done anything, it was that I could really feel that curve now—it was as vivid and tactile as the metal railing beneath my hands and the gusts of wind on my forehead. I turned my back to the just-risen sun. To the west, the earth made an arc to our home in California, and farther still, Papua and the Malay archipelago of Indonesia. To the north, an arc led to the Turks and Caicos and, farther on, to where I was born, New York City. To the east, another arc stretched thousands of miles to the Mediterranean and North Africa.

You know those toys for toddlers with round and square pegs that fit into matching holes? It was like that: the cognitive leap when the round peg fits in the round hole. An irreversible moment.

I'd finally gotten the shape of things, the mystery at the edge, the one that flickered through blinds that always seemed to snap shut too soon. That mystery, that beauty, it was calling me to a deeper, truer home. I'd finally come home in a way that would have been unfathomable before. It was "the place."

It was a little spinning sphere with a thin glaze of water held to it by gravity, punctuated by archipelagos of islands and mountains and tundra and plains and deserts. And that fluid, transparent medium, intermingled with sun and oxygen, that carved riverbeds through mountains and circulated through seas and pulsed through our veins: *that gives birth to life.*

Our clapboard house with musical instruments and travel photographs on the walls, where our dog likes to stretch out in a sunny spot on the oak floor and our greenhouse teems with seedlings—our little home—it was nested inside that bigger home within layers and layers and layers of life.

I'd learned to let a mystery be a mystery and a longing be a longing. Better to be inarticulate, but true. So I won't try to explain it too much except to say that I'm so glad I kept trying to listen to that mysterious longing. It brought me home and closer to others in ways I never would have imagined possible. I'll keep feeling that mystery, keep longing for it. I'll never want to extinguish it. It's life longing to be, to connect, reconnect, beat the odds, and push forward anew.

Toward the end of the day, we cautiously approached a mother and calf. The driver deftly maneuvered the boat as we timed their breaths. Then they surfaced together once more, exhaled with muffled bursts, and descended like a submarine and its companion submersible.

"Okay," said Gene. "Let's give this a try."

We slipped into the water. The mother was resting motionless at about sixty feet, and the calf had nuzzled itself right beneath her chin with the sleepy-eyed, soft-mouthed expression of a baby in a cradle. The water was suffused with peacefulness and an unthinkable energy I was at a loss to name.

Every few minutes, the calf stirred and rose, as if swimming in its sleep, outstretching its newborn fins in slow motion to propel itself to the surface and take a breath. Then it sank, as if tiptoeing back to bed in a trance-like slumber, and tucked itself under its mother's chin.

We floated like a loose-knit blob of jellyfish, gawking silently. There was just an hour or so of daylight left; the light cast angular, silvery threads through the darkening, violet-blue water. Once again the calf raised its head and slipped out from under its mother's chin. But this time it seemed to wake out of its slumber.

As it rose, it turned vertically in the water, revealing the soft-looking pleats beneath its throat and belly. "When a whale turns its belly toward you," Gene had told us, "it's actually positioning itself so it can see you with both eyes." The calf spread its fins, took a breath of air, and began to swim horizontally, bobbing just below the surface. The mother started to rise, steady as a slow-moving barge.

They both inched toward me, side by side, and eyed us curiously. Soon their heads were just a few feet away. The calf wobbled in the sea surge, its fins spread like the wings of a fledging sparrow. Right behind it was the mother's long head. Her eye, big as an apple, was filled with steady confidence and warmth.

"Bury me here," I mused. "When I die, bring my ashes to a moment like this and scatter them."

My god! I've never thought that before! What's got me by the throat?

It was so clear it seemed silly that I hadn't seen it before. That unthinkable energy that I was at a loss to name?

It was power.

Unthinkably massive power married to ... kindness. Forty tons of constant, attentive, steadfast care.

"Mummy" could break our necks with a casual flick of one of her fins. Our boat, half her size, wouldn't survive a breach on top of it.

But what was she doing? Gently approaching, careful that her fins didn't hit anyone, and slowly, as if trying not to startle us. Soon she would migrate north, navigate threats of ship strikes and fishing-gear entanglement and orcas attacking her calf. Despite all the changes in the seas that we have wrought, she would guide her calf north. She would forge on ahead.

Eva swam up beside me. We held hands as the whales nudged even closer. I felt Eva's soft, tiny hand in mine. I wove my fingers into her small, squirmy fingers and squeezed.

Bring out the best in me, kiddo. Bring out the best in me.

The calf turned slowly, as if on a spindle, and eyed us playfully. The pleats on its belly were unscarred, like the porcelain skin of a newborn baby. The mother calmly looked on. Our search was over. They were finding us now.

It's night. It's not in the past anymore. It's now. I hear Charlie's breathing shift to a soft snore as he drifts off to sleep. Tomorrow we will leave this underwater oasis and cross back over that fourteen-thousand-foot trench. We'll pack our bags and depart for different parts of the world, Brazil and Britain and Canada and, Charlie and I, home to California.

Outside, white caps are breaking; the dark sea is lit by the stars. The wind dropped at sunset, but now it's building back up. The mother and calf we saw today are perhaps still resting, breaths punctuating their synchronous sea-sleep. At some point in the next few weeks, something will shift in the blood or pulse or in the mind or the heart of that mother whale, and she'll begin the long migration north with her calf.

Right now is my now, as I write these words. But it's also yours. As you read these words, neurologists have discovered, the same neural pathways are firing in your brain as if you were speaking them. The words sound out as you read them. If not for that, if not for knowing that these words would be sounded out in the minds of others, I would not have written this.

There's an aboriginal saying that a true gift cannot be kept unless one gives it away. I need to write like that, at the edge of my existence, as the poet Turner wrote, with "nothing to lose and everything to give away."[111] I need to give away the gift of this journey, so I can keep it alive in myself.

And the gist of that gift? This moment! This vital, alive now. *The one you're in.* That's the magic juice! Where everything you are, everything you have been, everything you can be, comes to bear.

I can't hear them now, but I know the whales are singing beneath us. And I'm singing too, my octave divided into twenty-six letters—the alphabet. I arrange and rearrange them, searching for the truest chords I can find. You know that "desert island" list? Which songs you'd bring with you if you could bring only one or two? Well, if I could sing one thing, just one, it'd be this: find someone or something to save. Be specific. Now's the time.

Epilogue

I paddled past the breakers and drifted. The water was calm. Lying down on my surfboard, I rested my head on my arms. It was a beautiful August day, just a few days shy of when, eighteen years before at this spot, the rogue wave had slammed into me.

It'd been a little over a year since Charlie and I'd swum with the whales. Kind of funny—after all that coming to terms with the state of the world, I felt, deep in my heart, happier. I knew what I needed to do. I knew how lucky I was to be able to write, to make choices, to contribute to the world. And for the first time in my life, *I felt that I truly belonged to this world.* I was home. I knew where I belonged.

A bottle cap floated in the water. I tucked it inside the neck of my wet suit. One bottle cap? What difference would that make? I knew now: to the albatross or sea lion or turtle that might swallow it, a monumental one.

Before I left the house, I posted a card to Elisabeth in Paris with a Marine Mammal Center certificate, adopting a sea lion, named Chippy, in her honor. "I owe you one," I wrote. "Lunch on me sometime soon."

Sometimes one truth is so glaring it overpowers others. The truth of how much is being devastated can overpower the truth of how much we can do, how much is possible.

Every morning when I get up, I know one thing for sure. I know the whole of which I am a part, an ever-growing movement to preserve the life of this earth. I'm not so much a writer as a voice, not so much journalist as a person who puts her skills in service of that bucket chain of efforts, that gathered newcomers daily like magnetic filings. It's driven by an elemental force: survival.

Two sea lions swam by and glided into the lagoon. Peter

was now at Emory University. His work with Ronan, he said, revealed that sea lions can bob their heads in synch to music, something that'd only been seen in humans and birds capable of vocal mimicry, such as parrots.[112] Ronan's favorite music, Peter said, was disco.

Eiglys and Amdeep had released all of the baby turtles. In all the photographs I saw, Eiglys wore sunglasses. I didn't doubt she choked back tears. Rikardo had just finished his first year of studies in Kyoto. Naima was in the Galápagos Islands, studying sea lions. Mauricio invited Charlie and me to visit him and Emelina. I'd visited with Dave, Suzanne, and Eva two months back. We reminisced about our time with the whales.

In a groundbreaking gesture, Indonesia banned the hunting of manta rays, creating the largest manta ray sanctuary in the world. Secretary of State John Kerry had just unveiled his Ocean Action Plan—end overfishing by 2020; reduce nutrient pollution 20 percent by 2025; reduce carbon emissions; get at least 10 percent of the ocean protected by 2020. US-AID pledged $170 million for capacity building in coastal nations.[113] Things still hung in the balance and the issues had grown even more urgent in a year's time. But awareness of these issues was also spreading, along with, importantly, more signs of political will to address them.

I rode a wave in. The salt water stung my eyes. All around me—like a glove that I fit inside—blazing, bright light. As evening came, I roamed the shore and filled a plastic bag with debris.

The sun went around the bend in the peninsula and the beach was draped in shadow. A line of golden light persisted at the horizon. I hesitated to leave. Finally I headed for my car. I turned around for one last look. *You can come back here anytime, anytime you need to be reminded how precious this is: every moment you're alive.*

When I got to the car, I reached for my phone.

Charlie answered.

"It's me," I said. "I'm headed home."

Resources

There many ways to make a difference—below are a few areas directly related to ocean conservation. A more extensive list is on my website, www.lizcunningham.net.

EATING SUSTAINABLE SEAFOOD

Support restaurants and retailers that sell sustainable seafood. Letting them know that you care about sustainable seafood encourages them to keep up the good work. There are a number of great organizations that post updated lists of which fish are the most sustainably harvested—the Safina Center, the Monterey Bay Aquarium Seafood Watch program, Fish Choice, NOAA's Fish Watch, Sea Choice, SeaWeb Europe, the Marine Stewardship Council.

LOWERING YOUR CARBON IMPRINT

The Carbon Fund offers tips for reducing your carbon imprint, including simple things like carpooling, driving the speed limit, insulating your home, eating less meat, reducing food waste, and buying local. To learn more and help efforts to mitigate climate change, check out 350.org, NextGen Climate and The Climate Reality Project. Project Drawdown is developing an open-source database and digital platform describing how one hundred solutions deployed at scale can alter the composition of our atmosphere and help forge a path toward temperature decline.

MAKING YOUR VOICE HEARD

As with most problems, silence isn't a solution, and political will is key to a sustainable future. Share what you have learned. Help others understand why ocean conservation is so important. Many conservation organizations offer email lists that you can subscribe to that will forward petitions for you to considering signing. Write your local and national legislators—let them know that you think ocean conservation should be a priority and that you support marine protected areas and clean-water legislation.

VOLUNTEERING

For many people, volunteering is a tremendously rewarding experience. Find an organization you feel passionate about. It could be a marine-mammal rescue center, a park or marine sanctuary, or a group that cleans up streams, reservoirs, or beaches. Volunteering for even a few days a year can make a big difference.

REDUCING YOUR PLASTIC USE

The Plastic Pollution Coalition has a list of steps you can take to reduce plastic use. A great start is carrying your own reusable containers—water bottles, shopping bags, and coffee mugs. Something as simple as using bar soap versus soap from a plastic container makes a difference.

SUPPORTING CONSERVATION ORGANIZATIONS

Many people feel at a loss as to which organizations are best to support. A good start is to find one focused on something you feel passionate about. If you want to "peek under the hood" of an organization you are considering giving money too, Charity Navigator and Guide Star score nonprofit organizations for their financial transparency and for how they spend the funds they raise—how much goes to actual services and how much to fundraising, marketing, salaries, and general overhead.

Notes

1. BEAUTY

1 State of New York, U.S. Department of Commerce, U.S. Department of the Interior, "PCB Contamination of the Hudson River Ecosystem, Compilation of Contamination Data through 2008: Hudson River Natural Resource Damage Assessment (January 2013)," 1. The Environmental Protection Agency reported that between 1947 and 1977, General Electric (GE) dumped an estimated 1.3 million pounds of polychlorinated biphenyls (PCBs) into the Hudson River. PCBs are highly toxic—even very small amounts are considered hazardous. The New York State water quality standard for protection of human consumers of fish is 0.001 parts per trillion, 1/1,000th of a drop of PCBs in one trillion (1,000,000,000,000) drops of water.

3. WATER GARDEN

2 David Biello, "The Origin of Oxygen in Earth's Atmosphere," *Scientific American,* August 19, 2009. Some of the oldest fossils of photosynthetic cyanobacteria are found in the Archaean Sea from the Precambrian Era. They date back 3.45 billion years. Early in the Precambrian Era, the atmosphere was a toxic mix of carbon dioxide, nitrogen, hydrogen, and ammonia. With the proliferation of photosynthetic organisms, oxygen levels rose, and the earth witnessed a proliferation of multicellular life, from forms of algae to the first animals. Sylvia A. Earle, *National Geographic Atlas of the Oceans: The Deep Frontier* (Washington, DC: National Geographic, 2001), 91–92. See also David H. Milne, *Marine Life and the Sea* (Independence, KY: Wadsworth, 1995), 135.

3 "Arrest Warrant Issued for Michael Misick," *The Jamaica Observer,* March 19, 2012.

4 "California Creates a Globally Significant Network of Marine Protected Areas," *California Department of Fish and Wildlife News,* April 15, 2013. California's network of MPAs increased greatly with the passage of the Marine Life Protection Act (MLPA) in 1999. Approximately 9.4 percent of California waters have "no-take" protection and about 16 percent are now under some form of protection (some 124 designated areas including 119 MPAs and five recreational management areas), a dramatic increase.

5 "Michael Misick: The King of Sleaze in the Colonies," *The Independent,* March 25, 2009.

6 Megan Gambino, "A Coral Reef's Mass Spawning: Understanding How Corals Reproduce Is Critical to Their Survival," *Smithsonian Magazine,* December 2009.

4. THE TRUTHS OF THE ISLANDS

7 National Oceanic and Atmospheric Administration, National Climate Data Center, *State of the Climate Global Analysis,* June 2012.

8 Lauretta Burke, Kathleen Reytar, Mark Spalding, and Allison Perry, *Reefs at Risk Revisited* (Washington, DC: World Resources Institute, 2011), 21.

9 Toby A. Gardner, Isabelle M. Côté, Jennifer A. Gill, Alastair Grant, and Andrew R. Watkinson, "Long-Term Region-Wide Declines in Caribbean Corals," *Science* 301, no. 5635 (August 15, 2003): 958–60. A massive region-wide decline of corals was documented across the entire Caribbean basin. Evidence showed the average hard coral cover on reefs had been reduced by 80 percent, from about 50 percent to 10 percent in three decades.

10 As quoted in Tim McKee, "A More Perfect Union: Tom Hayden on Democracy and Redemption," *The Sun,* January 1, 2006, http://thesunmagazine.org/issues/361/a_more_perfect_union.

11 "Endangered Green Turtle Shyvonne Starts Epic Migration," *FP Turks and Caicos,* September 30, 2010.

5. SECOND THOUGHTS

12 Ben Block, "Coral Reef Loss Suggests Global Extinction Event," World Watch Institute, 2014.

13 "A Framework for Action on Biodiversity & Ecosystem Management," Johannesburg: World Summit on Sustainable Development (WEHAB Working Group), August 2002, 7.

14 "Deforestation in Decline but Rate Remains Alarming, UN Agency Says," United Nations News Centre, March 25, 2010.

15 C. D. Thomas, A. Cameron, R. E. Green, M. Bakkenes, L. J. Beaumont, Y. C. Collingham, B. F. N. Erasmus, et al., "Extinction Risk from Climate Change," *Nature* 427 (2004): 145–48.

9. Home

16 Stewart L. Pimm, "Ecology," *Encyclopedia Britannica,* August 5, 2014.

17 Joe Rosato, Jr., "Bay Area Oysters Show Symptoms of Climate Change, Researchers Claim," *NBC Bay Area,* September 10, 2014.

18 Alex Loorz, "Kids Speak Out," Public Radio International (PRI) Environmental News Magazine, May 29, 2009.

19 Boris Worm, Edward B. Barbier, Nicola Beaumont, J. Emmett Duffy, Carl Folke, Benjamin S. Halpern, Jeremy B. C. Jackson, et al., "Impacts of Biodiversity Loss on Ocean Ecosystem Services," Science 314, no. 5800, (2006): 787–90.

20 Brian Cheng, John Largier, and Kelley Higgason, eds., *NOAA Climate Change Impacts: Gulf of the Farallones and Cordell Bank National Marine Sanctuaries* (Executive Summary), June 2010, 2. The study states that "the observed rise in sea level at the mouth of San Francisco Bay over the last century is 20 cm, and this rise is expected to continue. The State of California is using a projection of 40 cm rise in sea level by 2050 and 140 cm by 2100 for planning purposes. However, the most recent sea level rise analysis projects 75 to 190 cm respectively." Among other

things, this is expected to increase flooding, shoreline erosion, saltwater intrusion into groundwater aquifers. Beaches, sand dunes, intertidal habitats and marshlands will be dramatically affected. As an example, the report explains that habitat loss and fragmentation will result from sea level rise as beaches narrow and become steeper. Beaches that were once continuous habitats in front of coastal cliffs will become isolated pocket beaches.

Development adjacent to the San Francisco Bay, including two international airports, the ports of San Francisco and Oakland, a naval air station, freeways, housing developments, and a sports stadium, have been built on landfill only a few feet above the highest tides. The San Francisco International Airport will begin to flood with as little as 40 cm of sea-level rise, a value that could be reached by mid-century. See Committee on Sea Level Rise in California, Oregon, and Washington; Board on Earth Sciences and Resources; Ocean Studies Board; Division; on Earth and Life Studies; National Research Council, *Sea-Level Rise for the Coasts of California, Oregon, and Washington: Past, Present, and Future* (Washington, DC: National Academies Press, 2012), 24. This report states, "Even if storminess does not increase in the future, sea-level rise will magnify the adverse impact of storm surges and high waves on the coast. For example, a model using the committee's sea-level projections predicts that the incidence of extreme high water events (1.4 meters above historical mean sea level) in the San Francisco Bay area will increase substantially with sea-level rise, from less than 10 hours per decade today to a few hundred hours per decade by 2050 and to several thousand hours per decade by 2100."

21 John M. Broder, "Climate Change Seen as Threat to Security," *New York Times,* August 8, 2009.

7. THE LONGING

22 Richard Thompson, "Plastic Entanglements Increase for Marine Animals," *Ocean Health Index,* August 22, 2013. Thompson notes that the 40 percent increase in "fatal entanglement" by ingestion of marine debris by marine animals is documented in a Convention on Biological Report he coauthored with Sarah Gall and Duncan Bury. They reviewed 280 scientific papers, and over half of them documented this phenomenon, which impacted 46,000 individual animals, spanning 663 species. The ingestion of plastic debris, including microplastics, is of special concern, because it can provide a pathway for harmful chemicals to get into the food chain. Research has show that plastic particles smaller than 1mm are consumed by animals and entering the food chain. See Mark Anthony Brown, Phillip Crump, Stewart J. Niven, Emma Teuten, Andrew Tonkin, Tamara Galloway, and Richard Thompson, "Accumulation of Microplastic on Shorelines Worldwide: Sources and Sinks," *Environmental Science and Technology* 45, no. 21 (September 6, 2011): 9175–79.

23 Jalal al-Din Rumi, *The Essential Rumi,* new expanded ed., trans. Coleman Barks with John Moyne, A. J. Arberry, and Reynold Nicholson (New York: HarperOne, 2004), 253–54.

24 Kurt Hahn, "Outward Bound: Address at the Annual Meeting of the Outward Bound Trust," *KurtHahn.org Archives*, July 20, 1960, 11.

25 Rainer Maria Rilke, *Rilke's Book of Hours: Love Poems to God,* trans. Anita Barrows and Joanna Macy (New York: Riverhead Books, 2005), 119.

26 Jacob Darwin Hamblin, *Poison in the Well: Radioactive Waste in the Oceans at the Dawn of the Nuclear Age* (Piscataway, NJ: Rutgers University Press, 2008).

27 Audie Cornish and Geoffrey Brumfiel, "Fukushima Nuclear Plant Leaking 300 Tons of Tainted Water Daily," *National Public Radio,* August 8, 2013.

28 "Fukushima Radiation on B.C. Coast Measured by Crowdsourcing: Scientists from Woods Hole Oceanographic Institution Recruit 'Citizen Scientists' to Collect Data," *Canadian Broadcasting Corporation News,* February 26, 2014. Ken Buesseler, senior scientist, specializing in marine chemistry and geochemistry at the Woods Hole Oceanographic Institution, stated that there was little data and incomplete monitoring for radiation in the Pacific coastal waters by American and Canadian governments, despite urges to do so. He stated, "I think it's important to get measurements, and since the governments aren't doing it, we thought the public has a large concern and we'd ask them help collect and fund the sampling."

29 Joanna Macy and Chris Johnstone, *Active Hope: How to Face the Mess We're in without Going Crazy* (Novato, CA: New World Library, 2012) 2.

30 Joanna Macy, *Despair and Personal Power in the Nuclear Age* (Gabriola Island, BC: New Society Publishers, 1983), 17.

31 Joanna Macy, "The Greatest Danger," *Yes Magazine,* February 1, 2008.

32 Macy, *Despair and Personal Power in the Nuclear Age,* 18.

33 Macy and Johnstone, *Active Hope,* 39.

8. THE FAMILY TREE

34. Brian Switek, "Deep Diving Sea Lions Squeeze the Air Out," *Science,* September 18, 2012. A California sea lion fitted with a data logger demonstrated that sea lions collapse their lungs to withstand water pressures and endure deep dives. Scientists used the data logger to keep track of the partial pressure of oxygen in the sea lion's arterial bloodstream—a proxy to detect lung collapse—throughout forty-eight dives in August 2011, each lasting an average of six minutes and reaching more than three hundred meters deep. Sea lion's hearing in air is slightly worse than that of human beings at most frequencies. But underwater it's much better than ours. Sound loses less energy per unit of distance when traveling underwater than in air, so, due to their good hearing underwater, they can likely hear very loud sounds from miles away. But distance isn't a good measure for sound in general, as it all depends on frequency of sound and amplitude and density of medium, for instance, sound travels farther at sea level in air than on a mountain.

35 Peter Cook, personal correspondence. The adjustment of the pupil controls for light availability. But it's the changing of the shape of the lens over the pupil (accommodation), and general eye shape that primarily affects the eye's ability to focus. Sea lions have two adaptations for seeing in low-light conditions: really

wide pupil opening, and a *tapetum lucidum* (cats and dogs have them too, reflective layer of cells at back of retina). Their ability to see underwater, however, is different and not fully understood. In brief, they have unique adaptations to the structure of their eye that allow them to see in both mediums.

36 Paul S. Buckmaster, Xiling Wen, Izumi Toyoda, Frances M. D. Gulland, and William Van Bonn, "Hippocampal neuropathology of domoic acid-induced epilepsy in California Sea Lions *(Zalophus californianus),*" *Journal of Comparative Neurology Research in Systems Neuroscience* 522, no. 7 (2014): 1691–706.

37 To learn more about this research, see the following papers. William Van Bonn, S. Dennison, Peter Cook, and A. Fahlman, "Gas Bubble Disease in the Brain of a Living California Sea Lion *(Zalophus californianus),*" *Frontiers in Physiology* 5, no. 5 (2013). P. Cook, A. Bernard, and C. Reichmuth, "Which Way Did I Go? Remote Training of a Spatial Memory Task," *Soundings* 36, no. 2 (2011). P. Cook, C. Reichmuth, and F. Gulland, "Rapid Behavioral Diagnosis of Domoic Acid Toxicosis in California Sea Lions," *Biology Letters* 7, no. 4 (2011): 536–38.

38 Peter Cook, personal correspondence. This basic alternation task can be learned with or without hippocampal damage. In Cook's final data, which involved the study of thirty animals, brain damage had no effect whatsoever on how many sessions it took to learn the alternation task. The real test is called "delayed alternation"—in that version, the animal has to wait in the pool for seven to twenty seconds at the beginning of each trial. The idea is that, when running freely through the maze, the correct choice can be made without really thinking about it. It's like riding a bicycle or tying your shoe. The animal has learned a "motor pattern," that is, a sequence of movements that can be repeated ad nauseam. You don't need the hippocampus for this really basic type of learning. But you do need it to remember, explicitly, what you just did. So, put in the delay, break the "motor pattern," and now the animal has to rely on explicit memory to figure out which way it went last time so it can do the opposite now. Cook's primary analysis was a comparison of how well the animals did, at the end of training, with and without the delay, and how this related to extent of brain damage, which was obtained in vivo as part of their medical work up. The prediction being that more hippocampal damage means more impairment on delay relative to non-delay trials. In the context of DA, sea lions can probably learn to navigate their environment sufficiently, even with hippocampal damage. But they should be heavily impacted when they need to be flexible. They can learn habit, but they can't remember recent behavior that hasn't been repeated over and over. So if they found some fish by the pier yesterday, they don't remember that today. If they always find fish there, eventually they'll get in the habit of going there and do just fine.

39 The Humane Society of the United States, "Questions and Answers about Biomedical Research," September 16, 2013. This estimate is of the use of vertebrate animals used annually in research, testing, and education in the United States. No comprehensive figures are available for the United States or worldwide. However, the U.S. Department of Agriculture compiles some animal use statistics, which appear annually as the USDA Animal and Plant Health Inspection Service's *Annual Report of Animal Usage by Fiscal Year.*

40 Judith Reitman, "From the Leash to the Laboratory," *Atlantic Monthly*, July 2000. Reitman documents how some of the biggest money made by puppy-mill breeders is in dogs sold to medical-research labs. Reitman describes visiting a "Trade and Sale Day" in Missouri where dogs were crammed into "dog cabs"— crates crammed with six to eight dogs. Many of the dogs were ailing and emaciated. Reitman witnessed a dog dealer, registered by the U.S. Department of Agriculture, purchase dozens of dogs in this condition. She quotes Patricia Jensen, a former USDA assistant secretary who testified in 1996 that one of the most "egregious problems in research" is the "introduction of stolen and fraudulently acquired pets into the process."

9. DIVESTITURE

41 Jürgen Freund and Stella-Chiu Freund, *The Coral Triangle* (Jakarta, WWF-Indonesia, 2011), 217.
42 World Conservation Monitoring Centre of the United Nations Environment Programme (UNEP-WCMC), 2004. Species Data (unpublished, September 2004). This ranking is based on the total number of amphibian, bird, mammal, reptile, and vascular plant species by country.
43 Campaign for Poverty Reduction Indonesia, "Water and Sanitation," April 2014. More than 70 percent of Indonesia's 240 million citizens rely on water from sources severely polluted by sewage, industrial effluent, and agricultural runoff. Few Indonesian cities possess waste-management systems. Many households rely on private septic tanks, which send waste into rivers and canals. There are over one hundred thousand infant deaths in Indonesia from cholera, dysentery, and typhoid per year. One hundred and twenty million people in Indonesia live on the equivalent of $1 or $2 a day.
44 United Nations Children Fund (UNICEF), "The State of the World's Children: 2014 in Numbers," January 2014, 18.

10. HEART

45 "Slaughter for the Marketplace: Huge Rise in Ray Hunting Threatens Ocean's 'Gentle Giants,' " *Daily Mail Online*, March 8, 2011.
46 Patricia Daniels, *Body: The Complete Human* (Washington, DC: National Geographic Books, 2007), 126.
47 Neil Lineback and Mandy Lineback Grizner. "Geography in the News: World Fisheries," *National Geographic NewsWatch,* July 28, 2013.
48 Sea Sanctuaries entered into a marine conservation agreement (MCA) with the local villagers rather than an MPA (marine protected area). There is a material difference between MCAs and MPAs: the former are private agreements between an NGO (such as Sea Sanctuaries) and the local community (which is supported by local government). Sea Sanctuaries spent more than a year "socializing" the idea of a marine conservation project before gaining the community's trust and agreement, which was then formalized in a written contract. Marine protected ar-

eas, on the other hand, are controlled and managed by the government along with the local communities. Sea Sanctuaries did not lease the no-take zones. The MCA just gave Sea Sanctuaries the right to undertake conservation work with the local community for twenty-five years. Sea Sanctuaries does not own or lease any land or ocean. That remains in the ownership of individuals and the local communities. (Simon Day, personal correspondence.)

49 Camilo Mora and Peter F. Sale, "Ongoing Global Biodiversity Loss and the Need to Move beyond Protected Areas: A Review of the Technical and Practical Shortcomings of Protected Areas on Land and Sea," *Marine Ecology Progress Series* 434 (2011): 251–66.

50 International Union for Conservation of Nature, "World Nearing 3% of Ocean Protection," October 24, 2013.

51 William D. Robbins, Mizue Hisano, Sean R. Connolly, and J. Howard Choat, "Ongoing Collapse of Coral-Reef Shark Populations," *Current Biology* 16, no. 23 (2006): 1–2.

52 Gerald R. Allen and Roger Steene, *Indo-Pacific Coral Reef Field Guide* (Singapore: Tropical Reef Research, 1996), 351.

53 Smithsonian Ocean Portal, reviewed by Nancy Knowlton, "Coral and Coral Reefs," Smithsonian National Museum of Natural History, September 2014. Coral reefs cover less than 1 percent of the earth's surface and less than 2 percent of the ocean bottom. But because they are so diverse, they are extremely productive. The article notes that the "value of coral reefs has been estimated at 30 billion U.S. dollars and perhaps as much as 172 billion U.S. dollars each year, providing food, protection of shorelines, jobs based on tourism, and even medicines."

54 E. Chivian and A. Bernstein, eds., *Sustaining Life: How Human Health Depends on Biodiversity* (New York: Oxford University Press, 2008), 129.

11. THE RIVER

55 Elizabeth Brundige, Winter King, Priyneha Vahali, Stephen Vladeck, and Xiang Yuan, "Indonesian Human Rights Abuses in West Papua: Application of the Law of Genocide to the History of Indonesian Control," (Allard K. Lowenstein International Human Rights Clinic, Yale Law School, 2004), 3–8. The list of documented abuses include arbitrary and mass detention, torture by electric shock, beatings, whipping, water torture, cigarette burns, confinement in steel containers for months on end, forced relocation and often uncompensated labor, mutilation, and acts of rape and sexual violence. The paper is a detailed examination as to whether Indonesia's conduct toward the people of West Papua constitutes genocide as defined by the 1948 Convention on the Prevention of the Crime of Genocide (the Genocide Convention). It studies policies and practices of the Indonesian government and military in West Papua through extensive reviews of primary and secondary factual sources and consultation with Papuan, Indonesian, and international human-rights experts. It states that "according to current understandings of the Genocide Convention, the pattern of acts and omissions documented by this paper supports the conclusion that the Indonesian government

has acted with the necessary intent to find that it has perpetrated genocide against the people of West Papua."

56 Ehito Kimura, *Political Change and Territoriality in Indonesia: Provincial Proliferation* (London: Routledge, 2012), 147. Papua has approximately 41.5 million hectares of forest, so the 27.6 million hectares classified as "production forest" is well over one half of all of Papua's forests.

57 Environmental Investigation Agency, "The Last Frontier: Illegal Logging in Papua and China's Massive Timber Theft," February 2005, 1–2. Papua contains some of the last virgin forest in Asia, which has lost 95 percent of its frontier forests. This trade benefits the people of Papua little. The report states, "Local communities in Papua are paid around $11 USD per cubic meter for merbau logs which are worth around $240 USD at the point of import in China." Illegally logged lumber moves via middlemen through Jakarta, Malaysia, Singapore, and Hong Kong. Indonesia is home to the worst deforestation rates in the world. Enforcement efforts have not been sufficient in stemming the tide. A Conservation International (CI) study concluded that the Papuan police interdicted only 3 percent of vessels carrying illegally logged lumber. The Environmental Investigation Agency recommends the following to counter illegal logging (along with a wide array of other recommendations): enact laws banning the import and sale of illegally logged timber and wood products in consuming countries; bilateral agreements, including the formation of a task force to counter illegal logging; make Papua a priority for enforcement; launch high-level enquiries into identifying timber barons and prosecuting key timber barons and officials involved in illegal logging; offer technical assistance for reforestation efforts; encourage the timber processing industry to pursue certification systems similar to the Forest Stewardship Council; and encourage consumers to purchase only timber and wood products certified as legally and sustainably sourced.

58 Diane Parker, "Former Cop to Face Charges in Illegal Logging Scandal, Indonesia Police Say," *Mongabay.com,* July 30, 2013. See also Yuliasri Perdani and Nethy Dharma Somba, "Papua Police Hand Over Labora Sitorus' Dossier to Prosecutors," *Jakarta Post,* July 26, 2013. Perdani and Somba report, "The Papuan Police have handed over the dossier on Chief Brig. Labora Sitorus to the Papua Prosecutors' office for processing. Labora has been accused of engaging in illegal logging, money laundering and fuel smuggling. The Labora Sitorus' case originated from his financial report first released by the Financial Transaction Reports and Analysis Center (PPATK). PPATK had spotted accumulative financial transactions totaling more than Rp 1.5 trillion (US$146 million), not in keeping with Labora's role as a police officer."

59 Forests Monitor, "Environmental Impact of Logging," 2012. See also D. Lamb, *Exploiting the Tropical Rain Forest: An Account of Pulpwood Logging in Papua New Guinea* (Nashville, TN: Parthenon, 1990). Lamb's study contains some of the central findings from the fifteen-year UNESCO "Man and the Biosphere" research program, which was supported by scientists from over one hundred nations.

60 Jane Perlez and Raymond Bonner, "Below a Mountain of Wealth, a River of Waste," *New York Times,* December 27, 2005.

61 Craig Vogt, "International Assessment of Marine and Riverine Disposal of Mine Tailings" (United Nations Environment Programme/London Protocol International Maritime Organization, November 30, 2012), 14. The report also documents the effect of this on the rainforest. "In the Ajkwa River downstream of the Grasberg mine, 130 square kilometers of new flood plain had been created by 2002 and it is expected to increase to 220 square kilometers before the targeted time for mine closure. This resulted in dieback and a long term problem of acid rock drainage. In 2002, the mine at Ok Tedi was reported to have caused dieback from riverine disposal of mine tailings impacting approximately 480 square kilometers of rainforest."

62 Perlez and Bonner, "Below a Mountain of Wealth, a River of Waste."

63 "Indonesia: Papuan Copper Miners End Freeport Strike," *BBC News,* July 13, 2012.

64 Linda Hunter, "Pollution Leads to Greater Number of Dead Zones," *Upwelling: The Newsletter of the Farallones Marine Sanctuary Association,* October 2006. Hunter states that "the number of 'dead zones' in the world's oceans may have increased by a third in just two years, threatening fish stocks and the people who depend on them, according to a report released by the United Nations. Fertilizers, sewage, fossil fuel burning and other pollutants have led to a doubling in the number of oxygen-deficient coastal areas every decade since the 1960s. Scientists have found 200 'dead zones' in the world's oceans." The steps that need to be taken to prevent and repair dead zones are reducing nutrient runoff, improving water quality, and restoring natural ecosystems, such as watersheds. Hunter quotes the United Nations Undersecretary-General, Achim Steiner, who states, "An estimated 80% of marine pollution originates from the land. And this could rise significantly by 2050 if, as expected, coastal populations double in just over 40 years time and action to combat pollution is not accelerated."

65 Doug Moss and Roddy Scheer, "What Causes Oceanic 'Dead Zones'?" *Scientific American EarthTalk,* September 25, 2012.

66 "The 2012 Chesapeake Bay Summer Dead Zone," Maryland Department of Natural Resources, 1. The Maryland Department of Natural Resources offers a "Citizen Guide to Restoring the Bay: What Every Resident Can Do," with specific steps for developers, farmers, and homeowners.

67 World Resources Institute, "Global Forest Watch Project," March 6, 2014. See also "Deforestation in Decline but Rate Remains Alarming, UN Agency Says," United Nations News Centre, March 25, 2010.

13. IT'S TIME

68 Alexandra Di Stefano Pironti, "Jakarta's Rich Get Richer and Poor Get Poorer," *Jakarta Globe,* July 4, 2012.

69 Rosamond L. Naylor, David S. Battisti, Walter P. Falcon, Marshall Burke, and Daniel Vimont, "Assessing Risks of Climate Variability and Climate Change for Indonesian Rice Agriculture," *Proceedings of the National Academy of Sciences (PNAS)* 104 (May 8, 2007): 7752–57. See also Marshall Burke, Program on Food

Security and the Environment, "Climate Change a Threat to Indonesian Agriculture, Study Says," *Stanford University News Service,* May 1, 2007. The findings of *Proceedings of the National Academy of Sciences (PNAS)* study show that Indonesian rice agriculture is greatly affected by short-run climate variability and could be significantly harmed by long-run climate change. Indonesia is the fourth most populous country in the world, one of the largest producers and consumers of rice. The rural poor depend on rice agriculture for their livelihood. "Agriculture is central to human survival, and is probably the human enterprise most vulnerable to changes in climate," notes lead author Rosamond Naylor, director of the Program on Food Security and the Environment at Stanford. She adds, "This is particularly true in countries such as Indonesia, with large populations of rural poor." David Battisti, coauthor and atmospheric scientist at the University of Washington, says, "Most models predict that the rains will come later in Indonesia, it will rain a little harder once the monsoon begins, and then it will really dry up during the summer months. So Indonesia could be looking at a much shorter rainy season, with an almost rainless dry season in some areas, squeezing rice farmers on both ends." See also Rosamond L. Naylor, *The Evolving Sphere of Food Security* (New York: Oxford University Press, 2014).

70   Charles Clover, *The End of the Line: How Overfishing Is Changing the World and What We Eat.* (Berkeley: University of California Press, 2008), 282.

71   Ed Davies, "Indonesia Counts Its Islands Before It's Too Late." Reuters, May 16, 2007. Indonesia is an archipelago nation. Its territory contains so many islands that for many years there was no exact count. In 2012, Indonesia submitted an exact "island count" to the United Nations—13,466 coral and volcanic islands spattered across the equator, including Sulawesi and West Papua, the western half of New Guinea. Before that official survey, over half of islands were uninhabited and unnamed. Alex Retraubun, the leader of the survey, states, "with the majority of small islands in the country only one meter above sea level, there was little Indonesia could do if sea levels rose dramatically." Indonesia's environment minister Rachmat Witoelar said, "the country could lose about two thousand islands if sea levels continued to rise."

72   A 2012 World Bank report projects sea-level rises of around 110 centimeters (1.2 yards) by 2080–2100. Because South Asian coastlines are closer to the equator, sea-level rise is generally 10–15 percent higher than the global mean. See Hans Joachim Schellnhuber, et al., *Turn Down the Heat: Climate Extremes, Regional Impacts, and the Case for Resilience—Full Report* (Washington DC: World Bank, 2012), 77. Peer-reviewed scientific studies around the world echo the same findings. WWF and the University of Queensland published report presents somber findings and warns that immediate action needs to be taken: "In one world, based on the Intergovernmental Panel on Climate Change (IPCC) A1B scenario, our attempts to stabilize the Earth's climate fail, as does our resolve to deal with the multitude of local threats to the coastal ecosystems in the Coral Triangle. In this world, temperatures soar and the current rich coral reef and mangrove ecosystems disappear, with huge impacts on food security, human survival and regional security. This is a world that we must avoid at all costs. In the other world, based

on a modified version of the B1 scenario of the IPCC, the international community takes decisive and effective action, which rapidly reduces greenhouse gas emissions, and resolves to assist countries like the Coral Triangle nations develop effective solutions to the growing problems they face. These actions, while not without challenges, limit the impacts of the changing climate and maximize the resilience of biological, ecological and socioeconomic systems to those climate change impacts that are currently unavoidable. This is a world in which the poorest people are not abandoned to the impacts caused by the developed world." *The Coral Triangle and Climate Change: Ecosystems, People and Societies at Risk, A Comprehensive Study Involving Over 20 Experts and Based on 300 Peer-Reviewed Scientific Articles* (Sydney: WWF Australian and The University of Queensland, 2010), 4. See also Lauretta Burke, Kathleen Reytar, Mark Spalding, and Allison Perry, *Reefs at Risk Revisited* (Washington DC: The World Resources Institute, 2011), 21. An additional report by the same authors focuses on the Coral Triangle. See Lauretta Burke, Kathleen Reytar, Mark Spalding, and Allison Perry, *Reefs at Risk Revisited* (Washington DC: The World Resources Institute, 2012).

73 Simon Busch, "And the World's Most Polluted City Is...." *CNN Travel*, January 13, 2014.

74 *The Coral Triangle and Climate Change: Ecosystems, People and Societies at Risk, A Comprehensive Study Involving Over 20 Experts and Based on 300 Peer-Reviewed Scientific Articles* (Sydney: WWF Australian and The University of Queensland, 2010), 3.

14. ULAR LAUT

75 Ellen MacArthur Foundation, *The Circular Model—An Overview,* 2014.

76 Ellen MacArthur Foundation, *The Circular Model—An Overview.* An example of this is that in 2014 the European Commission adopted a communication outlining a plan to establish a common and coherent EU framework to promote the circular economy. Turning Europe into a more circular economy is listed as meaning: boosting recycling and preventing the loss of valuable materials; creating jobs and economic growth; showing how new business models, eco-design, and industrial symbiosis can move us toward zero-waste; and reducing greenhouse emissions and environmental impacts. As part of the circular economy package, the commission adopted a legislative proposal to review recycling and other waste-related targets in the European Union and annex. Achieving the new waste targets would create 180,000 new jobs, while making Europe more competitive and reducing demand for costly scarce resources. See European Commission, *Towards a Circular Economy: A Zero Waste Programme for Europe, Communication from the Commission to the European Parliament, the Council, the European Economic and Social Committee and the Committee of the Regions* (Brussels, February 7, 2014).

77 Mark Best and Duncan Neuhauser, "Ignaz Semmelweis and the Birth of Infection Control," *BMJ Quality & Safety: The International Journal of Health Care Improvement* 13, no. 3 (2004): 233–34.

78 Jeff Smith, "Low-Cost Solar Brightens Lives in the Developing World," Nation-

al Geographic News, June 6, 2012. Low-cost solar power can have wide-reaching impacts. Smith recounts how a family's life in Uganda was profoundly changed—they prospered by selling more eggs, because the chickens lay more eggs when they have more light. Because of that, over time they bought a cow, a goat, and a pig. They even started a school and women's literacy club. Efforts to bring more low-cost solar power to developing world communities are growing. The Scandinavian furnishing company IKEA has partnered with UNICEF and Save the Children to bring solar power to children in India and Pakistan; the International Organization for Migration provided thousands of solar lamps to people displaced by the 2010 earthquake in Haiti; a Philippines organization called Isang Litrong Liwanag (A Liter of Light) helped install more than thirty thousand solar "bottle bulbs" in poor areas. Students at MIT created the design for the "bottle bulb," which was pioneered by Alfredo Moser, a Brazilian mechanic who was looking for a way to light his workshop.

15. THE ISLAND

79 Jean-Michel Cousteau with Daniel Paisner, *My Father, The Captain: My Life with Jacques Cousteau* (Washington DC: National Geographic Society, 2010), 29.

80 Susan W. Fair, *Alaska Native Art: Tradition, Innovation and Continuity* (Fairbanks: University of Alaska Press, 2007), 63–64. Fair describes that Asiatic Native peoples used whalebone ribs for architectural framing and public monuments with mythic associations, such as the marking of a shaman's grave site. Whalebones were used among traditional structures of the Yu'pik and Inupiaq peoples on the Bering Strait. "Whales and other sea mammals," Fair writes, "are treated with deep respect by northern villages. A single large whale, shared in a specific ritual manner, can provide food for an entire village for several months."

81 Janine M. Benyus, "Recognizing What Works: A Conscious Emulation of Life's Genius," in Stephan A. Goldsmith, Lynne Elizabeth, and Arlene Goldbard, *What We See: Advancing the Observations of Jane Jacobs* (Oakland, CA: New Village Press, 2010), 195–196. Benyus writes that she realized that "biology's technological feats were best kept secrets outside of specialized journals," how organisms "match and make their places," such as leaves that tilt toward the sun, sperm whales that change the density of their oil to dive deep, and flowers that avoid too much UV light through fiber-optic leaf hairs. See also Janine M. Benyus, *Biomimicry: Innovation Inspired by Nature* (New York: HarperPerennial, 2002), 195–96.

82 Ellen MacArthur Foundation, *The Circular Model—An Overview.*

83 Lisa M. Krieger, "A Cut Above: The Stone that Built Paris also Building Stanford," *San Jose Mercury News,* October 24, 2010. Much of Notre Dame is built from Lutetian limestone, from quarries beneath Paris. Close examination of the limestone with reveal coquillages—traces of shellfish fossils from coral reefs that populated the sea that filled the Paris Basin forty-five million years ago. Lutetian limestone is known for its resistance to erosion—enduring for centuries—and that it can be cut into very precise sections. It is known as "the stone that built Paris."

84 Elaine Sciolino, "Heroic Tale of Holocaust, with a Twist," *New York Times,* October 3, 2011. There were many North African Sephardic Jews in France during the 1940s, who spoke Arabic and shared daily traditions and habits with Arabs, such as circumcision and abstaining from eating pork. The rector of the Grand Mosque of Paris, Si Kaddour Benghabrit, provided refuge and certificates of Muslim identity to a small number of Jews to allow them to evade arrest and deportation. See also Robert Satloff's *Among the Righteous: Lost Stories from the Holocaust's Long Reach into Arab Lands* (New York: Perseus, 2006).

85 Edward Rolf Tufte, *Beautiful Evidence* (Cheshire, CT: Graphics Press, 2006), 9

86 Tufte, *Beautiful Evidence,* 9.

16. PLUS SIGNS

87 Elisabeth Vallet, personal correspondence. SeaWeb Europe is entirely dedicated to marine conservation and in particular sustainable seafood. Created in 2006, SeaWeb Europe has seen the need to inform seafood buyers about the sustainability of the species they buy, and the necessity of creating a new type of collaboration with and between stakeholders. SeaWeb Europe does this by creating opportunities for dialogue amongst stakeholders, helping them to develop sustainable practices and promoting their engagement in seafood sustainability. SeaWeb Europe works with the whole seafood supply chain, from fishermen and fish farmers to suppliers, fishmongers and chefs, as they all have a key role to play in sustainability through the species that they choose for their clients. They can initiate changes in the supply chain for more sustainability. SeaWeb Europe informs buyers about the sustainability of the species based on scientific data and creates opportunities for meetings and exchanges of experiences around these issues; they also help the buyers to develop sustainable practices and their own seafood policy. They work with future generations of chefs and fishmongers in catering schools and training centers to inform them of these issues, so that they are able to take them into consideration as soon as they have their own fish shop or restaurant.

88 United Nations Food and Agriculture Organization (FAO), *World Review of Fisheries and Agriculture (SOFIA) 2010,* 8–9. According to this report 53 percent of the world's fisheries are fully exploited, and 32 percent are overexploited, depleted, or recovering from depletion. "In 2008, 39.7 percent (56.5 million tonnes) of total world fish production was marketed as fresh, while 41.2 percent (58.6 million tonnes) of fish was frozen, cured or otherwise prepared for direct human consumption." The top ten marine fisheries, which account for about 30 percent of all capture fisheries production, are fully exploited or overexploited. Unless the current situation improves, stocks of all species currently fished for food are predicted to collapse by 2048. See also Boris Worm, Edward B. Barbier, Nicola Beaumont, J. Emmett Duffy, Carl Folke, Benjamin S. Halpern, Jeremy B. C. Jackson, et al., "Impacts of Biodiversity Loss on Ocean Ecosystem Services," Science 314, no. 5800, (2006): 790.

89 Sophie Laggan, "Mediterranean Fish Stocks at Point of Collapse," World Research and Innovation Congress Oceans, 2014. The European Commission re-

leased its findings for 2015 at the Congress. "In a stark warning, the EC draws attention to the 'dismal picture' of Mediterranean fish stocks, noting that 96% or more of bottom-dwelling fish are overfished and 71% of middle-water stocks, such as anchovy and sardines, have been brought to the brink of extinction. And the Black Sea has not fared any better, seeing 33% of pelagic stocks and all of its bottom-living fish overexploited. European Commissioner for Maritime Affairs and Fisheries, Maria Damanaki, echoed this concern: 'The time of denial is over,' she exclaimed. 'The Mediterranean Sea is heavily overfished.' To overcome the uphill struggle, Damanaki prescribes more research and the adoption of regional fishing plans to secure sustainable extraction."

90 "U.S. Could Feed 800 Million People with Grain that Livestock Eat, Cornell Ecologist Advises Animal Scientists," *Cornell Chronicle,* August 1997. Professor David Pimentel, of Cornell University's College of Agriculture and Life Sciences, reported at the 1997 meeting of the Canadian Society of Animal Science that "If all the grain currently fed to livestock in the United States were consumed directly by people, the number of people who could be fed would be nearly 800 million." Tracking food-animal production from the feed trough to the dinner table, Pimentel found broiler chickens to be the most efficient use of fossil energy, and beef, the least. Chicken meat production consumes energy in a 4:1 ratio to protein output; beef-cattle production requires an energy input to protein–output ratio of 54:1. See also David Pimentel and Marcia Pimentel, "Sustainability of Meat-Based and Plant-Based Diets and the Environment," *American Journal of Clinical Nutrition* 78, no. 3 (September 2003): 660–61.

91 CBC Digital Archives, "Cod Fishing: 'The Biggest Layoff in Canadian History' " Canadian Broadcasting Corporation, 1992. For over five hundred years, cod was the king of global fisheries, but when it collapsed, it was deemed the largest layoff in Canadian history. Charles Clover documents how the "Grand Banks disaster" was an example of a failure to be truly open with the public about fisheries data. "Positive news makes people happy. Bad news is not always appreciated." Charles Clover, *The End of the Line: How Overfishing Is Changing the World and What We Eat* (Berkeley: University of California Press, 2008), 115.

92 As of 2013, Atlantic and Mediterranean bluefin tuna stocks had been hunted nearly to the point of extinction. Bluefin stocks in the Pacific were in slightly better shape, but still severely endangered. The best reference on the status of Atlantic bluefin is updated and published yearly. For 2014, see the ICCAT Executive Summary for Atlantic Bluefin Tuna (*8.5 BFT—Atlantic Bluefin Tuna*). ICATT refers to the International Commission for the Conservation of Atlantic Tunas, which is an intergovernmental fishery organization responsible for the conservation of tunas and tuna-like species in the Atlantic Ocean and its adjacent seas. For Pacific Bluefin, see the International Scientific Committee for Tuna and Tuna-like Species in the North Pacific Ocean's report of the Pacific Bluefin Tuna Working Group (PBFWG). See also International Scientific Committee for Tuna and Tuna-Like Species in the North Pacific Ocean, *Stock Assessment of Pacific Bluefin Tuna,* 2014. An example of the power of the "sum of cumulative efforts" to save bluefin is well described by Carl Safina in "Bluefin Tuna Finally Catch a Break,"

National Geographic NewsWatch, October 7, 2014. Safina documents the National Marine Fisheries Service (NMFS) prohibition on longlining in bluefin-tuna spawning grounds in the Gulf of Mexico and that this was "hard-fought victory borne out over decades." Safina describes how the importance of these spawning areas were first documented by Stanford University's Barbara Block, who caught and tagged spawning bluefin, providing scientists with data about migration and spawning patterns. The organizations that joined in Block's effort were Earthjustice, the Blue Ocean Institute (now the Safina Center), the Natural Resources Defense Council (NRDC), Oceana, and the Pew Charitable Trusts. Safina states, "Spawning bluefin tuna will still be vulnerable to Gulf longlines. The new gear restricted areas cover two months and two hotspots, but bluefin spawn throughout the northern Gulf for six months of the year. Even so, when bluefin tuna gather in the Gulf of Mexico to spawn in 2015, there will finally be a safe haven waiting for them, making decades of work well worth the effort."

93 Martin Hickman, "Revealed: The Bid to Corner World's Bluefin Tuna Market," *Independent,* June 3, 2009. Hickman describes how the corporate conglomerate Mitsubishi had a 40 percent share of the global bluefin market and was importing thousands of tones of bluefin, despite populations plummeting toward extinction. Hickman draws attention to Mitsubishi's calculation in freezing bluefin was that it "could be sold in several years' time for astronomical sums if Atlantic bluefin becomes commercially extinct as forecast." In the documentary *The End of the Line,* inspired by Charles Clover's book, Roberto Mielgo, a former bluefin fishermen who now researches the industry, claims that Mitsubishi buys and sells 60 percent of the bluefin market and has expanded its freezer capacity to hold extra fish. Mitsubishi responded to that claim that it handled "only between 35–40% of the Atlantic and Mediterranean bluefin imported to Japan."

94 ICCAT Executive Summary for Atlantic Bluefin Tuna (*8.5 BFT—Atlantic Bluefin Tuna 2014*). "What is said about incipient recovery holds for the East Atlantic and Mediterranean stock of bluefin, the most important one" (Sergi Tudela, personal correspondence).

95 Google Hangout celebrating Jane Goodall's eightieth birthday, April 3, 2014.

17. THE RING IN THE FISH

96 Simon Jennings, Michael J. Kaiser, and John D. Reynolds, *Marine Fisheries Ecology* (Oxford: Blackwell Science, 2001), 297.

97 The needed derogations to the current law need to be justified by a scientific study in order to ensure that there is no negative impact to other species and habitats (Susana Sainz-Trápaga, personal correspondence).

98 Ivor Clucas, "Discards and Bycatch in Shrimp Trawl Fisheries," United Nations Food and Agriculture Organization *Fisheries Circular,* (928 FIIU/C928), 1997.

18. LA SEMILLA

99 Luís Trias Martín explained that they used to get food and other things without paying for them, and once they had the money, they paid for them. The Spanish word for this practice is *fiar*, which is different from *borrow*. It is the case of the owner of a shop who knows you giving you something because he or she trusts that as soon as you have the money, you will pay for it (Susana Sainz-Trápaga, personal correspondence).

100 *Cofradias* are still in place and manage fisheries within its competence area in addition to the general national and European Union rules (Susana Sainz-Trápaga, personal correspondence).

101 The system was like it is today, but from shore, and the role of the machine was done by the people pulling the net out of the water. At that time, the sandeel was used as bait for longlines on hooks (Susana Sainz-Trápaga, personal correspondence).

102 Jordi Lleonart, Montserrat Demestre, Paloma Martín, Jordi Rodón, Susana Sainz-Trápaga, Pilar Sánchez, Itziar Segarra, and Sergi Tudela, "The Co-Management of the Sand Eel Fishery of Catalonia (NW Mediterranean): The Story of a Process," *Scientia Marina* 78 (2014). This paper details how the management plan for the boat seines, called *sonsera*, used in Catalonia to target sand eels *(Gymanammodytes cicerelus* and *G. semisquamatus)* and transparent gobies was drawn up in accordance with European Union rules. A Sand Eel Co-Management Committee was formally created with the specific mission of ensuring a sustainable fishery. The committee is composed of public administrations, fishermen's associations, researchers, and NGOs. The process has two phases: first, a comprehensive study of the fishery and subsequent advice for the establishment of a management plan, and second, the implementation and monitoring of the management plan. The study of the fishery included the analysis of the ecosystem impacts of the fishery (mainly stock status, impact on sensitive habitats, and by-catch) and was carried out in the wider context of an adaptive co-management process to respond to the requirements of an ecosystem approach to fisheries. See also S. Sainz-Trápaga, R. Allue, M. Demestre, J. L. Guarga, J. Lleonart, P. Martín, C. Ojeda, J. M. Pulido, J. Rodon, P. Sánchez, I. Segarra, L. I. Trias, S. Tudela, and Borja Velasco, "The Co-management Committee of the Catalan Sand-Eel Fishery: A Bottom-Up Approach Successfully Delivering on Sustainability for Fish and Fishing Catalan Sand-Eel Fishery Co-management Committee," delivered at the First Regional Symposium on Sustainable Small-Scale Fisheries in the Mediterranean and Black Sea: Malta, November 2013.

19. THOUSANDS OF SELVES

103 Olivier Schlama, "Un forage pour percer les secrets du Golf du Lion," *Midi Libre*, 2014.

104 Steven A. Berkeley, "Pacific Rockfish Management: Are We Circling the Wagons around the Wrong Paradigm," *Bulletin of Marine Science* 78 (2006): 665–68. "West Coast rockfishes are managed with traditional fishing-mortality and spawn-

ing stock biomass-based control rules, the objectives of which are to maintain a specific biomass of mature females, regardless of their size or age. The implicit assumption is that larvae produced by all females are equivalent in their probability of survival, but recent research on black rockfish indicates that larvae of older mothers are far more likely to survive than those of younger females. Using a simple deterministic equilibrium model that incorporates the influence of maternal age on larval survival, I compared population age structure, fishery yield, effective larval output, and recruitment for four different management strategies: status quo, slot limit, marine reserves, and reduced fishing mortality. Results of these simulations indicate that a 35 percent reduction in fishing mortality would achieve increases in effective larval output and yield comparable to a 20 percent marine reserve option. If recruitment is proportional to effective larval output, a 20 percent marine reserve would increase yield at equilibrium by 9 percent relative to the status quo. These results suggest that managing for age structure can increase both resilience and yield." See also Steven A. Berkeley, Colin Chapman, and Susan M. Sogard, "Maternal Age as a Determinant of Larval Growth and Survival in a Marine Fish, *Sebastes Melanops*," Publications, Agencies and Staff of the U.S. Department of Commerce, Paper no. 429, 2004.

105 Seagrass are flowering saltwater plants. Their meadows are so large in places that that astronauts can see them from outer space. A "productive seagrass meadow will fizz with oxygen bubbles, looking like champagne." Seagrass Watch, *Seagrass Recovery Newsletter,* October 2008, p. 1. Seagrass have gas-filled tissues called aerenchyme. "Daytime photosynthesis charges aerenchyme with a high gas pressure. Sometimes during the day seagrass beds can be heard sizzling as oxygen bubbles are released from the surface of the blade." George Karleskint, Richard Turner and James Small, *Introduction to Marine Biology,* (Boston: Cengage Learning, 2012), p. 174.

106 A. Peirano, C. Nike Bianchi, D. Savini, and G. Farina, "A Long-Term Monitoring Activity on a *Posidonia oceanica* Meadow at Monterosso al Mare (Ligurian Sea)." *Archo Oceanogr. Limnol. Istituto di Biologia del Mare* 22 (2001): 145–48.

107 Sylvia A. Earle, "My Wish: Protect Our Oceans," transcript of the TED Conference talk given in February of 2009.

108 Paul Hawken, *Blessed Unrest* (New York: Penguin Books, 2007), 3.

109 Paul Ray and Sherry Ruth Anderson, *The Cultural Creatives: How 50 Million People Are Changing the World* (New York: Harmony Books, 2000), 44.

110 Hawken, *Blessed Unrest,* 3.

23. SONG

111 Frederick Turner, *Beauty: The Value of Values* (Charlottesville: University of Virginia Press, 1991), 6.

EPILOGUE

112 P. Cook, A. Rouse, M. Wilson, and C. Reichmuth, "A California Sea Lion *(Zalophus californianus)* Can Keep the Beat: Motor Entrainment to Rhythmic Au-

ditory Stimuli in a Non-Vocal Mimic," *Journal of Comparative Psychology,* American Psychological Association, 2013.

113 U.S. Department of State, "Our Ocean Action Plan," Washington, DC, June 17, 2014.

Selected Bibliography

Abrams, David. *The Spell of the Sensuous.* New York: Vintage Books, 1996.

Allen, Gerald R., and Roger Steene. *Indo-Pacific Coral Reef Field Guide.* Singapore: Tropical Reef Research, 1996.

Augier, Henry. *Guide des fonds marins de Méditerranée: Ecologie, flore, faune, plongées.* Paris: Delachaux et Niestlé, 2010.

Austin, Bryant. *Beautiful Whale.* New York: Harry N. Abrams, 2013.

Barlow, Maude. *Blue Covenant: The Global Water Crisis and the Coming Battle for the Right to Water.* New York: New Press, 2009.

———. *Blue Future: Protection Water for the People and the Planet Forever.* New York: New Press, 2014.

Basho, Matsuo. *The Narrow Road to the Deep North and Other Travel Sketches.* New York: Penguin, 1967.

Baxter, Charles, and Judith Connor. *Kelp Forests.* Monterey, CA: Monterey Bay Aquarium, 1990.

Benyus, Janine M. *Biomimicry: Innovation Inspired by Nature.* New York: HarperPerennial, 2002.

Berman, Phillip L. *The Journey Home: What Near-Death Experiences and Mysticism Teach Us About the Gift of Life.* New York: Simon & Schuster, 1996.

Berta, Annalisa, James L. Sumich, and Kit M. Kovacs. *Marine Mammals: Evolutionary Biology.* Durham, NC: Academic Press, 2005.

Blair, Richard, and Kathleen Goodwin. *Point Reyes Visions.* Inverness, CA: Color & Light Editions, 2002.

Bonnefis, Jean, and Michel Pathé. *Le monde sous-marin du plongeur biologiste en Méditerrané.* Challes-les-Eaux: Editions Gap, 2010.

Borden, Richard J. *Ecology and Experience: Reflections from a Human Ecological Perspective.* Berkeley, CA: North Atlantic Books, 2014.

Bortolotti, Dan. *Wild Blue: A Natural History of the World's Largest Animal.* New York: Thomas Dunne Books, 2008.

Bottignolog, Bruno. *Celebrations with the Sun: An Overview of the Religious Phenomena among the Badjaos.* Manila, Philippines: Ateneo de Manila University Press, 1995.

Braungart, Michael, and William McDonough. *Cradle to Cradle: Remaking the Way We Make Things.* New York: North Point Press, 2002.

———. *The Upcycle: Beyond Sustainability—Designing for Abundance.* New York: North Point Press, 2013.

Breidbach, Olaf. *Art Forms from the Ocean: The Radiolarian Prints of Ernst Haeckel.* Munich: Prestel, 2005.

Calcagno, Robert, and André Giordan. *Méditerranée: Splendide, fragile, vivante.* Monaco: Editions du Rocher, 2010.

Carson, Rachel. *The Sea around Us.* New York: Oxford University Press, 1961.

——. *The Sense of Wonder.* New York: Harper & Row, 1965.

Chautard, Sabine. *Carnet de mouillages.* Boutigy Prouais, France: Archilivres, 2012.

Cheng, Brian, John Largier, and Kelley Higgason, eds. *NOAA Climate Change Impacts: Gulf of the Farallones and Cordell Bank National Marine Sanctuaries.* Washington, DC: National Oceanic and Atmospheric Association, 2010.

Clover, Charles. *The End of the Line: How Overfishing Is Changing the World and What We Eat.* Berkeley: University of California Press, 2008.

Cousineau, Phil. *The Art of Pilgrimage: The Seeker's Guide to Making Travel Sacred.* Berkeley, CA: Conari Press, 1998

Cousteau, Jacques. *The Silent World.* New York: Harper & Brothers, 1953.

Cousteau, Jacques, and Susan Schiefelbein. *The Human, the Orchid, and the Octopus: Exploring and Conserving Our Natural World.* New York: Bloomsbury, 2010.

Cousteau, Jean-Michel, and Daniel Paisner. *My Father, the Captain: My Life with Jacques Cousteau.* Washington, DC: National Geographic, 2010.

Cox, Lynne. *Grayson.* New York: Harvest Books, 2008.

Cramer, Deborah. *Great Waters: An Atlantic Passage.* New York: W.W. Norton, 2002.

——. *Smithsonian Ocean: Our Water, Our World.* Washington, DC: National Geographic, 2008.

Crawford, Peter. *Nomads of the Wind: A Natural History of Polynesia.* London: BBC Publications, 1994.

Daniels, Patricia. *Body: The Complete Human.* Washington, DC: National Geographic Books, 2007.

Danson, Ted, and Michael D'Orso. *Oceana: Our Endangered Oceans and What We Can Do to Save Them.* New York: Rodale Books, 2011.

Darwin, Jacob Hamblin. *Poison in the Well: Radioactive Waste in the Oceans at the Dawn of the Nuclear Age.* Piscataway, NJ: Rutgers University Press, 2008.

Davis, Frederick. *The Man Who Saved Sea Turtles: Archie Carr and the Origins of Conservation Biology.* New York: Oxford University Press, 2007

Diamond, Jared. *Collapse: How Societies Choose to Fail or Succeed.* New York: Viking, 2005.

Dubos, Réne. *So Human an Animal: How We Are Shaped by Surroundings and Events.* New York: Scribner, 1968.

D'Vincent, Cynthia, Delphine Haley, and Fred A. Sharpe. *Voyaging with the Whales.* Danville, VA: Boulton, 1989

Earle, Sylvia A. *Sea Change: A Message of the Oceans.* New York: Ballantine Books, 1996.

——. *National Geographic Atlas of the Oceans: The Deep Frontier.* Washington DC: National Geographic, 2001.

——. *The World Is Blue: How Our Fate and the Ocean's Are One.* Washington DC: National Geographic, 2001.

Ehrlich, Gretel. *Islands, the Universe, Home.* New York: Penguin Books, 1992.

Eiseley, Loren. *The Immense Journey.* New York: Random House, 1957.

——. *The Star Thrower.* New York: Mariner Books, 1979.

Ellis, Richard. *The Empty Ocean.* Washington, DC: Island Press, 2004.

————. *Men and Whales.* New York: Lyons Press, 1999.

————. *Tuna: A Love Story.* New York: Knopf, 2008.

Erlande-Brandenburg, Alain. *Notre-Dame de Paris.* New York: Harry N. Abrams, 1999.

European Commission. *Towards a Circular Economy: A Zero Waste Programme for Europe, Communication from the Commission to the European Parliament, the Council, the European Economic and Social Committee and the Committee of the Regions.* Brussels: European Commission, 2014.

Fair, Susan W. *Alaska Native Art: Tradition, Innovation and Continuity.* Fairbanks: University of Alaska Press, 2007.

François, Icher. *Building the Great Cathedrals.* New York: Harry N. Abrams, 1998.

Freund, Jürgen, and Stella-Chiu Freund. *The Coral Triangle.* Jakarta: WWF-Indonesia, 2011.

Fromm, Erich. *The Forgotten Language: An Introduction to the Understanding of Dreams, Fairy Tales, and Myths.* New York: Grove, 1957.

Glover, Linda K., and Sylvia A. Earle, eds. *Defying Ocean's End: An Agenda for Action.* Washington DC: Island Press, 2004

Goldsmith, Stephan A., Elizabeth Lynne, and Arlene Goldbard. *What We See: Advancing the Observations of Jane Jacobs.* Oakland, CA: New Village Press, 2010.

Goleman, Daniel, Lisa Bennett, and Zenobia Barlow. *Ecoliterate: How Educators Are Cultivating Emotional, Social, and Ecological Intelligence.* San Francisco: Jossey-Bass, 2012.

Goodall, Jane, and Phillip Berman. *Reason for Hope: A Spiritual Journey.* New York: Grand Central, 2000.

Goodall, Jane, Gail Hudson, and Thane Maynard. *Hope for Animals and Their World: How Endangered Species Are Being Rescued from the Brink.* New York: Grand Central, 2009.

Gore, Al. *The Future: Six Drivers of Global Change.* New York: Random House, 2013.

————. *An Inconvenient Truth: The Planetary Emergency of Global Warming and What We Can Do about It.* New York: Rodale Books, 2006.

Greenberg, Paul. *Four Fish: The Future of the Last Wild Food.* New York: Penguin, 2011.

Griffin, L. Martin. *Saving the Marin-Sonoma Coast: The Battles for Audubon Canyon Ranch, Point Reyes, and California's Russian River.* Healdsburg, CA: Sweetwater Springs, 1998.

Grudin, Robert. *The Grace of Great Things.* New York: Mariner Books, 1991.

Harmelin, Jean-Georges; and Frédéric Bassemayousse, *Méditerranée: A la découverte des paysages sous-marins.* Glénat, 2008.

Harrigan, Stephen. *Water and Light: A Diver's Journey to a Coral Reef.* San Francisco: Sierra Club Books, 1992.

Harrison, R. J. *The Behavior and Physiology of Pinnipeds.* New York: Appleton-Century-Crofts, 1968.

Hart, John. *An Island in Time: 50 Years as Point Reyes National Seashore.* Mill Valley, CA: Pickleweed Press, 2012.

Havel, Václav. *The Art of the Impossible*. New York: Knopf, 1997.

———. *Living in Truth: 22 Essays Published on the Occasion of the Award of the Erasmus Prize to Vaclav Havel*. London: Faber & Faber, 1990.

Hawken, Paul. *Blessed Unrest: How the Largest Social Movement in History Is Restoring Grace, Justice, and Beauty to the World*. New York: Penguin Books, 2007.

———. *The Ecology of Commerce: A Declaration of Sustainability*. New York: HarperBusiness, 2012.

Heller, Peter. *The Whale Warriors: The Battle at the Bottom of the World to Save the Planet's Largest Animals*. New York: Free Press, 2008.

Helvarg, David. *50 Ways to Save the Ocean*. Novato, CA: New World Library, 2006.

———. *The Golden Shore: California's Love Affair with the Sea*. New York: Thomas Dunne Books, 2013.

Henley, Thom, Geo Klathalay, and Jok Klathalay. *Courage of the Sea: Last Stand of the Moken*. Phuket, Thailand: Thai Nature Education Books, 2013.

Hobman, Robert. *Sarimanok*. Paris: Éditions Grasset, 1989.

Hope, Sebastian. *The Outcasts of the Islands: The Sea Gypsies of South East Asia*. New York: HarperCollins, 2001.

Howard, Carol J. *Dolphin Chronicles: One Woman's Quest to Understand the Sea's Most Mysterious Creatures*. New York: Bantam, 2009.

Humann, Paul, and Ned DeLoach. *Reef Coral Identification: Florida, Caribbean, Bahamas, 3rd ed*. Jacksonville, FL: New World Publications, 2013.

———. *Reef Fish Identification: Florida, Caribbean, Bahamas, 3rd ed*. Jacksonville, FL: New World Publications, 2014.

Ivanoff, Jacques. *Moken: Sea-Gypsies of the Andaman Sea*. Banglamung, Thailand: White Lotus Press, 1997.

———. *Rings of Coral: Moken Folktales (Mergui Archipelago Project)*. Banglamung, Thailand: White Lotus Press, 2002.

Jennings, Simon, Michael J. Kaiser, and John D. Reynolds. *Marine Fisheries Ecology*. Oxford: Blackwell Science, 2001.

Jones, Burt, and Maurine Smimlock. *Diving Indonesia's Birds Head Seascape*. Denpasar, Indonesia: Saritaksu Editions, 2011.

Jung, Carl. *The Collected Works of C. G. Jung*. London: Routledge & Kegan Paul, 1960.

Karleskint, George, Richard Turner, and James Small. *Introduction to Marine Biology*. Boston: Cengage Learning, 2012.

Kaufman, Paul, and Philip Zaleski. *Gifts of the Spirit*. New York: HarperCollins, 2009.

Keener, Victoria, John J. Marra, Melissa L. Finucane, Deanna Spooner, and Margaret H. Smith, eds. *Climate Change and Pacific Islands: Indicators and Impacts: Report for the 2012 Pacific Islands Regional Climate Assessment*. NCA Regional Input Reports, 2013.

Keller, Catherine. *Apocalypse Now and Then*. Minneapolis, MN: Augsburg Fortress, 2004.

———. *The Face of the Deep: A Theology of Becoming*. New York: Routledge, 2003.

Kennedy, Robert F., Jr. *Crime against Nature*. New York: HarperCollins, 2004.

Keogh, Martin, ed. *Hope beneath Our Feet: Restoring Our Place in the Natural World.* Berkeley, CA: North Atlantic Books, 2010.

King, Peter. *West Papua and Indonesia Since Suharto: Independence, Autonomy or Chaos?* Kensington: University of New South Wales Press, 2004.

Kirksey, Eben. *Freedom in Entangled Worlds: West Papua and the Architecture of Global Power.* Durham, NC: Duke University Press, 2012.

Klein, Naomi. *The Shock Doctrine: The Rise of Disaster Capitalism.* New York: Picador, 2008.

_____. *This Changes Everything: Capitalism vs. the Climate.* New York: Simon & Schuster, 2014.

Klimley, A. Peter. *The Biology of Sharks and Rays.* Chicago: University of Chicago Press, 2013.

Knowlton, Nancy. *Citizens of the Sea: Wondrous Creatures from the Census of Marine Life.* Washington, DC: National Geographic, 2010.

Kolbert, Elizabeth. *Field Notes from a Catastrophe: Man, Nature, and Climate Change.* New York: Bloomsbury, 2006.

_____. *The Sixth Extinction: An Unnatural History.* New York: Henry Holt, 2014.

Kowalski, Gary, and John Robbins. *The Souls of Animals.* Novato, CA: New World Library, 2007.

Kübler-Ross, Elisabeth. *On Death and Dying.* New York: Routledge, 1969.

Kulansky, Mark. *Cod: A Biography of the Fish that Changed the World.* New York: Penguin, 1998.

Lederach, John Paul. *The Moral Imagination: The Art and Soul of Building Peace.* New York: Oxford University Press, 2010.

Lieske, Ewald, and Robert Myers. *Coral Reef Fishes: Indo-Pacific and Caribbean.* Princeton, NJ: Princeton University Press, 2002.

Louisy, Patrick. *Guide d'identification des poissons marins: Europe et Méditerranée.* Paris: Éditons Ulmer, 2002.

Lovins, Amory, and Michael Braungart. *A New Dynamic—Effective Business in a Circular Economy.* Isle of Wight, UK: Ellen MacArthur Foundation, 2014.

Lynch, Kevin. *What Time Is This Place?* Cambridge, MA: MIT Press, 1972.

Macy, Joanna. *Despair and Personal Power in the Nuclear Age.* Gabriola Island, BC: New Society, 1983

———. *Widening Circles: A Memoir.* Gabriola Island, BC: New Catalyst Books, 2001.

———. *World as Lover, World as Self.* Berkeley, CA: Parallax Press, 1991.

Macy, Joanna, and Chris Johnstone. *Active Hope: How to Face the Mess We're in Without Going Crazy.* Novato, CA: New World Library, 2012.

Macy, Joanna, and Molly Young. *Coming Back to Life: The Updated Guide to the Work that Reconnects.* Gabriola Island, BC: New Society, 2014.

Maggio, Teresa. *Mattanza: The Ancient Sicilian Ritual of Bluefin Tuna Fishing.* New York: Penguin, 2001.

Matsen, Brad. *Jacques Cousteau: The Sea King.* New York: Vintage 2009.

McCalman, Iain. *The Reef: A Passionate History of the Great Barrier Reef from Captain Cook to Climate Change.* New York: Farrar, Straus and Giroux, 2014.

McKibben, Bill. *Eaarth: Making a Life on a Tough New Planet.* New York: St. Martin's Griffin, 2008.

———. *Oil and Honey: The Education of an Unlikely Activist.* New York: St. Martin's Griffin, 2014.

Moltmann, Jürgen. *The Spirit of Life: A Universal Affirmation.* Minneapolis, MN: Fortress Press, 2001.

Morton, Nelle. *The Journey Is Home.* Boston, MA: Beacon Press, 1985.

Mouthe, P. Clavreul. *Paysages et fleurs des îles de Port Cros et Porquerolles.* Paris: Editions du Rouergue, 2000.

Mowat, Farley. *Sea of Slaughter.* New York: Atlantic Monthly Press, 1984.

Murphy, Susan. *Minding the Earth, Mending the World: Zen and the Art of Planetary Crisis.* New York: Picador, 2014

Myers, Robert F. *Micronesian Reef Fishes: A Practical Guide to the Identification of the Coral Reef Fishes of the Tropical Central and Western Pacific.* 2nd ed. Guam: Coral Graphics, 1991.

Naylor, Rosamond L. *The Evolving Sphere of Food Security.* New York: Oxford University Press, 2014.

Nichols, Wallace J. *Blue Mind: The Surprising Science That Shows How Being near, in, on, or under Water Can Make You Happier, Healthier, More Connected, and Better at What You Do.* New York: Little, Brown, 2014.

Nicklin, Charles. *Among Giants: A Life with Whales.* Chicago: University of Chicago Press, 20011.

O'Donohue, John. *Anam Cara: A Book of Celtic Wisdom.* New York: HarperPerennial, 1998.

———. *Beauty: The Invisible Embrace.* New York: HarperPerennial, 2005.

Orr, David. *Hope Is an Imperative: The Essential David Orr.* Washington DC: Island Press, 2010.

Palumbi, Stephen R., and Carolyn Sotkay. *The Death and Life of Monterey Bay: A Story of Revival.* Washington DC: Island Press, 2012.

Parsons, E. C. M. *An Introduction to Marine Mammals: Biology and Conservation.* Sudbury, MA: Jones & Bartlett Learning, 2012.

Payne, Roger. *Among Whales.* New York: Scribner, 1995.

Peter, Kimley A. *The Biology of Sharks and Rays.* Chicago: University of Chicago Press, 2013.

Quirk, Joe. *Call to the Rescue: The Story of the Marine Mammal Center.* San Francisco: Chronicle Books, 2009.

Ray, Paul, and Sherry Ruth Anderson. *The Cultural Creatives: How 50 Million People Are Changing the World.* New York: Harmony Books, 2000.

Riedman, Marianne. *The Pinnipeds: Seals, Sea Lions, and Walruses.* Berkeley: University of California Press, 1991.

Rigsby, Michael A. *A Natural History of the Monterey Bay National Marine Sanctuary.* Monterey, CA: Monterey Bay Aquarium Press, 1999.

Rilke, Rainer Maria. *Rilke's Book of Hours: Love Poems to God.* Translated by Anita Barrows and Joanna Macy. New York: Riverhead Trade, 2005.

Rumi, Jalal al-Din. *The Essential Rumi*. Translated by Coleman Barks. New Expanded Edition. New York: HarperOne, 2004.

Safina, Carl. *Song for the Blue Ocean: Encounters along the World's Coasts and beneath the Seas*. New York: Owl Books, 2000.

———. *The View from Lazy Point*. New York: Henry Holt, 2010.

———. *Voyage of the Turtle: In Pursuit of the Earth's Last Dinosaur*. New York: Holt Paperbacks, 2007.

Salzberg, Sharon. *Faith: Trusting Your Own Deepest Experience*. New York: Riverhead Trade, 2003.

Satloff, Robert. *Among the Righteous: Lost Stories from the Holocaust's Long Reach into Arab Lands*. New York: Perseus Book Group, 2006.

Schmitt, Catherine. *A Coastal Companion: A Year in the Gulf of Maine, from Cape Cod to Canada*. Thomaston, CT: Tilbury House, 2008.

Schoenherr, Allan A. *A Natural History of California*. Berkeley: University of California Press, 1995.

Sewall, Laura. *Sight and Sensibility: The Ecopsychology of Perception*. New York: Tarcher, 1999.

Sheppard, Charles R. C., and Simon K. Davy. *The Biology of Coral Reefs (Biology of Habitats)*. New York: Oxford University Press, 2009.

Shiva, Vandana. *Earth Democracy: Justice, Sustainability, and Peace*. Cambridge, MA: South End Press, 2005.

Shubin, Neil. *Your Inner Fish: A Journey into the 3.5-Billion-Year History of the Human Body*. New York: Vintage Books, 2008.

Spotila, James R. *Saving Sea Turtles: Extraordinary Stories from the Battle against Extinction*. Baltimore, MD: Johns Hopkins University Press, 2011.

———. *Sea Turtles: A Complete Guide to Their Biology, Behavior, and Conservation*. Baltimore, MD: Johns Hopkins University Press, 2004.

Stevenson, Andrew. *Whale Song: Journey into the Secret Lives of North Atlantic Humpback Whales*. Guilford, CT: Lyons Press, 2011.

Suzuki, David. *The Sacred Balance: Rediscovering Our Place in Nature*. Vancouver, BC: Graystone Books, 2007.

Tufte, Edward Rolf. *Beautiful Evidence*. Cheshire, CT: Graphics Press, 2006.

Turner, Frederick. *Beauty: The Value of Values*. Charlottesville: University of Virginia Press, 1991.

United Nations Children Fund (UNICEF). "The State of the World's Children: 2014 in Numbers." New York: UNICEF, 2014.

United Nations Food and Agriculture Organization (FAO). *World Review of Fisheries and Agriculture (SOFIA)*. New York: United Nations, 2010.

Wallace, Alfred Russel. *The Malay Archipelago: The Land the Orang-Utan and the Bird of Paradise*. Oxford: John Beaufoy, 2011.

Watts, Alan. *Nature, Man and Woman*. New York: Vintage, 1991.

West, Page. *Conservation Is Our Government Now: The Politics of Ecology in Papua New Guinea (New Ecologies for the Twenty-First Century)*. Durham, NC: Duke University Press, 2006.

White, Walter G. *The Sea Gypsies of Malay*. London: Seeley, Service, 1922.

Whitty, Julia. *Deep Blue Home: An Intimate Ecology of Our Wild Blue Ocean.* New York: Mariner Books, 2010.

————. *The Fragile Edge: Diving and Other Adventures in the South Pacific.* New York: Mariner Books, 2008.

Wiesel, Elie. *Ani Ma'amin: A Song Lost and Found Again.* Translated by Marion Wiesel. New York: Random House, 1973.

————. *From the Kingdom of Memory: Reminiscences.* New York: Schocken Books, 1990.

Wilson, Edward O. *Biophilia.* Cambridge, MA: Harvard University Press, 1986.

————. *The Diversity of Life (Questions of Science).* Cambridge, MA: Belknap Press, 2010.

Wong, Kathleen M., and Ariel Rubissow Okamoto. *Natural History of San Francisco Bay.* Berkeley: University of California Press, 2011.

World Summit on Sustainable Development. "A Framework for Action on Biodiversity and Ecosystem Management." Johannesburg, South Africa: WEHAB Working Group, 2002.

Index

A

aboriginal culture, 132, 134, 275. *See also* hunter-gatherer cultures

Aboucaya, Annie, 251, 255, 256

acidification. *See* ocean acidification

Active Hope (Johnstone and Macy), 89

activism: as the basis for social change, 43, 50, 244, 190; efforts of, the sum of, xi, 211–12, 216, 258; inspired by Cousteau, 90, 191; leading to the termination of dredging operations, 30; and petitions, 43, 210, 265, 279; which prevented the dumping of radioactive waste, 90; and the reduction in dead zones, 151; and saving whales, 265; success of, in creating the Point Reyes National Seashore, 69; working to save bluefin tuna, 210–11. *See also* volunteers

Aeolus, 4

Africa, 5, 21, 64–65, 237, 256, 272

afterlife, 194

Agricultural Revolution, 160, 184, 197

agriculture: livestock feed, 202, 219, 294*n*90; rice, 142, 163, 290*n*69. *See also* droughts

air: gases which compose, 7; pollution, in "killer cities," 174. *See also* oxygen

airplanes, righting, during a nosedive, 74

albatross, 277. *See also* seabirds

algae, 27, 29, 247; blooms, 100; and domoic acid toxicosis, 100; fish that feed on, 38; overgrowth, 38, 39, 41, 42, 49, 143; and nutrient runoff, 42; percentage of oxygen that comes from, in each breath, 27, 152, 248; and photosynthesis, 65; which has a symbiotic relationship with coral, 41–42, 145

Algeria, 251

Allen, Gerald, 143

alternation exercises, 107, 285*n*28

alternative energy, 5, 62. *See also* solar energy

Amazon rainforest, 26, 118. *See also* forests; rainforests

amnesiac shellfish poisoning, 100, 105. *See also* domoic acid toxicosis

ancestors (elders), listening to the voices of, 163, 164–65, 175

anchoring techniques, 40, 248, 253–54

anchovies, 107, 131–32, 135, 139

Anderson, Sherry Ruth, 257

anemonefish, 126

anemones, 68–69, 126, 242

anguish, 10, 75, 89, 91. *See also* despair

animal(s): and biomedical research, 111, 285*n*39, 286*n*30; coral as a type of, 33–36, 39; entanglement of, in fishing gear, 82–83, 265, 274; humane/inhumane treatment of, 108–12, 285*n*39, 286*n*30; ingestion of plastic debris by, 50, 84–85, 109, 277, 283*n*22; inner lives of, 109–10; intelligence of, 99–112, 122, 128, 136, 181, 182; kinship with, 6, 34, 35, 80, 109, 181–82, 194, 250; as "lacking a soul," belief in, 108; rights, 108–9, 254. *See also* animal cognition; *specific species*

animal cognition: and alternation exercises, 107, 285*n*28; and dogs,

M

R

radioactive waste, 89–90, 284*n*28. *See also* nuclear bombs

rainforests, 26, 118, 149, 248, 289*n*61. *See also* forests

Raja Ampat, 115, 128–46; as the epicenter of marine biodiversity, 129, 132, 135, 142; first settlers of, 134; limestone pinnacles in, 131, 132, 137, 192; as a migration corridor, 142; as a species factory, 135

Ray, Paul, 257

recession, 221. *See also* economy

recycling, 23. *See also* plastic pollution

Red List, for species at risk of extinction, 243

Reddick, Laura, 92

Reef Ball Foundation, 33

reef balls, 33–34. *See also* coral reefs

Reeve, Christopher, xix

Reichmuth, Colleen, 101

Relais et Châteaux, 203, 204

remoras, 49, 93–94

Renault, 257

renewable energy, 5, 62, 152, 183, 184, 292*n*78

rescue: CPR procedures, xxiv; drills, for scuba diving, xxiii–xiv; of marine mammals, 78–79, 81, 83, 85; passion for, 87, 96–97, 244

rice agriculture, 142, 163, 290*n*69

Richmond Bridge, 61, 62, 77

rights: of animals, 108–9, 254; human, 147–50, 151, 228, 287*n*55

ring, metaphor of, 223–24, 227

Rio (sea lion), 101–2

ripple effects, 55, 64, 71, 89, 204. *See also* interconnection

risk(s): and a second innocence, 249; of failure, courage to take, xxiv

river(s), 40, 42; dead zones in, 150–51; and estuaries, relationship of, 62; and logging runoff, 147–53; the ocean as a vast, 86, 152; PCBs

in, 10, 86, 281*n*1; and the water cycle, 198. *See also* Hudson River, Mississippi River, Seine River

river otters, 69

Rodríguez, Naima Andrea, 217–18, 225–32, 235, 238–39, 257; coining of the expression "thousands of selves" by, 244, 249; in the Galápagos Islands, 278

Rodeo Beach, 79

Roellinger, Olivier, 204

Rogers, Barb, xxvi

role to play, having a, 208–9, 227

Roman conquest, 197

Ronan (sea lion), 99–102, 106, 112, 277–78

Ronny, 123–25, 162

Roosevelt, Theodore, 248

Rubik's cube, 94

Rumi, 86

Russia, 89–90

Rwandan genocide, 72, 148. *See also* genocide

S

Sadar, 161, 163

sadness. *See* despair

safety sausages, 135, 137, 144, 156

safety stops, 6–7, 137, 138, 144–45, 155–56

Sainz-Trápaga, Susana, 217, 226, 233, 257

Salamanca, Eric, 31

Salawati, 129

Saliki, Rikardo, 161–63, 169–72, 174, 176–78, 190, 205, 278

salmon, 219

salt trade, 4

San Francisco Bay, 53, 61–62, 71, 89; oxygen-depleted dead zones in, 151; and sea-level rise, 117, 282*n*20

Sánchez, Pilar, 221, 222, 233, 241

sandeel fishery, 217–39

Acknowledgments

My first thanks go to those whose voices and actions illuminate these pages with insight and hope: Alizee Zimmermann, Amdeep Sanghera, Annie Aboucaya, Arman, Arnaud Vanhamme, Bryan Manco, Cybèle Idelot, Dorman, Eiglys Trejo, Elisabeth Vallet, Emily Howgate, Enci Wahab, Eric Salamanca, François Pasteau, Gene Flipse, Helen Newman, Ii Rosna Tarmidji, Itziar Segarra, Jenny Stock, Joanna Macy, John Walch, Lindsay Olsen, Lormeka Williams, Luís Trias Martín, Marsha Pardee, Mauricio Pulido, Michel Mouisel, Nicolas Gérardin, Peter Cook, Pilar Sánchez, Robert Hobman, Ronny, Sabine Chautard, Sergi Tudela, Stéphanie Mathey, Sugi Sugiyanta, Susana Sainz-Trápaga, and William Van Bonn.

Beneath the web of these voices, a large herd of helping hands helped me to find the best areas of study and to assure the scientific accuracy of the material: Debbie Crockard and Peter Richardson of the Marine Conservation Society, Catherine Kilduff of the Center for Biological Diversity, Lynette Koftinow of the American Cetacean Society, Karen Garrison of the National Resources Defense Council, Lida-Pet Soede of the World Wide Fund for Nature, Catherine Plume of the World Wildlife Fund, Coleen Reichmuth of the Pinniped Cognition and Sensory Systems Laboratory, Stacie Steensland of the TCI Environmental Club, Peter Mous of the Indonesia Marine and Climate Support (IMACS) project, and Wesley Clerveaux of the Turks Caicos Department of Environment and Maritime Affairs.

I am extremely grateful to the following organizations for their assistance: the American Cetacean Society, Conservation International, the Cordell Bank National Marine Sanctuary, Long Marine Lab, NOAA (the National Oceanographic at Atmospheric Association), the Marine Conservation Society,

The Marine Mammal Center, Parc National de Port-Cros, the Pinniped Cognition and Sensory Systems Laboratory, the Reef Ball Foundation, SeaWeb Europe, the School for Field Studies, the Sea Sanctuaries Trust, Sustain (sustainweb.org), the Turks and Caicos Department of the Environment and Maritime Affairs, WWF-Indonesia, and WWF-Spain.

Helen Newman's insightful words play a key role in the chapter entitled "Heart," as she addresses the importance of marine biodiversity. She tragically passed away just before the book was completed. Her steadfast dedication to coral-reef conservation will be an enduring source of inspiration to many around the world.

Much of the dialogue in this book was rendered into English by the hard work of my translators, Naima Andrea Rodríguez and Rikardo Saliki. I am indebted to Naima for the phrase she coined, "we have thousands of selves," which inspired the chapter title "Thousands of Selves."

Kathy Borsuk, managing editor of *Times of the Islands* magazine, offered crucial feedback in the early phases and edited much of the manuscript. I am grateful as well to Maureen Nandini Mitra, managing editor at *Earth Island Journal,* for her insight and encouragement, and to Kai Lord-Farmer for his research on traditional ecological knowledge and biomimicry. A special thank you to Lynn Morton, Laura Cohn, and Cathy Conner for their advice and help with travel arrangements. Also to John Claydon who made it possible to visit the School for Field Studies. My thanks to Anne Napier for her guidance a long time ago and her vivid descriptions of aviation adventures. Naomi Epel peppered my journey with insight into the creative process, and similarly, Cary Sheldon introduced me to new avenues of awareness regarding music and the nature of vocalization.

This book benefited greatly from the expertise of a team of readers, many of whom I am also grateful to for their remarkable friendship—Eve Aldridge, Peter Allison, Constance Anderson, Richard Borden, Ann Britt Bosson, James Bosson,

David Bricker, Laura Cohn, Simon Day, Richard Green, Phyllis Greene, Bridget Hedderman, David Helvarg, Dana Jiacolleti, Catherine Keller, Susan Klee, Elizabeth Anglin Knox, Uldis Kruze, Manuel Fernández López, Susan Murphy, Barbara Rogers, April Sayre, Arlene Ustin, and Ann Zoeller. A special thanks to Miller Wise, Elizabeth McAnally, and Laura Reddick for their exceptional help with proofreading.

Toward the end of this journey the staff at North Atlantic Books brought renewed focus and energy to envisioning how *Ocean Country* could make a contribution. I am grateful to all of them for their hard work, picking up where I left off and ferrying this book across the finish line and out into the world. Many thanks to all the staff at North Atlantic Books, including Emily Boyd, Susan Bumps, Jasmine Hromjak, Janet Levin, Julia Kent, Doug Reil, and Kim Westerman. The manuscript benefited immensely from Jennifer Eastman's meticulous and in-depth copyediting. I am especially grateful to Tim McKee for his expansive vision and tireless editing and to Leslie Larson for her wise and good-natured shepherding of this book through production.

I would like to also thank specific individuals whose inspiring words are quoted in this book—Coleman Barks, for his beautiful translation of a poem by Rumi, as well as Jane Goodall, Paul Hawken, Tom Hayden, and David Orr.

I am greatly indebted to Dr. Reuben Ziegler, whose extraordinary care helped me through the lengthy healing process after the kayak accident.

Dana Jiacolleti provided much needed assistance with describing the technical details of diving techniques along with steady doses of encouragement. Catherine Keller's inspired work and her sage advice spurred me on through some of the most difficult periods. Elizabeth Anglin Knox, Ana Patel, and Arlene Ustin offered much insight into the philosophy of Outward Bound. Susan Klee provided editorial support and good-natured cheerleading throughout, not to mention a few one-hour crash courses in French. Uldis Kruze was an astute and, on occasion, ruthlessly funny sounding board. Trudy Neuhaus's savvy and humor regarding the book-making process kept me laughing and taught me to take things one day at a time. April Sayre offered much insight into the challenges of keeping one's writing true and soulful. Barbara Rogers lent an ear and helped so many times I can't remember them all. And she always managed to put a smile on my face, even when driving me to the emergency room in the middle of the night. Teresa Villegas stunned me with her soulful illustrations, which she made as gifts for me to carry with me as I traveled.

A special thanks to friends in the wonderful neighborhood that my husband and I live in for their support—Sally Adams and Dave Krinkel, Bob Dering and Gay Gale, and Claudia Lewis and Miller Wise. To Ann Britt and James Bosson, my heartfelt thanks for their constant support and soulful friendship.

I am especially grateful to the members of my writers and illustrators group, whose wisdom and joyousness helped this book find its way into being—Eve Aldridge, Constance Anderson, and Kieren Dutcher. Last, but not least, I am immensely grateful to my family for their love and support.

My thanks to my professors at College of the Atlantic—Richard Borden, JoAnne Carpenter, William Carpenter, Susan Lerner, Steven Katona, and Richard Davis. They instilled in me an intellectual and emotive flexibility that allowed me to maintain something at the very core of this book's enterprise: a teachable spirit.

These acknowledgments would not be complete without thanks to all the strangers who helped me along the way—in airports, ferry terminals, and train stations, in villages small and large. Their help and friendly gazes got me through many a difficult day.

In the age of the sixth mass extinction, it is all the more appropriate to express gratitude to the nonhuman creatures of our earth and acknowledge how deeply they have inspired me. Much of this book was written in the company of our dog, Zack, who has taught me so much about love and what it means to cherish another creature on a daily basis. The list of species that have inspired me is too long to assemble. But today I voice thanks to the bluefin tuna, the California sea lion, the dusky grouper, the green sea turtle, the humpback whale, and the oceanic manta ray.

Most of all, I am grateful to the man I barely know how to thank, my husband, Charlie. His good cheer, incisive editing, unflinching support, and wisdom sustained me in ways I'll never be able to express. Authors often thank their spouses for their patience during the time spent away from them. My gratitude has an added twist—gratitude for the gift of his faith in me in the face of formidable uncertainties. He knew how important it was to let me go into an unknown labyrinth and—despite its vicissitudes and my frailty—trust that I'd find my way back home to him.

About the Author

Photo by Dana Davis

LIZ CUNNINGHAM is the author of *Talking Politics: Choosing the President in the Television Age* (Praeger), which analyzes the impact of television news on the outcome of presidential campaigns. It features probing oral-history interviews with top television journalists such as Tom Brokaw, Larry King and Robin MacNeil. Her writing has been published in *Earth Island Journal, The East Bay Express, the Marin Poetry Center Anthology, The Outward Bound International Journal, Times of the Islands,* and the *San Francisco Chronicle.* She has collaborated with institutions such as the Academy for Educational Development, the Constitutional Rights Foundation, the Tides Foundation, and the Smithsonian Institution. She is the cofounder of KurtHahn. org, the web archive for the founder of Outward Bound and serves on the board of Outward Bound Peacebuilding. She holds a B.A. in Human Ecology from College of the Atlantic.

ABOUT CARL SAFINA

Carl Safina is the author of seven books and roughly 200 scientific and popular publications, including features in the *New*

York Times and *National Geographic*. He is the founding president of the Safina Center. *Audubon* magazine named him one of the "100 Notable Conservationists of the 20th Century" and the *Utne Reader* listed Safina among "25 Visionaries Changing the World."